Stunned In
America

Sub-Crime Mortgage Crisis

Mary Tootikian

authorHOUSE®

AuthorHouse™
1663 Liberty Drive
Bloomington, IN 47403
www.authorhouse.com
Phone: 1-800-839-8640

First published by AuthorHouse 9/11/2009

ISBN: 978-1-4490-0838-3 (e)
ISBN: 978-1-4490-0837-6 (sc)

Printed in the United States of America
Bloomington, Indiana

This book is printed on acid-free paper.

Table of Contents

Section I: The Story - Who Did It?
Where We Are and How We Got Here

Section II: The Secret - How to Fix It!
What They Don't Want You to Know

Section III: The Start - Workbook

Section IV: Supplemental

Thank You

When I started this project in July of 2008, it was in response to my utter frustration at the constantly unfolding changes in the mortgage lending industry. I am not a reporter telling a story....I live this story. As such, emotions can run high and a state of irritability is often the result. My first thank you is to my family, friends, clients and business associates who have endured my crankiness through these last couple of tough years.

I could not have finished this book without the ongoing assistance of Heather Tootikian, my daughter-in-law and assistant. She prepared all of the many charts and support data that went into this book. From day one, she has read, proofed and fixed all of my mistakes (no easy task). She is invaluable to me as an assistant, daughter (in-law or not) and sometimes my best friend. I love you Heather.

Nancy Cozens has contributed significantly to this project. She is my greatest critic and my most loyal supporter. When she read the first draft of this book, she told me to quit ranting and write it. She has read and reread every word that I wrote, offering me priceless advice all along the way. I don't know how I could ever survive without her, as she is my sister and friend. I love you too.

A big thank you goes out to Doug Olson who patiently read the final manuscript and offered me so many ways to make it more readable. I thank you and I'm sure my readers will as well.

Eleanor Garrod has been my friend for almost forty years. Many years ago we started a project that never quite came to fruition. Two of the poems and many of the witticisms in this book are the result of her handiwork and a testimony to her cleverness. I learned a lot from you and my life has been blessed just knowing you.

Several people, in and out of the lending industry, have been kind enough to read through this book and offer me their feedback. A warm thank you goes to Terry McCall who gave me very useful advice in the early stages of this work. I send to you and Gwenda a great big hug for being there for me in more ways than I could ever thank you for. A special thanks to Zaven Tootikian, Lisa Voegele, Celeste Szot, Bill and Connie Bailey, Sandi Kane, Carl Giese, Dannette Prancevic, and Bonnie McGavock. I really appreciate your feedback and support.

I first met Gary Spangler in 1982 when he was a Vice President at Home Federal Savings and Loan. He started in the lending industry when it was still a people-helping-people business. Gary can tell many stories (and does) of how they not only originated loans, but also showed up at people's doorsteps to collect on any late payments. Although he could have continued up the corporate ladder, he chose to work in the field as an originator. His office is his car or someone's kitchen table as he is always available to assist a client with understanding their loan options. His clients value his knowledge and expertise in this constantly changing lending environment. I have learned a lot from Gary, as he is a true veteran in the industry. His assistance with this book has been invaluable and I am proud to have him as a business associate and close friend. If our mortgage industry had more people like Gary Spangler, we would not be in crisis today.

I thank you all.
Mary Tootikian

Who Am I?

Author's Preface

They call me the "Queen of Hugs & Kisses". They, being my grandchildren: Kaelyn, Quintin, Makenna, Vincint, Isabelle, Kody and Asher. I'm not even old enough for most senior discounts, but I am proud of being a senior level mom. I believe that grandchildren are God's way of compensating us for growing up (or for not killing our kids when they were teenagers). Kaelyn and Quintin are the oldest of my grandchildren, both born in 2001. In fact Quintin was born two days before the now infamous September 11th. What a scary and troubled time that was! I couldn't even get out of bed, watching in horror as the twin towers collapsed on the very day my grandson was coming home from the hospital.

As a nation we were rocked to the core and our future was very uncertain. In the days that followed that fateful day in September we banded together. We were not Republicans or Democrats, not rich or poor, we were Americans and proud of it. That horrible attack from without brought us together in ways we had not experienced before. It is time for us to come together again, in unity, and fight this insidious financial battle that threatens to bring us down. This is a battle not fought with weapons of war, but weapons of reason and common sense. I'm speaking of course about our current housing and lending crisis.

The mortgage industry has been home to me since 1980. I started out in the business as an underwriter working for a mortgage banking firm. It was during these early years that I learned what credible lending was. I'm thankful for these years of training. Many people have entered the housing industry in the last few years and have left without ever knowing what real loan documentation is. They knew nothing of the mountainous paperwork that we had to obtain and analyze in order to determine borrower creditworthiness. Yes, it was human underwriters not computers who determined a borrower's ability to repay.

I have watched the industry pendulum swing from paperwork necessitating a forest to be cut down, to no-documentation loans, where the only requirement was to bring a pen to the signing table. Well the pendulum has swung once again and this time to a different extreme. I hope this book will be the moving force to bring the pendulum back to a resting position where it belongs.

Over five years ago I started warning people of an impending real estate correction in prices. Ridiculous I was told, but I remembered all too well the crash in the early 90s after the Savings & Loan debacle. During that time many people also lost their homes, as values of properties dropped and loan programs dried up. Short sales (the selling of a property for less than what is owed against it) were commonplace as lenders worked with homeowners to unload their properties and avoid foreclosure. Everything is cyclical. Nothing goes up forever. That *crash* of the 90's looks like a fender bender compared to today's multi-car pile-up.

I based my assumptions, then and now, on basic "common sense". Common sense is defined as rational behavior. The opposite of rational is irrational, even insane. What was happening in the housing industry during the early 2000s and up until 2006 was pure insanity. Each home sale was higher than the one preceding it, home loans for everyone whether they could afford it or not, renters becoming homeowners with 100% financing, irresponsible lending practices that were destined to fail, people using their homes as ATM machines and spending all the proceeds on excessive living. Insanity……….? You bet!

This book was written for three reasons. First, I want to see our current housing crisis solved and that will only happen if the decision makers understand why we are in this mess to start with. We need concrete solutions in the lending industry, both with underwriting standards and with realistic loan programs. It is my sincere hope that our legislators in Washington will educate themselves about the mortgage industry and listen to the real problems. Excessive tightening of our credit standards has only thrown more fuel on this out of control fire storm that we face. I will explain in detail what basic common sense underwriting is and why we need to return to human underwriters once again.

Secondly, it is my desire that this book will educate you, the consumer, on the principles of real estate lending and help you in your own quest for a mortgage loan. For most of us our homes represent our personal security, our primary asset and our greatest financial liability. Many people losing their homes today did not fully understand the loans they were being placed in. In fact, many of the loan officers didn't even understand the loans they were selling to the public.

Finally, and most importantly, I have designed a loan program that is not currently offered by the lending industry. *It needs to be.* This stable loan gives initial low monthly payments with the security of a fixed interest rate. It is outlined in chapter 15 and you will see how it compares to other loan products. We desperately need this loan to restore affordability to our housing payments once again.

Why this housing crisis has taken everyone by surprise is a mystery to me. An even greater mystery is why the people in charge are having such a tough time solving this fiasco. We customarily look to the leaders in the industry to guide the way. They seem to be lost. Those of us, who work in the trenches everyday, see the impact of ineffective legislative decisions and how these decisions affect human lives. We see the individual trees in this forest of life.

Who Am I? – First and foremost I am a mom and grandma and as such I care deeply about our tomorrows and whether we are mortgaging our children's future. I am also the owner of a small loan processing company in Southern California where I provide processing services to both banks and mortgage brokers. My almost thirty years in the business has afforded me the opportunity to review and analyze thousands of people's loans. I may be a Queen to my grandkids but within the lending industry, I'm just a worker bee. No degrees, no titles, but from down here at the bottom my perspective is different. Don't overlook us little people who do the little jobs.

Common people have common sense! - Let's use some.

Section I:

The Story

Who Did It?

Where We Are and How We Got Here

1

Greedonomics 101

Is It Our Fault?

Hippies, Yuppies, Preppies and DINKS (double income, no kids) are all labels that the "Baby Boomers" have been saddled with. The later-born Boomers have been called Generation Jones (how fitting). We produced Generation X & Y and now they are making little Z's. We survived the Cold War, Vietnam, and black and white TV. We wore poodle skirts, did the hula hoop and enjoyed a Beatle invasion. We have watched a man walk on the moon and then surfed the globe via the internet. What a wonderful time to be alive on planet earth! However, we are also a "NOW" generation and patience is not our strongest virtue.

Through reality TV we have become exposed to the lifestyles of the rich and famous. We see where they live, what they drive, and certainly what they wear. We forget they are being paid millions of dollars to visit our living rooms. All we know is – we want it: the homes, the cars, the clothes and oh yes, the lifestyle. Gotta have it! They say the average American lives better than royalty in many countries. We take our lifestyle for granted and don't seem to know when enough is enough. We fear not getting *ours* when everyone else is getting *theirs*. And, we have taught our kids by example. I was informed by a chipper sales clerk in the Macy's department store in Orange County, California, that she had worked her entire summer, prior to her first year in college, just to acquire designer handbags. Someone should tell her - it's what's *in* the purse that counts.

True Religion is no longer a spiritual experience; it is a brand of very expensive designer jeans. In fact, I saw a five-year-old at my granddaughter's school a few months back wearing a pair of these jeans. Sure hope this kid has a college fund.

In the past, working-class people were not as aware of famous designers and their brands as it was an exclusive club for those who could *afford* to stand out from the crowd. Now it is not uncommon to see teenagers sporting $1200 Louis Vuitton handbags. I didn't even know that a "Louis" existed until four years ago when my now daughter-in-law just had to have one. I found out that apparently Jessica Simpson, in the "Newlyweds" reality series, made this famous brand a household name. To my amazement, this company has been around since 1854 and still uses the same fabric design today. I sure felt like I had been living under a rock. Perhaps some of you reading this are feeling the same way – go ask your kids, they will know. Wonder what the truly rich crowd is using today to satisfy their *status quo* now that the common people have invaded their territory?

Levi's, Keds, Calvin Klein and even *Liz Claiborne* have been replaced by *Gucci, Dolce and Gabbana, Burberry, Prada* (the devil wears this), *Versace*, and *Chanel* (isn't that a perfume?). We want what is *in* and these brands are. They have become the new necessities of life.

Necessities

Johnny has a paper route,
And Susie sits for two;
Mary's flipping hamburgers
While Mother teaches school.

I am sweating at three jobs
To keep this family fed;
Since keeping up with necessities
Won't let me get ahead.

Eleanor Garrod

For many years, "To have and to hold, for richer or poorer" has been a part of the vows that we take during a marriage ceremony. The new vows are "To have and to hold onto, for richer and in wealth". We don't do poorer. The housing boom of the early 2000's gave us a false sense of wealth. Home prices rising disproportionately to income made many of us "instant millionaires" or "thousandaires", as the case may be. The continuous spending from this new-found wealth (*the House of ATM*) created a *Saks Fifth Avenue* of luxury living for many. Designer jeans, famous name handbags, exotic vacations, fine dining and gas guzzling vehicles became the norm for average income people. It started with purchasing homes that stretched the budget, to "keeping up with the Joneses" or today "keeping up with the Kardashians", an age old problem. Driven to infectious proportions, because everyone was and is doing it, made each of us competitors in having the latest and greatest. The peer pressure of being "up and coming" has strained many to fear becoming the "down and out". You don't have to drive a *BMW* to be a big wheel, nor wear a *Rolex* to know the time. Do we know that self-worth is not determined by net-worth?

Greed is defined by the Merriam-Webster Dictionary as "a selfish and excessive desire for more of something than is needed." Greed is insidious and insatiable and causes us to redefine our value system. Our yearning for more can lead us to bending the rules or to abandoning them altogether. Our kids think "values" are something on sale. We seem to have forgotten some of the old adages like: "A penny saved is a penny earned", "Take care of the pennies and the dollars will take care of themselves", or "Put something away for a rainy day". We don't have to save – we have credit. The flow of easy money has made everything so accessible to us. Buy today – pay tomorrow. Well, tomorrow has finally arrived with a vengeance and it is time to pay up!

Many of our parents (well, in some cases, grandparents) used to purchase their homes with cash or financed it over a very short period of time. They lived in this home, raised their kids there, and then retired in it. After death, it was often passed on to one of their heirs, because they *owned* it. Our current generation is more likely to want to move up in house every five or so years as the call to "bigger and better" comes.

We all heard the many radio and TV commercials encouraging us to purchase houses or refinance our homes and buy more "stuff": Bad Credit, <u>no problem</u>. One day out of bankruptcy, <u>no problem</u>. Can't prove you make enough income, <u>no problem</u>. No cash reserves, <u>no problem</u>. No money for a down payment, <u>no problem</u>. We'll finance 100%. No paperwork needed...............

Guess What? The "<u>No Problem</u>" has become a "<u>Big Problem</u>"!

<u>How Big?</u>

Historians can't quite agree on the one major cause of the Great Depression but the following are generally accepted as to the probable causes:
1. The stock market crashed
2. Bank failures
3. Massive unemployment, reaching 25%

4. Damaging legislation by Congress that served to lengthen the time for recovery (Smoot-Hawley Tariff)
5. Drought conditions leading to poverty

The "Roaring Twenties" came to a screeching halt with the sudden crash of the stock market in 1929. It ushered in a ten year period of poverty not seen since. Bread lines had to be established so poor people could get food and not starve to death. There was no question as to what was a *necessity*. People were willing to work at anything that would provide an honest day's wage.

Everyone didn't become poor on October 29th, 1929, the day we now know as Black Tuesday. No one knew on that fateful day that they were in a *depression*. The term recession and depression are used when looking back at the economic numbers for the past several months or years. Although economists differ in their definitions, a recession is generally defined by two or more quarters of negative growth as evidenced by GDP (Gross Domestic Product) numbers. A depression is a recession gone bad. There is a progression of events that transpire to create a recession or depression. First, people stop spending. Whether from fear or necessity, if people don't buy things then companies must downsize or go out of business. This leads to unemployment. More people stop spending and more companies lay off workers fueling a vicious cycle that leads to greater economic decay. We are currently in a recession since our financial hardships have lasted long enough for this to be defined. Are we facing a depression? Going back to the historically defined causes of the Great Depression, are there any similarities?

1. Stock market crash – yes
2. Bank failures – yes
3. Massive unemployment - yes
4. Damaging legislation – oh yes
5. Drought – no, Thank God

We are currently experiencing four of the five causes of the Great Depression with only the severity yet to be addressed. Are we done yet or is there more to come?

What was the Cause of the Cause of the Great Depression?

The 1920's, when things were truly roaring, was a time of unbelievable prosperity. Most of the wealth came from the stock market explosion. Many people became investors in this fast-moving treasure hunt and found ways to speed up the riches by buying stocks on margin. Using borrowed money, investors were able to acquire more shares than their finances should have allowed. These credit-driven purchases were empowered by banks willing to loan using securities (stocks) as collateral. No one in those days thought the market would ever go down. The frenzy of stock buying continued until the market suddenly crashed. No ability to repay the loans caused the banks to fail. Companies, whose value diminished overnight, started to lay off workers and the whole cycle began. Congress, in an attempt to fix the problem, only made things worse with faulty legislation. Sound familiar?

In 1929 the stock market crashed – in 2007 the housing market crashed. Both were economic firestorms fueled by massive spending from free-flowing credit. But what was the underlying cause? Did greed play a role in the financial collapse of America, then and now? How many shortcuts were taken to accumulate massive profits at the expense of future economic stability? Did corruption play a role? Will we ever learn?

The yuppie generation of baby boomers has erroneously judged success by what they possess. Our major corporations and our country are primarily being run by baby boomers, a group in which I find myself. Former President George W. Bush is a baby boomer, most of our legislators are baby boomers, and President Barack Obama and his wife Michelle are later-born boomers, making them Generation Jones boomers. The boomers are the movers and shakers in this country. In fact, the last movement that we felt would have hit an "8" on the Richter scale as we saw century-old institutions come crashing down. But what was behind the "crash"? As we sit here "Stunned in America", we are looking for answers. Who did it? How did it happen? Who is to blame? How do we fix it? These are the questions that will be addressed in this book. As you read through the next chapters, you may want to have your anti-anxiety medication handy, as the facts behind this economic crisis will anger you. And it should.

If greed is the root cause of our current economic decline, did it originate with us or did it trickle down like molten lava being spewed from an erupting volcano? Our generation X and Y 'ers' are just now coming into their own and will soon be replacing the old baby boomers, who are leaving us a legacy that we won't soon forget. I only pray that we are NOT entering the next *Great Depression*. Let us hope that the *Now* Generation will be replaced by the *Future* Generation who will seek to better their world for the children.

It is for the benefit of the little Z's that I write this book.

<u>**Living on Easy Street**</u>

The Ogle family got a raise, and decided it was time
To move into the suburbs where life was more sublime,
They bought a large five bedroom house on classy Easy street
Believing that the mortgage loan was not too large to meet.

As they drove into the driveway in their little yellow Volks,
Jack said, "A nicer car we need, as we're advancing folks,
And just look at all the neighbors' yards, manicured with care,
I want our home to be the best, the money we'll not spare."

So the Ogle's crew got busy with changes not a few,
Rock garden, bushes, palm trees, a couple grand now due.
"Repainting and repapering will add a finished touch,
And I am sure when it is done, it will not cost that much."

"Why not do the whole house? It'll be cheaper in the end."
So they signed the Ogle name for the extra they must spend.
Thirty easy payments won't be hard to meet,
Anyway, it's worth it - living on this street.

With Susie's music lessons, and Johnny's baseball game,
"We really need a second car, " Mrs. Ogle claimed.
Mothers in this neighborhood all car-pool kids to school,
Each one takes a turn a week, according to the rule.

It doesn't need to be brand new; an older car will do,
Large enough to transport all the kids to private school.
It'll help with all the church work I do in my spare time
Since I'm not working anymore in all that city grime.

A pool would also be so nice, to help enjoy the sun
Increasing our house value and give the kids some fun.
It may relieve the tension and pressures that we face
Since you have to work so hard in keeping up this pace.

Patio furniture, don't forget, will make our pool a splash;
Let's put it on our Mastercard – that's just as good as cash.
Eighteen easy payments won't be hard to meet,
And anyway, it's worth it – living on this street.

One day the Ogles noticed the plumbing not too strong;
First one thing and then the next, things started to go wrong.
Toilets ran, faucets leaked, and bathtubs would not drain,
It wasn't very long until the Ogles felt the strain.

Could we take another loan, to fix this awful mess?
We've borrowed to the limit, would be my dreaded guess.
18% compounded, I was told by the lending man
Would lesson all our burdens on a consolidation plan.

"Your credit seems to indicate a late payment now and then,
And Continental Bank reports you've bounced some checks again.
Statistics indicate that with customers like you
We must increase the interest rate to over 22."

What Ogles didn't allow for, an emergency or more
So they were unprepared when a knock came at their door.
That Saturday afternoon, they both were so alarmed
When Little League brought Johnny home with a broken arm.

Then Susie had an accident, upon the gymnast bar
Which cracked her two front teeth, pushing them out too far.
Doctor bills began to mount, with dentist ones still climbing,
Two-thousand dollar braces, oh, what awful timing.

With payments due, and some behind, they began to really fuss;
What in the world is happening, dear, to the both of us?
The nights began to drag along; when morning sun shone through,
It did not shed a ray of light, on the problems of these two.

The lights are being turned off the morning after next,
They haven't had a phone for days, leaving them perplexed.
The house is in foreclosure now, oh, what an awful mess,
To think that it would end like this would not have been their guess.

The cars in repossession, back to the bank must go
All credit cards and doctor bills in collection, also.
The creditors, all one by one, have taken back their wares,
Leaving Ogles all alone, exchanging angry stares.

Looking back, in deepest thought, to where they had gone wrong,
Was it because of foolish whims and egos ultra-strong?
Pay raise that should have brought them joy, ended up in waste
And now with bankruptcy ahead, the Ogles feel disgraced.

Easy street is not a place where average people live
And payment plans called "easy" can only trouble give.
The Ogle family learned a lesson through very trying days,
That dealing on 'cash only' basis is what really pays.

Written in 1983 by:
Eleanor Garrod & Mary Tootikian
Some things never change

2

Housing Boom and Bust

History of our Current Housing Crisis

The failure of over 700 lending institutions cost the Federal government and in turn, we the taxpayers, approximately $124 billion dollars. This loss has been attributed to unsound, high risk, real estate lending practices and the failure of regulators to take notice. It was laden with fraud, insider transactions, and opportunistic executives who profited greatly at the expense of the general public. Wall Street investment firms found ways to profit from this fiasco as they purchased real estate secured loans for a fraction of their worth, repackaged and then sold them for significant profits. I am *NOT* referring to our current credit crisis, but to the Savings and Loan Crisis of the 1980's and 1990's. **If we do not learn from our mistakes, we are destined to repeat them.** We have all seen the classic movie, "It's a Wonderful Life". Who will rise up, like good old George Bailey and preserve the lending institutions against the greedy Mr. Potters of this world?

Property prices, greatly suppressed from this lending debacle of the Savings and Loans, didn't start improving until the late 1990's and as most upward movements go, it was fast and dramatic. The market for single family homes became a feeding frenzy, as the insatiable desire for bigger and better got the best of us. New homes emerged faster than there was land to build on. Where once open spaces graced us with beautiful trees and singing birds, we found clear cut parcels of land, waiting for future homes to occupy them. The building rush of the early 2000's is unprecedented in any recorded history.

Builders were anxious to get back into the game, and they started building with fervor. Flags and dancing signs marked the entrance to the grand openings of the newest home developments. The appetite of the American consumer was for larger homes with more amenities, and so came the mega-mansions. Even young couples buying their first starter home wanted four or five bedroom houses with bathrooms to match. Smaller homes, built in earlier days, were also in more demand, as less of them were available. The most modest of homes became unaffordable for many. Even former apartment buildings evolved into condominiums as the renting public sought to become homeowners.

It is customary for builders to build homes in phases, a few at a time, so they can have guaranteed sales of those homes before moving on to the next phase. A development might consist of thirty custom built homes or 300 pre-designed homes with four or five models. Checking out the newest model homes became the weekend pastime for many, as these homes were decked out in the finest of designer touches, posh furniture, and upgrades galore. A trip through these professionally decorated homes served to entice our imaginations to see what this house of sticks could really become, with a little imagination and a whole lot of money. If we couldn't afford to purchase a new home, then we certainly could refinance our existing home, taking out sufficient cash to remodel, and make our home look like these "star-quality" dwellings. After all, this building bonanza was driving up the value of real estate to new heights, making all of us homeowners wealthier.

Developers, early in the designing stage, would often create waiting lists so potential buyers could be assured of a call when the first homes began selling. As opening sales would start, people rushed to secure a home, months before they would actually be built. Builders, assured of guaranteed sales, started additional developments as the appetite for more homes could not be satisfied. The demand became so great that many people ended up on multiple waiting lists, hoping for cancellations. It became apparent, after a while, that homes built in the early phase of a development gained in value even before that house was built. Savvy buyers knew that if they were lucky enough to get in on the first phase, they were going to profit. Many people began signing their name to the dotted line before even putting their current home on the market. No problem there; you could sell a home over a good weekend with housing prices on the rise and no end in sight.

Soon, many people became speculators and started securing spots on these ever growing waiting lists, knowing they could sell the house for a profit without ever taking possession of the property. Every new development seemed to face this speculator-driven rush to get on the lists to the point where builders were insisting that any person buying a house be the occupant of the house. Most developers even required that you sign an affidavit (unenforceable) that you would live in the house for at least one year before potentially using it as a rental or selling it for a profit.

Speculators, fueling the already hot real estate market, made it even more difficult for the true home buyer to get on the lists, while homes were still reasonably priced. People became afraid that they would lose out on home ownership as prices for properties were escalating at an insane rate. If you weren't first in line when a property went on the market, chances are you were out of luck. Prices were going through the stratosphere. Average wage earners were quickly being priced out of the already overheated market.

Lenders rose to the occasion with a vast assortment of loans. As home prices soared, it was necessary to have loans that had lower monthly payments for the consumers. Interest-only loans became very popular as they lessened the minimum monthly payment and therefore allowed the buyer to purchase even more home than they normally would be able to afford. Loans that had teaser payments for the first few years of the loan also became extremely popular. These loans offered minimum monthly payments that were even less than the interest due on the loan (negatively amortizing loans). It was assumed that home prices would continue to rise and you would gain on the appreciation of the home, even if you were adding unpaid interest to your principal balance.

Wall Street investment firms, like the former Bear Stearns and Lehman Brothers, had been the investment source of jumbo and specialized loans for many years. They too, got into the action in a big way, introducing very risky loans for a premium price, to people who might otherwise be turned down for conventional financing. These risky subprime loans allowed everyone to venture into the home buying market. With no down-payment needed, they offered loans to even the least credit-worthy people. As time went on and the prices of homes continued to rise, the underwriting criteria for these subprime loans became less and less. In the end, everyone could get a loan for any amount that they desired. After all, you could always sell the house for a profit, and quickly at that.

Low interest rates also helped fuel this very hot real estate market. Rates that had at one time been in the double digits were now the lowest in our lifetimes. As the rates would fall, and home values increased, homeowners could refinance in order to drop their payments or take out some cash. The refinance craze of the early 2000's was unbelievable. Individuals who purchased homes with zero down-payment could refinance and take cash out of their homes as the inflated values of their property earned them an instant profit. It was not uncommon for people to refinance multiple times as the interest rates continued to hit new lows. Houses became an instant source of cash, like the ATM machines, as people started utilizing their equity for all of the things that they deemed "necessary".

Many people used their primary residences' equity to put down payments on investment properties and became real estate moguls.

The housing industry itself became the new *golden goose* as everyone seemed to want to profit from this "get rich quick" business. There were realtors on every corner, each competing for the new listings. These new ambitious agents would even go door to door trying to persuade us to sell and list with them. Every night at dinner time the phone would ring with telemarketers begging you to refinance. Mortgage companies were springing up overnight hiring anyone willing to learn how to peddle loans. There were people in the industry who were part timers, moonlighting on their regular jobs, so they too could be part of the craze. I was in a Red Lobster restaurant waiting for my daughter to join me for lunch. The waiter walked up, and during "small talk" advised me that he was a loan officer. I was buying groceries at a local organic market and the checker did mortgage loans on the side. I went to my son's birthday party, only to discover that over half the room was filled with loan officers, all knowing so much more than I, who had made this business my life's occupation. Everyone was in the business and making money hand over fist. If you weren't driving a BMW, a Mercedes, or a Range Rover, there was something wrong.

It was certainly the time of plenty as everyone was employed and spending like there was no tomorrow. We all felt rich as our home equity grew faster than the cash we were taking out of it. What a wonderful gravy train! The economy was fantastic and there was no foreseeable end to the upward movement of home prices in sight.

UNTIL . . . .

Little by little, the fervor settled and homes that were once selling before the sign even hit the front lawn were now staying on the market longer. The fanatic building of new homes had finally caught up with the demand and there was a surplus. Oops! Builders, who at one time had waiting lists full of buyers, now faced a dilemma. Houses were not selling over the weekends any more. Many of their future homeowners still had their current residences to sell before they could finalize the purchase of the new home. Lenders, unaware that the market was cooling, provided the solution with 100% financing, so these buyers of new homes just went ahead with their purchases, with zero down payment, while waiting for their former residences to sell. This scenario became somewhat common and soon many average income people became the owner of two homes.

The speculators, who had no intention of taking possession of that newly built house in the first place, also caused problems for the builders. As fewer buyers were available, and prices began to drop, they couldn't resell the newly built homes fast enough. They began walking away from their earnest money deposits and letting the property go back on the market. Now, builders with houses completely built, needed to find buyers quickly. The best way to sell a home quickly is to add a lot of incentives to the deal or just drop the price. As more cancellations occurred, there was more surplus and prices dropped further. So many homes - so few buyers.

A new problem was beginning to raise its ugly head. With property prices dropping, people were unable to either sell quickly or refinance when the need arose. The individuals who had financed with the subprime mortgages in the past two years needed an answer quickly. All subprime mortgage loans were written as 2/28's or 3/27's. That meant that for the first two or three years of the loan, the payment was fixed at an affordable interest rate. At the adjustment period that would follow, the remaining 27 or 28 years would be fully adjustable at an interest rate significantly higher. To make matters worse, all of these subprime loans carried a stiff prepayment penalty during the fixed portion of the loan. That meant that a very narrow window existed where you needed to get out of that loan after the prepayment penalty went away, and before the monthly payments rose to unaffordable heights. Imagine to your horror that the time period in which you need to refinance your home coincides with a drop in market prices. Since you possibly purchased the home with 100% financing, you now have a negative equity position. Negative equity doesn't do so well in the selling market either. One of the common characteristics of the borrowers in the subprime market was that they had a poor credit history. Maybe they just had a history of poor decision making. However, in a situation where you cannot refinance your loan, cannot sell your home for what you owe, cannot afford the newly adjusted payments, what do you do? You walk away, and why not, you had nothing invested . . . . and the surplus of housing inventory continued to grow.

Builders, who made huge profits during the peak years, continued to lower prices in order to secure more buyers for their houses already built. This lowered the prices of the existing neighboring properties as well. Since many of their committed buyers couldn't sell their current homes, more cancellations ensued. More lower prices, more falling values, and even more cancellations. As builders started to wholesale out their remaining inventory, they lowered the market prices for all homes in their areas. Now, the regular owners of properties had to compete with the builders for the sales of their existing homes and were forced to drop their prices even further. The cycle continued.

Supply and demand has always set the pricing criteria. More demand, higher prices - more supply, lesser prices. As more homes than buyers were available, it was an economic fact that prices would drop until the supply had corrected itself. Under normal economic conditions, this would not necessarily be a disaster.

HOWEVER . . . .

Wall Street's creative subprime mortgages were an enigma that no one seemed to anticipate (the greatest mystery of all since I had figured it out a few years earlier). **Mortgages that only have affordable payments for two or three years do not give the consumer time to wait out a correction in pricing.** Not being able to sell or refinance is a recipe for disaster. Buyers were unaware that the strings pulled by the builders and bankers to move them into that new house with no down payment would later become the noose around their necks.

The American dream has now become a frightening nightmare that we find ourselves desperately trying to wake up from.

3

<u>Nightmare on Every Street</u>

<u>State of Foreclosure – Housing Crash</u>

The nightmare on Elm, Oak, Main and every other street in the city is marked by "Foreclosure Sale" signs that scream to us of the financial disaster we are facing. Many wish they could just wake up from this bad dream. The media is having a field day as everywhere you turn the dial or page some reporter or commentator is talking or writing about the state of our current housing crisis. The media tends to prey on the misfortunes of people to sensationalize their tales. As you listen to them recount story after story, you assume that they are telling the whole truth. After all, it's on TV or it's in print. It is unfortunate that, for many of us, this is the only source of our education on current events. We falsely assume that we can become authorities on various subjects since we have watched the extended coverage on television. It certainly gives us a lot to talk about around the water coolers at work.

My mother-in-law, along with thousands of other naive individuals have faithfully purchased the national tattlers every week so they can be kept up to date on the most current information. We would like to assume that reporters do enough research to tell us the cold hard facts. Maybe it is a good thing for them that they are not under oath. Facts don't sell stories, or advertising. It would seem that reporters care more about how their hair looks on camera than the plight of the lives that they are telling us about. As we sit and listen to the devastating accounts of how these poor, innocent people in foreclosure got "taken" by their cunning loan officer and deceptive mortgage broker, we empathize with them. How could all of this destruction of peoples' lives be happening? Are we so gullible that we can be that easily taken advantage of? Did we play a role in this dilemma ourselves? Or, do we really know who the true villains are?

A San Diego woman chained herself to her home in order to gain media coverage of her predicament in losing her home of 20 years to the foreclosure monster. What was briefly glossed over by the media, as they clamored for someone to stop these mammoth home eating banks, was that she had refinanced three times in the past five years and drew out so much cash that she now owed more on her home than it was worth. She had also stopped making her mortgage payments. DUH! Do we want the banks to let us live for free in the homes that we technically sold to them? Didn't they pay us in cash?

Here are the facts:

As of July 2008, 1 in every 171 households in the United States of America received a foreclosure filing during the 2nd quarter of that year. WOW, how scary is that! There were a total of 739,714 foreclosures filed during this one 3-month period alone. It was the eighth straight quarter that we had seen an increase in filings. In California, where I live, there were 202,599 filings in this same quarter, representing 1 in every 65 households. That number looks even worse when you look at individual cities' statistics. This information is reported each quarter by RealtyTrac, Inc. an online resource for the listing of foreclosure properties. I am using somewhat dated statistics as ever since that quarter there have been ongoing moratoriums placed from time to time on the foreclosure filings based on federal and state mandates. The actual number of foreclosure filings currently may be higher than those being reported due to these freezes that have been imposed.

The initial wave of foreclosure filings started to rise in 2006. Most of these early filings came on the heels of the cooling of the previously hot real estate market. Many of the early foreclosures were clearly the people who could not afford to buy their homes in the first place. As property prices started to drop, those individuals who purchased their homes with "creative financing" or 100% financing found themselves immediately upside down. This meant that their homes were no longer worth as much as they owed on them.

As a side note, there is a category of loans in foreclosure that were purely fraudulent from the start, with use of straw buyers (buyers who were paid to lend their name to the transaction but in reality were not the real buyer), etc. Default usually happens from the very first payment and these loans have certainly added numbers to the foreclosure statistics.

Also included in this early phase of foreclosures are homes that were mortgaged with reset interest rate loans. These are adjustable loans that have an initial fixed interest rate that later adjusts to a potentially higher rate. All subprime loans had this provision, with either two or three years of initial low rates followed by a reset that sent payments significantly higher. Other mortgages, including interest-only loans and negatively amortizing loans also have this reset provision, once the initial fixed period ends. No equity, no motivation and no reason to even try to hang on.

As more properties went on the market in a time of descending home prices, fewer sales happened. First of all, there was a surplus of homes and secondly, smart buyers wanted to wait for a bottom. Resale homes have been trying to compete for the past two years with builder inventories, all to no avail. Builders have been quick to wholesale out their remaining homes so they can tuck tail and run. Individuals, in trouble and needing to sell their homes quickly, have had to drop prices further and further in an effort to avoid foreclosure. Each month in a down market brings a lesser price than the month before, an inverse of what was happening in the hot market preceding it.

Real estate investors are traditionally those individuals or companies who acquire houses as long-term investments. They normally have deep enough pockets to wait out a market correction and make their money in the rental arena. During the housing boom era, too many individuals who didn't have the capital or knowledge invested in real estate holdings other than their primary residence. In fact, "flipping homes" became quite popular and there were even a few television shows devoted to this topic. Flippers were people who bought a home cheaper than the market price because it needed some work, did the remodel or repairs, then turned around and resold the property for a higher price. These people were making quick profits during the rising market. With any investment, however, timing is everything, and if you don't sell at a high, you must wait out the lows. Some of the real estate investors of the 2000's didn't have the capital to hold on to their real estate holdings. Many of these investor properties also became a part of the foreclosure statistics.

The snowball effect of lowering home prices has taken with it all of those people who were in their homes by the skin of their teeth, those with adjustable rate mortgage loans where the interest rate escalated their payments to heights they couldn't afford, and those investors who were struggling to keep up with more than one property worth of payments. As the snowball of lowering property values continues to grow, it picks up more momentum in its downward fall.

Casualties of this foreclosure nightmare are not only the individuals who are losing their homes, but the banking institutions who granted the mortgage loans. According to ML.impode.com, as of September 2008, there had been 286 major lender implosions since late 2006. This is a website that was tracking the fate of lenders since foreclosures started their ascent. It is estimated that we may see another 200-300 such implosions before this crisis is truly over. Despite what homeowners may think, banks do not want your properties back. They are not in the business of owning real estate and must sell foreclosure properties, often for pennies on the dollar.

As mortgage lenders closed up shop and went out of business, the loans they once offered also disappeared. In August of 2007, I went to my office only to discover that there were no more jumbo mortgages. These are the mortgage loans that were over the lending limits of Fannie Mae and Freddie Mac. Overnight, they were gone. If you had a HELOC (Home Equity Line Of Credit) loan on your property, chances are it has been frozen by your lender. These are the 2nd trust deed lines of credit that people use for emergencies. Lenders have stopped granting them and are also closing the ones currently in place, as fear has gripped the industry. Gone too, are any sources of hard money loans, such as the subprime loans of the previous few years. Fannie Mae and Freddie Mac, the primary purchasers of home mortgages have also fallen on hard times. These once publically traded companies are now under conservatorship of the United States government, or you and I the taxpayers, as they face multiple billions of dollars in mortgage related losses.

Mortgage loans are no longer the "darling of Wall Street", as they are now viewed as the riskiest of all investments. Wall Street, before its recent implosion, had moved on to new investment vehicles, leaving the rest of us to deal with the devastation of their subprime loans. They made their fortune in the subprime lending markets and then, profits in hand, started playing the oil markets. As if we weren't in enough trouble already, they profited as the ever increasing gas prices drove us closer to the edge. Must we also face higher costs of just about everything, since the elevated price of oil has made products and services more expensive? Shipping costs, transportation costs, food, heating costs, etc. have caused us to face potential inflation fears. As inflation fears rise, so too do the chances of interest rates being raised by the Federal Reserve Board in order to keep things under control. Higher interest rates mean even less affordable mortgage payments, and more foreclosures. Vicious cycle isn't it? ......and the snowball continues to grow.

To review where we stand right now in the overall scheme of things: the economy is shaky, inflation fears loom over us, banks are failing, Wall Street is collapsing, the cost of basic services and food is way up, home prices are down, few homes are selling unless they are bargain priced, foreclosures continue to rise and we can't find a loan to save our financial lives. This is truly a nightmare scenario.

If we do not solve our current credit crisis soon, there will be more casualties. Unemployment rates are beginning to rise to levels not seen in many years. Remember, millions of people earned their living through some aspect of the housing industry. How many of these people are surviving and how many of them are now being included in the latest foreclosure data?

How can realtors survive when no homes are selling? The National Association of Realtors boasts of 1.3 million members. With almost 300 major lending institutions imploding and thousands more of smaller operations gone, where are their staff? Who is paying all of the loan officers, processors, underwriters, clerical staff and all the others? What has happened to appraisers, escrow officers, title representatives and that whole part of the lending industry? Who is paying their salaries? Where are all of the people involved in building the houses? Who is paying the roofers, tilers, painters, drywallers and the likes? Their homes are in jeopardy too. At one point it was said that 75% of the people in Orange County, California were employed in some capacity in the housing market. California also housed most of the nation's mortgage lenders. Why do you think California has one of the highest foreclosure rates in the nation? I'm sure now that Wall Street is suffering from the consequences of their irresponsibility, maybe New York will see more foreclosures also.

Who is subsidizing the gardeners, housekeepers, interior designers, appliance salespeople, window covering people, and the list goes on and on. With many thousands of people employed in some capacity tied to the housing industry, how long until all of us stop spending entirely? No Starbucks, no new cars, no Coach purses, not even a Wal-Mart visit. Which industry is thriving so much that it can afford to absorb all of us into it and pay our salaries?

Many of us in the housing industry are surviving by using our savings and our credit cards. This gives all of us a limited shelf life. How long until we expire and add to the current thousands of foreclosure filings? …….and the snowball definitely grows.

The initial foreclosures may have involved people who deserved to lose their homes. That is a judgment call that can only be made looking at individual cases. However, many of the people in foreclosure now could afford their homes when they purchased them. What of them? In my job, I see many of these casualties. Countless of my associates have lost most, if not all of their income and can't see a way out if this credit crisis doesn't pass soon. They certainly don't have the ability to hang on much longer. Answers have been slow in coming and credit has tightened to the point where only the people who don't need the financing, can get it. This snowball is growing and taking on more momentum every day. It won't be long until it affects more and more lives.

Are you in the path as this snowball grows into an avalanche that is threatening to bury the United States of America?

The following charts are reprinted with the permission of RealtyTrac, Inc.

Terms Defined for US Foreclosure Data Charts

NOD: Notice of Default

LIS: Lis Pendens

NTS: Notice of Trustee Sale

NFS: Notice of Foreclosure Sale

REO: Real Estate Owned by banks

Legal processes and terms vary by individual states. Some states file a Notice of Default whereas other states use a Lis Pendens (lawsuit pending) document. Both indicate that the homeowner has been notified that they are in default of their mortgage note.

Some states file a Notice of Trustee Sale and others file a Notice of Foreclosure Sale. This is notice of a public auction.

REO is Real Estate owned by the bank after the process of foreclosure has been completed.

U.S. Foreclosure Market Data by State – Q2 2008

				Properties with Foreclosure Filings						
Rate Ran k	State Name	NOD	LIS	NTS	NFS	REO	Total	1/every X HH (rate)	%Change from Q1 08	%Change from Q2 07
--	United States	161,162	157,094	139,955	59,112	222,391	739,714	171	13.82	121.36
43	Alabama	3	0	680	0	1,146	1,829	1,154	7.59	-0.76
32	Alaska	1	0	445	0	60	506	547	5.20	75.69
3	Arizona	18	0	25,431	0	11,781	37,230	70	35.86	272.26
25	Arkansas	168	0	2,488	0	818	3,474	367	-7.41	226.50
2	California	119,836	0	19,968	0	62,795	202,599	65	19.29	197.78
5	Colorado	22	0	10,331	0	5,881	16,234	129	-14.54	50.69
19	Connecticut	0	3,872	2	845	226	4,945	290	-35.21	7.95
36	Delaware	0	0	0	308	297	605	633	12.66	178.80*
	District of Columbia	226	0	728	0	221	1,175	241	7.90	3,163.89*
4	Florida	0	74,968	28	18,379	16,058	109,433	78	24.51	181.83
8	Georgia	107	0	17,522	0	10,124	27,753	140	-2.63	85.12
41	Hawaii	61	0	385	0	50	496	1,008	33.69	82.35
20	Idaho	1,142	0	693	0	251	2,086	295	15.25	148.63
10	Illinois	0	18,302	30	1,912	6,646	26,890	193	15.83	57.99
11	Indiana	0	4,048	29	5,021	4,792	13,890	198	-0.33	59.40
39	Iowa	1	0	751	0	630	1,382	955	-11.75	33.14
34	Kansas	0	273	5	735	948	1,961	616	40.47	131.25
42	Kentucky	0	415	8	814	597	1,834	1,030	15.93	0.60
40	Louisiana	0	3	2	1,432	455	1,892	967	-2.37	73.10
38	Maine	369	0	389	0	67	825	838	40.55	2,257.14
16	Maryland	0	6,881	17	1,357	1,197	9,452	243	-17.04	130.20
9	Mass.	0	6,734	22	4,345	5,072	16,173	168	-1.18	285.71*
7	Michigan	5,114	0	12,526	0	15,228	32,868	137	11.25	73.18
27	Minnesota	80	0	2,777	0	2,816	5,673	403	34.08*	119.71*

22

#	State									
46	Mississippi	0	0	366	0	313	679	1,828	48.25*	81.33*
18	Missouri	3,289	0	1,932	0	4,455	9,676	271	9.42	85.36
44	Montana	7	0	299	0	30	336	1,286	-20.19	13.90
33	Nebraska	0	68	6	973	227	1,274	608	71.70	86.80
1	Nevada	13,831	0	2,110	0	8,716	24,657	43	25.83	146.77
22	New Hampshire	0	0	952	0	786	1,738	339	-2.80	1,748.94*
12	New Jersey	0	11,725	8	3,694	1,862	17,289	201	31.94	140.33
37	New Mexico	0	877	0	73	200	1,150	739	-2.71	59.94
30	New York	0	11,101	7	2,292	2,625	16,025	493	11.46	61.66
26	North Carolina	6,521	0	444	0	3,546	10,511	383	2.22	57.97
49	North Dakota	0	0	0	1	50	51	6,035	2.00	-25.00
6	Ohio	0	11,716	78	10,131	15,764	37,689	134	20.60	26.93
29	Oklahoma	1,182	0	1,434	0	1,270	3,886	414	19.98	72.10
23	Oregon	2,504	0	1,645	0	460	4,609	344	9.69	118.44
31	Pennsylvania	0	3,199	7	4,653	2,548	10,407	524	76.36*	62.76*
17	Rhode Island	0	0	1,150	0	510	1,660	271	5.00	444.26*
35	South Carolina	0	305	11	397	2,466	3,179	621	63.95*	211.97*
47	South Dakota	0	0	1	80	12	93	3,794	45.31	1,450.00*
13	Tennessee	2,935	0	4,189	0	4,884	12,008	223	-3.08	105.19
21	Texas	308	0	14,781	0	14,020	29,109	317	-13.61	40.47
14	Utah	516	0	2,744	0	721	3,981	226	21.04	113.23
50	Vermont	0	0	7	0	30	37	8,366	1,133.33*	236.36*
15	Virginia	2,882	0	6,483	0	4,811	14,176	228	7.79	278.43
24	Washington	39	0	5,805	0	1,876	7,720	350	16.30	87.11
48	West Virginia	0	0	136	0	59	195	4,501	36.36	22.64
28	Wisconsin	0	2,607	17	1,670	1,921	6,215	408	9.57	157.88
45	Wyoming	0	0	86	0	73	159	1,504	-3.05	87.06*

*Actual increase may not be as high due to data collection changes or improvements

23

Top 100 U.S. Metro Foreclosure Market Data – Q2 2008

Rate Rank	State	Metro Name	Props with Filings	1/every X HH (rate)	%Change from Q1 08	%Change from Q2 07
-- _		U.S. Total	739,714	171	13.82	121.36
1	CA	STOCKTON	9066	25	19.92	170.63
2	CA	RIVERSIDE/SAN BERNARDINO	43,600	32	17.08	193.42
3	NV	LAS VEGAS/PARADISE	21742	35	25.53	143.66
4	CA	BAKERSFIELD	6,431	41	25.78	294.78
5	CA	SACRAMENTO	15505	49	11.01	125.46
6	FL	FORT LAUDERDALE	15,558	51	42.39	215.26
7	AZ	PHOENIX/MESA	31613	51	36.65	306.81
8	CA	OAKLAND	15,904	60	25.56	237.31
9	CA	FRESNO	4806	62	26.08	178.13
10	FL	MIAMI	15,260	62	30.39	112.86
11	CA	SAN DIEGO	17343	65	13.24	206.52
12	MI	DETROIT/LIVONIA/DEARBORN	12,826	66	3.42	52.91
13	FL	ORLANDO	11809	72	12.23	247.94
14	FL	SARASOTA/BRADENTON/VENICE	4,690	82	9.1	163.34
15	CA	ORANGE	12439	82	29.69	276.71
16	CA	VENTURA	3,177	85	34.62	228.88
17	FL	TAMPA/ST PETERSBURGH/CLEARWATER	14960	87	26.66	158.51
18	FL	PALM BEACH	7,141	88	50.69	188.29
19	CA	LOS ANGELES/LONG BEACH	36955	91	14.85	168.24
20	GA	ATLANTA/SANDY SPRINGS/MARIETTA	22,484	91	-0.31	77.05
21	OH	TOLEDO	3253	92	73.31	121.44
22	OH	AKRON	3,283	93	58.68	24.4
23	CO	DENVER/AURORA	10829	95	-18.99	44.71
24	CA	SAN JOSE/SUNNYVALE/SANTA CLARA	6,437	97	35.66	343.32
25	TN-MS-AR	MEMPHIS	5141	105	3.75	95.33
26	OH	CLEVELAND/LORAIN/ELYRIA/MENTOR	8,735	108	-2.61	-3.69
27	DC-MD-VA-WV	WASHINGTON/ARLINGTON/ALEXANDRIA	15569	109	3.05	250.97*
28	MI	WARREN/FARMINGTON HILLS/TROY	9,312	113	17.22	100.26
29	OH	DAYTON	3304	115	21.47	18.68
30	IN	INDIANAPOLIS	6,058	122	-4.3	30.87
31	OH	COLUMBUS	6285	122	17.74	39.11
32	MA	ESSEX	2,418	122	1.77	365.90*
33	FL	JACKSONVILLE	4540	125	-0.37	73.35
34	IN	GARY	1,980	144	10.61	61.11
35	IL	CHICAGO	21488	144	22.08	58.3

36 MA	WORCESTER	2,156	146	-14.24	188.62*
37 AZ	TUCSON	2820	148	51.29	138.18
38 NJ	NEWARK	5,458	154	26.25	170.47
39 IL	LAKE/KENOSHA	1573	159	5.93	61.66
40 MA	BOSTON/QUINCY	4,719	159	-1.34	333.33*
41 OH-KY-IN	CINCINNATI	5601	161	15.6	16.49
42 NJ	CAMDEN	1,588	177	40.04	137.37
43 WA	TACOMA	1732	179	14.4	112.78
44 WI	MILWAUKEE/WAUKESHA/WST ALLIS	3,545	184	16.23	208.8
45 MO-KS	KANSAS CITY	4643	187	38.1	94.84
46 MO-IL	ST LOUIS	6,357	192	-4.05	76.73
47 MA	SPRINGFIELD	1449	195	-24.57	198.15*
48 MA	CAMBRIDGE/NEWTON/FRAMINGHAM	2,994	197	9.59	337.08*
49 TX	DALLAS	7638	202	-8.38	10.11
50 TX	FORT WORTH/ARLINGTON	3,785	203	-17.7	27.44
51 TX	HOUSTON/BAYTOWN/SUGARLAND	9827	214	-21.18	83.96
52 UT	SALT LAKE CITY	1,768	217	17.16	89.29
53 OK	TULSA	1772	222	41.65	69.57
54 MD	BETHESDA/FREDERICK/GAITHERSBURG	1,939	229	-9.69	167.45*
55 NC-SC	CHARLOTTE/GASTONIA	2923	232	-5.65	25.45
56 TN	NASHVILLE/DAVIDSON	2,626	238	0.69	126.18
57 CT	NEWHAVEN/MILFORD	1452	240	-36.81	-3.33
58 NY	POUGHKEEPSIE/NEWBURGH/MIDDLETOWN	1,015	241	210.40*	423.20*
59 MN-WI	MINNEAPOLIS/ST PAUL/BLOOMINGTON	5120	256	28.64	106.04
60 CA	SAN FRANCISCO	2,778	263	28.43	203.94
61 NC	RALEIGH/CARY	1515	270	8.45	64.5
62 AR	LITTLE ROCK/NORTH LITTLE ROCK	1,074	270	-16.42	167.16
63 RI	PROVIDENCE/NEW BEDFORD	1660	271	5	444.26*
64 CT	BRIDGEPORT/STAMFORD/NORWALK	1,283	272	-31.68	43.19
65 NJ	EDISON	3367	276	25.26	54.1
66 OK	OKLAHOMA CITY	1,826	282	5.86	75.58
67 OR-WA	PORTLAND/VANCOUVER/BEAVERTON	2961	295	10.57	132.05
68 TX	SAN ANTONIO	2,452	301	-5.66	39.08
69 NY	SUFFOLK/NASSAU	3298	304	-1.61	82.41
70 NC	GREENSBORO/HIGHPOINT	1,007	304	-4.73	75.44
71 NE-IA	OMAHA/COUNCIL BLUFFS	1075	322	113.29	97.97
72 PA	PHILADELPHIA	4,977	324	62.43	46.6
73 MD	BALTIMORE/TOWSON	3389	325	-19.65	105.64*
74 CT	HARTFORD	1,470	333	-35.67	-0.14
75 TN	KNOXVILLE	856	354	-17.77	108.78
76 NY	ALBANY/SCHENECTADY/TROY	1,062	356	74.67	276.6
77 SC	COLUMBIA	813	373	47.82*	354.19*

78 TX	AUSTIN/ROUND ROCK	1,611	381	-3.19	12.42
79 PA	PITTSBURGH	2880	383	73.29	87.74
80 NY	ROCHESTER	1,124	392	13.77	10.63
81 LA	NEW ORLEANS	1127	398	-1.31	83.85
82 NM	ALBUQUERQUE	857	405	-6.13	64.81
83 WA	SEATTLE/BELLEVUE/EVERETT	2616	411	25.89	69.1
84 NY-NJ	NEW YORK/WAYNE/WHITE PLAINS	10,189	432	16.61	66.19
85 VA	RICHMOND	1104	456	-6.6	804.92*
86 KS	WICHITA	548	466	56.13	122.76
87 DE-MD-NJ	WILMINGTON	576	483	-9.29	244.91
88 SC	GREENVILLE	536	492	40.68	587.18*
89 KY-IN	LOUISVILLE	1032	523	3.72	-21.22
90 VA-NC	NORFOLK/VIRGINIA BEACH/NEWPORT NEWS	1,081	551	-1.28	170.25*
91 TX	EL PASO	408	611	65.85	2.77
92 TX	MCALLEN/EDINBURG/PHARR	392	612	-25.62	276.92
93 SC	CHARLESTON	437	627	21.39	67.43*
94 PA	SCRANTON/WILKES/BARRE/HAZLETON	360	715	115.57	56.52
95 NY	BUFFALO/CHEEKTOWAGA/TONAWANDA**	680	765	0.44	77.55
96 LA	BATON ROUGE	400	780	13.96	132.56
97 AL	BIRMINGHAM/HOOVER	574	798	48.7	-43.39
98 NY	SYRACUSE	331	860	5.75	154.62
99 PA	ALLENTOWN/BETHLEHEM/EASTON	317	972	1168	10.84
100 HI	HONOLULU	250	1,331	61.29	63.4

*Actual increase may not be as high due to data collection changes or improvements
**Actual Total and Rate may be higher because of limited data coverage

4

The Golden Rule-Makers and Breakers

Who Are the Investors and What are the Rules?

We all know the *Golden Rule*, "Do unto others as you would have them do unto you." Fabulous words to live by. There is another rule of gold that dominates our world. "**He who has the gold makes the rules**."

Who Are the Rule Makers for the Mortgage Industry?

The rules that govern mortgage loans are set by the investors or buyers of these mortgage loans. At least, that is how it was.

- ✓ Fannie Mae- buys conforming loans (loans under $417,000)
- ✓ Freddie Mac- also buys conforming loans
- ✓ Ginnie Mae- buys FHA loans, insured by the US Government
- ✓ Banks, Savings & Loans, Credit Unions, Mortgage Banks – provide portfolio loans & sell conforming loans to Fannie Mae and Freddie Mac
- ✓ Wall Street Investment Firms – buy jumbo, niche and subprime loans
- ✓ US Government- (or various agencies) rule through legislation, and now govern Fannie, Freddie, FHA, and soon half of the banks and Wall Street

He who has the gold to loan sets the rules of getting that gold. Since they are now using our gold (taxpayer dollars) shouldn't we have a voice in the rule making?

Most of us do not know who really **owns** our mortgage loans. Lenders, in the form of either banks or mortgage companies, supply us with loans. Faithfully every month we send them our money, assuming that they hold the mortgage note to our property. Seldom is this true. Before the ink is even dried on the vast amount of papers we sign to encumber our homes, these loans are sold to investors. Loans are usually sold with servicing rights, given to the banks that originate the loans. This means that the entity that receives your money each month is being paid by the **owner** of the loan to collect on it for them. Banks generally own a very small percentage of the loans that they originate, those that we refer to as *portfolio* loans. We are now discovering that through the use of *collateralized debt obligations (CDO's)*, our loans are possibly owned by multiple entities including sovereign governments like China and Russia. No wonder we are in trouble!

Fannie Mae and Freddie Mac are by far the largest buyers of home mortgages. They currently have approximately 5 trillion dollars in loans that they guarantee. They are the buyers of what is known as conforming loans. Currently, the conforming loan limit is $417,000. This lending limit generally goes up incrementally as the need for higher lending limits is established annually. In order for loans to be sold to Fannie and Freddie, they must conform to the rules and guidelines set forth by these institutions. There are general rules that apply to all loans and then specific rules that apply to various programs. For example, they offer community programs to allow first-time homebuyers to get into the market. These unique loan products have requirements or rules that may differ from other loan programs.

FHA loans are purchased by Ginnie Mae and insured by the United States Government (you and I, the taxpayers) and they have different rules from that of Fannie and Freddie.

As mentioned, many lending institutions also offer portfolio loans. These are the loans that the bank chooses to keep and not to sell. Maybe they just swap them. Often, these are the loans that do not meet the lending criteria required by investors. For example, the negatively amortizing loans were once considered to be portfolio loans of the few institutions who granted them. The bank gets to set the rules that they want for these products.

Wall Street investment firms have long been suppliers of funding for loans that exceed the Fannie Mae and Freddie Mac lending limits. These loans are called jumbo loans and can go up into the millions of dollars. Jumbo loans are generally priced higher than that of their conforming counterparts. Loans that are outside of the requirements for sale to

Fannie and Freddie are often included in the "niche" loans offered by Wall Street. Most notable to this buyer of mortgage loans is the now infamous "subprime loans". Wall Street investment firms bought, packaged and then resold these loans to other investors who depended on the integrity of credible underwriting standards to ensure a solid investment portfolio. Some of these end buyers of mortgage loan products are our pension funds, or you and I the hopeful retirees.

Historically, or in the "olden golden days" before the S&L Crisis, housing lenders were generally community based banks, savings & loans and credit unions that had an interest in the community where they provided the loans. It might be interesting to note that many of the S&L failures happened after these companies decided to go outside of their native area to purchase speculative or risky loans in order to generate higher yields on their portfolios. Traditionally, mortgage loans have not been highly profitable, as the spreads that banks make on them have been relatively small. Mortgage lending was designed to be a service to the homeowners in the community and as such, affordability has been the primary concern. Spreads are the difference between what a bank pays for its money compared to what it loans it out for. Depositors (you and I) loan our money to banks, S&L's and credit unions and in return expect to borrow this money back, at a premium.

For many years, the rules of mortgage lending have been prudent and served us well.

What Were the Rules - Historically?

Traditionally, the rules or guidelines that governed mortgage lending were based on four underwriting criteria that determined the credit worthiness of any borrower seeking a mortgage loan. By analyzing **ALL** of these four areas, it could be decided as to how much a person was able to borrow and what the risk factors were.

1. **CREDIT HISTORY:** An analysis of a person's credit history can predict their desire to repay a loan by their overall previous debt repayment history. It also indicates how much debt a person is currently carrying and is used to indicate whether they can handle a new loan request.

2. **INCOME:** A person's income determines their ability to repay the loan that they have requested. It is wise that only a designated portion of a person's income should be allocated to their housing expense and to total debt repayment.

3. **RESERVES:** This is the amount of cash/ liquidity that a borrower has left after the transaction is completed. It shows the borrower's ability to survive a short-term income interruption. It also shows their ability to save and not spend to the full extent of their income.

4. EQUITY: The amount of money that a homeowner invests in a new home, or the amount of the existing home that is not encumbered by a mortgage loan is a major factor in determining credit worthiness and evaluating a person's motivation for repayment.

By reviewing all of the above lending criteria one can make an informed decision as to whether a person is "credit worthy" or not. It can also be determined if they are strong in one area, but weak in another. For example, a person may not have much in the way of income, but could have huge amounts of cash in the bank and be a good credit risk. Another person may have stumbled onto bad times with their credit history but have loads of equity in their property and also be viewed as a good risk. Not all factors have to be excellent to make a person worthy of a loan. A person may make significant income, but have a history of slow payments on their credit because they were too busy to pay their bills on time. Thus, the rules and guidelines of lending have always taken *all* of these factors into consideration when granting mortgage loans. These factors have also been used in pricing loans so that the higher risk loans generated a higher return to the investor.

So what went wrong ...... who changed the rules?

Who Are the Rule Breakers?

Institutions do not make rules. People make rules. People can change rules.

During the boom years of the housing market, the rules of lending began to relax as more *players* entered the market. People wanted larger loans to fulfill their need or lust for bigger homes. Builders wanted more buyers for their mega-mansions. Banks wanted their stock prices to soar as they played their roles in the housing bonanza. And let's not forget about Wall Street investment firms. They smelled profits and went after them with a vengeance. So the new rules of real estate lending began....... or should I ask: where did the rules go?

1. **CREDIT HISTORY:** – bankruptcy OK, slow pays OK – who cares?
2. **INCOME:** – no need to verify as stated income loans became the norm
3. **RESERVES:** – no need to verify with the no-documentation loans
4. **EQUITY:** – 100% loans – also OK – sometimes, no appraisal even needed

Subprime lenders sprung up overnight and became more aggressive than the traditional mortgage lenders. According to HUD, there were over 210 primary subprime lenders that reported on the Home Mortgage Disclosure Act (HMDA) forms during 2005. With no-documentation loans it was effortless to obtain financing. Some people, who would otherwise qualify through traditional paths, went with the subprime loans just because they could close the loan faster and with no headaches. Realtors, builders and loan agents pushed for quicker closings and pressured buyers into loans that were not in the buyer's best interest. As traditional lenders started losing out on this market share, many of them also entered the world of the subprime. It seemed that every bank had a subprime subsidiary company. Fannie and Freddie also relaxed their lending standards as the need for profits outweighed the need for caution. And certainly let us not forget the political pressure brought to bear by self-serving legislators whose mantra it was to make every American a homeowner.

Mortgage investors eventually set the bar so low that the only requirement to obtain a mortgage loan was that "you were breathing". This actual statement was issued by IndyMac Bank to their wholesale brokers in 2007 in an attempt to persuade brokers to send in every kind of imaginable loan possible. I know, because I received this notice personally. IndyMac was the 9th largest mortgage lender in the nation and one of the primary lenders involved in the subprime lending fiasco. In July of 2008 IndyMac was seized by the FDIC and its subsequent failure was one of the largest in US history. IndyMac Bank, a "spin-off" of its parent – Countrywide Financial (hmmm), was headed by the once golden boy Michael W. Perry. In a public letter from IndyMac in 2006, when Perry signed his new employment contract, he was promoted as having "the highest level of ethics" as they announced that his base salary would be $1,250,000 per year and proposed income for 2007 would be almost 9 million dollars. This was just prior to his company nose-diving into insolvency. Is anyone going after his millions to pay back the casualties of his bad decision making? Isn't he a rule breaker?

Who Are the Other Rule Breakers?

As stock prices soared for the many financial institutions of America, so too did the salaries of those running these companies. Just to list a few:

Angelo Mozilo was the Chairman of the Board of Countrywide Financial, the largest mortgage lender in the nation. Named as one of the "Ten Most Wanted Culprits" of the 2008 financial collapse by CNN, he is reported to have earned over 100 million dollars in

2007 as his company lost 1.6 billion. Countrywide was "sold" (sold, acquired, stabilized for stock holdings, whatever term was convenient for the time) to Bank of America in 2008 and Mr. Mozilo is now basking in the sun, increasing his leathery tan. As of April, 2009, the name of Countrywide has been retired. I guess Bank of America doesn't want to be tainted by the scandalous actions of their acquiree, although, according to CNNMoney. com, Kenneth Lewis, the CEO of Bank of America earned a total compensation of $28.8 million in 2007. Didn't Bank of America get TARP funds?

On March 7th of 2008, Mr. Mozilo, along with Charles Prince of Citigroup and E. Stanley O'Neal of Merrill Lynch (another Bank of America acquisition) were called before a congressional hearing in Washington to justify their excessive earnings in light of the massive losses that the industry was sustaining. According to the opening statement of Representative Henry Waxman:

"Mr. O'Neal left Merrill Lynch with a $161 million retirement package; Mr. Prince was awarded a $10 million bonus, $28 million in unvested stock options, and $1.5 million in annual perquisites when he left Citigroup; and Mr. Mozilo received over $120 million in compensation and sales of Countrywide stock."

I have witnessed many of these congressional hearings since this crisis has picked up steam, however, I never hear of anything coming of them. Are these just "sound bites" for the next round of elections? All three of these former CEO's have left a debris trail for their successors to clean up but none of their millions have been confiscated to pay back either homeowners or investors. Shouldn't they be paying back the US Government (you and I) for the tax dollars that we have dumped into their companies in order to make amends for their horrific decisions?

The CEO's of Fannie Mae and Freddie Mac have also fared well. According to ABC news, Daniel Mudd, CEO of Fannie Mae, earned a whopping $12.2 million in 2007 and Freddie Mac CEO Richard Syron earned nearly $19.8 million. What is wrong with this picture? As of September 8th 2008, both CEOs were relieved of their duties and the two lending giants, Fannie and Freddie, have been seized by the US government (you and I, the taxpayers). How do we, the stock holders of publically traded enterprises, including banks, Wall Street investment firms, Fannie, Freddie and all, allow these CEOs and their hand-picked executive staffs to garner such huge salaries? Do the compensation packages of these executives influence their decision making to short-term profits over prudent long-term strategies? So what if they get fired? Most of them have golden parachute clauses that make them richer – fired than hired????? T. Boone Pickens, a legendary executive in the oil industry has famously stated: "Far too many executives have become more concerned with the "four P's" – pay, perks, power and prestige – rather than making profits for shareholders."

The list of exorbitant executive compensation packages could go on and on, to show how the many Emperors of Wall Street prospered personally to the point of gluttony, during the lending boom. These fat compensation checks didn't stop the minute the profits dried up either. Did personal gain influence decision making to the point of a potential destruction of the American economy, the obliteration of century old institutions, and insolvency of its citizens? How much money does it take to look the other way while rules are abused and abandoned? How many lobbyists can you afford while billions roll your way? Seems like the Emperors were fiddling while Rome was burning!

Where is the gold now?

5

Who Stuck the Pin in the Bubble?

Who Caused this Credit Crisis?

The Wall Street gang of thugs and robbers have left us beaten, bruised and bleeding, clutching to the doorsteps of our homes. We don't want to leave. Their malicious romp on our sacred rights as homeowners have proven them incapable of restoring order to the chaos they have created. While they were rewriting the rules of mortgage lending, they forgot the first and foremost rule - "**Do No Harm**".

A crime spree has taken place and we, the American people are the victims. It's not just about people losing their homes, as if that isn't bad enough. It's about all of us, as Americans, who have seen our economy suffer, our home equity erode, and our incomes plummet or totally disappear. I personally know people that have broken lives resulting from the credit crisis that we are now experiencing. Retirement accounts or, what is left of them, are being tapped to fill in the void from lost income. Marriages have been destroyed by the stress. Teenagers are acting out in rebellion as they watch the stability of their home life collapse. Health issues are surfacing as the stress of trying to hold life and limb together pulls us apart. I dare say there have probably been suicides that can be attributable to this disaster. Is this 1929 revisited?

Subprime loans should be called "sub-crime" loans. These loans were flawed by design and destined to explode. An assortment of ticking time bombs was put into the hands of inexperienced homeowners and, right on time, their explosions could be heard around the world. Who designed these loans anyway? Where were the regulators?

Mr." know-it-all" Alan Greenspan, the top Fed dog, was on watch while this debacle unfolded. He acknowledged in a 60 Minutes interview that he "didn't really get it" that the subprime lending trend was significant enough to hurt the economy until very late in 2005. Sure he didn't! The Wall Street Journal reported in June of 2007:

"Edward Gramlich, who was Fed governor from 1997 to 2005, said he proposed to Mr. Greenspan in or around 2000, when predatory lending was a growing concern, that the Fed use its discretionary authority to send examiners into the offices of consumer-finance lenders that were units of Fed-regulated bank holding companies."

Mr. Greenspan has denied any recollection of this conversation and flatly refused to crack down on subprime lending practices. WHY? Anyone for mandatory retirement before you hit 75 years old? Did he create the "Age of Turbulence"?

Subprime loans used to be called "band-aid loans" as they were used to give someone time to fix a "boo-boo" (typically, a credit issue). In all of my years in this business, I have only processed three of these loans for clients that needed the "band-aid" fix. I flatly refused to even consider putting regular people in these loans as I could see how explosive they were. Couldn't everyone? Remember, these are the loans that only have a two or three year initial teaser payment and then instantly convert to an ugly adjustable loan with a very high interest rate and payments that few can afford. No band-aid is going to fix a severed artery. There is bleeding in the streets. Call the paramedics!

This organized crime spree has been headed up by Wall Street Godfathers like the Angelo Mozilo's of Countrywide and the Michael Perry's of IndyMac Bank. The sad thing is that none of these criminals are in jail. They put Martha Stewart in jail for selling stock – what crime did she commit that would parallel these crimes against society? I guess now that Elliot Spitzer has been caught with his pants down, we are left with no one to prosecute these white collar criminals. Sure, we watch as they march the low life brokers into the slammer, but what of those who put the loaded weapons in their hands?

Just to set the record straight (from an insider), subprime loans were handled very differently from traditional mortgage loans. Traditional loan applications are fully processed and then submitted by the loan officer/broker to the underwriting department of the lender/bank that they believe has the best rates and terms for their clients. The lender then renders a decision of approval or decline. In recent years, the process of submitting loans has become quite streamlined as computer programs have often replaced the function of human underwriters. Most lenders have a website where you can upload your application and a computer will tell you if the loan is approved and what documentation needs to be obtained. As long as you could supply what "R2D2" told you, your borrower was approved. And just for the record….. the software program that approves most of these borrowers is straight from the GSE's of Fannie Mae and Freddie Mac. GSE is government sponsored enterprise, which leads you to believe that these two entities are backed by the full faith of the United States government, and I guess they are living up to this designation since our government is now their conservator. They were publically traded, for profit, enterprises that were up to their nipples in hot water. Hank Paulson, former Treasury Secretary under President Bush, gave the CEO's Mudd and Syron their pink slips and two new Wall Street-types have assumed the control. Some may find it interesting that prior to his position as Treasury Secretary, Mr. Paulson was the CEO of Goldman Sachs. Didn't he know what was going on?

As previously stated, the procedures for handling subprime loans were quite different. Lenders, which included banks, mortgage companies, thrifts, and all of their sub-chapter companies, hired representatives who were paid on commission to solicit our business directly. Almost daily, phones would ring with multiple reps from multiple companies, calling to see what potential business we had to offer them. These very aggressive lender-paid representatives would offer to "look- see" any application that you had and offer you ways to get it approved. From my experience, you always sent your subprime loan applications directly to the representative of the lender who would then tell you what THEY wanted to see and THEY worked with the underwriters in getting the "job done". Most of these extremely well paid reps had little experience in the business and knew only what they had been taught. Remember, they worked on commission and were fighting the vast competition also. Just ask any of these now unemployed former reps if their bank employers were asking for numbers or quality? Was there fraud? You bet…….but who committed the act? Did the borrower misstate their information on the application? Did the loan officer make any "needed" corrections? Did the lender's representative input the information as they knew it needed to be presented in order to be approved? Everyone was just following the rules as set up by the lenders and investors. No smoking gun here!

In submitting a loan to IndyMac Bank on behalf of a long-term client, I was severely chastised for putting the applicant's income on the application. It seems the investor buying those loans wanted absolutely no income or assets disclosed. We were to leave those areas of the application blank. I'm an old dog and it takes time to learn new tricks. By the way, this was not a subprime loan and the client was fully qualified. This just happened to be a special program for investment properties (high risk) that offered an exceptionally low interest rate. Do you think many unqualified people took advantage of these "tell nothing" loans? No liar loans here!

You can only imagine how "shell shocked" we in the industry were to discover that overnight all of these loan programs were gone. I'm not speaking figuratively, I mean literally overnight. We went to our offices that fateful morning in August of 2007 to discover that ALL lenders were no longer offering any jumbo loans. They were just gone. I'll always be curious as to what major event happened to cause competing banks and Wall Street firms to shut it down so abruptly. In answer to the first wave of explosions, Wall Street brought the lending industry to a virtual stop. Pin in the bubble – **<u>KABOOOMMMM</u>.**

Mortgages that were once plentiful and available on every corner were all of a sudden risky investments that nobody wanted. August of 2007 ushered in the beginning of the fall of the house of cards. Overnight, the flow of easy money became a trickle and soon offices all across this country closed up shop and went home permanently. Staff members of these firms, with pink slips in hand and mouths wide open, hit the streets and joined the ranks of the unemployed.

Is it becoming clear who caused the housing prices to bubble and then burst?

<u>THE PLAN</u>

In the beginning there was a plan to fix the lending crisis
And then came the assumptions of what would work
And the assumptions were without form and they were wrong
And the plan was completely without substance
And darkness was on the face of home owners
And they spoke among themselves, saying
"It is a crock of shit and it stinks"
And the home owners went to the loan officers and said
"It is a pile of manure and no one will be able to live with the odor of it"
And the loan officers went to their managers and said to them
"It is a container of excrement and it is very strong such that no one will be able to live with it"
And the bank managers went to the legislators and said to them
"It is a vessel of fertilizer and no one will be able to live with its strength"
And the legislators went to the Federal Reserve and said
"The contents of the plan will aid growth and it is very strong"
And the Federal Reserve went to the Administration and said
"The plan will promote growth and it is very powerful"
And the Administrators went to President and said to him
"This powerful new plan will actively promote the growth and efficiency of the housing market"
And the President looked upon the plan and saw that it was good
And the plan became policy

Adapted by: Nancy Cozens

6

<u>Bring in the Body Bags</u>

<u>*Damaging Legislation – Will it Usher in Depression?*</u>

One of the first responders to the housing crash was our government, passing H.R. 5140 or the Economic Stimulus Act of 2008. This bill was introduced by Speaker of the House Nancy Pelosi, and was signed into law on 2/13/08 by President George W. Bush. The bill had basically three parts: Part one of the bill offered cash rebates to us, the taxpayers of this country. Yippee! Part two gave money as incentives to businesses. Part three raised the lending limits of Fannie Mae, Freddie Mac and FHA up to 125% of the area median price for homes.

Everyone loved the free money and we were instructed to spend it. The idea of the cash rebate was to prop up our economy and avoid (postpone) an economic recession. What a fabulous idea! Let's borrow money from ourselves and put it on the national debt, then go out and have a spending spree! Too many Baby Boomers in Washington? Isn't reckless spending part of what got us into this mess in the first place? Unless the government intends to send us a check every month to compensate for the lost wages of this economic crisis, let's make better use of our federal tax dollars.

The economic incentive to businesses was to allow them to depreciate a larger amount of their equipment, etc. and write it off their taxes. In other words, spend and spend some more. Thanks, Uncle Sam, for the free money. Short-term massive spending may have postponed a recession until after the elections, but it would not stop this potentially fatal crash that has resulted from the credit crisis.

The third part of the stimulus package and the section that interested me and my beleaguered colleagues the most was the increase in the lending limits of Fannie Mae, Freddie Mac and FHA. Yes! Way to go! That's it! You guys finally got one right! – NOT.

Nobody ever reads these bills, do they? Well, I did. The first thing that I noticed was that the increase in the Fannie Mae and Freddie Mac loan limits was retro-active back to July 1st of 2007. Why? This bill didn't go into law until February of 2008. Hmmm! Remember the jumbo loans, those over the Fannie and Freddie loan limits that disappeared overnight in August of 2007? (a mere coincidence, I am sure). That meant that the banks had no way to sell the loans that they had already funded. Wall Street, the buyer of the jumbo loans, pulled a "David Copperfield" and disappeared entirely, leaving the banks with an empty hat. Brilliant, our government found a way to allow the banks to dump these loans into Fannie, Freddie and FHA, all the while telling us, the US taxpayers, that this stimulus package was NOT a bank bailout. Again, who reads this stuff?

I live and do business in the very expensive housing area of southern California, which is one of the areas hardest hit by the foreclosures, so this bill was very welcomed and should have been a major solution for the many homeowners who were desperate for assistance. It was about time that us "regular" folks, who are forced to pay more for our housing, finally had a break and were going to enjoy the same loans that everyone else in this country enjoys. Wrong again. It is interesting to note that Hawaii, Alaska and the U.S. Virgin Islands already have 50% higher loan limits than those of us in these regular states. They must have some powerful lobbyists working for them. We in California have the likes of Nancy Pelosi. We used to have former Congressman Randy "Duke" Cunningham, but he is serving his last remaining years being supported by us taxpayers in a secure government facility (prison). It seems Mr. Cunningham got caught using his position as a house representative to award government contracts to the very individual who was padding his personal coffers. Anyone want to offer us Californians a trade?

The intent of this increase in the Fannie, Freddie and FHA lending limits was to allow people in the higher priced areas, like California, to refinance and /or purchase loans in order to buy some of the surplus and also to get out of the riskier loans. In theory, this was a great provision, but it could not be upheld in practice due to the application of H.R.5140 by Fannie and Freddie.

Fannie & Freddie – Can't Get the Ambulance out of the Driveway:

The implementation of the higher loan limits was immediately rolled out to the lending institutions as follows:

1. All loans that exceeded the $417,000 loan limit were NOT to be treated equally, but classified separately as a different loan with different pricing and different loan-to-value requirements. Let us call these new loans "agency jumbo", as every lender seemed to call them something different. I have my own name for them …….. There was nothing about segregating these loans in the bill. Who made that decision?

2. The rules for the higher loan limits were so restrictive that very few potential borrowers even qualified to take advantage of them, as I will show in an example to follow.

3. The loan amount limits were set by very large geographical areas and did not allow all of the truly higher priced areas to enjoy the full extent of the potential $729,750 loan limit. For example, the San Diego median price was established based on the entire county and did not differentiate the low cost housing areas close to the border from the higher priced coastal regions.

4. If your home was identified in an area where home prices were declining (and what area was not declining?) then your appraised/purchase value was diminished automatically by an additional 5%. (this has since been dropped from the guidelines as it was so blatantly injudicious)

5. New risk-based pricing has been attached to all of the "conforming" loans and has forced interest rates up by default, thus negating any potential savings to assist in rewriting these faulty loans. They even added an "adverse market" charge to the pricing. Talk about hitting us while we are down. Detailed information about this addition to pricing will be discussed in full in a later chapter. What you will discover is sufficient to make a saint start cursing.

The intent of this bill was to assist homeowners in need. The delivery of the final version is scandalous and whoever made this decision to implement it in this manner should be fired or voted out of office. Most homeowners have been hurt and not helped by this bill. To give a simple example:

Let us assume that you are a homeowner in a high priced area and you paid $600,000 for your very average home in a very average neighborhood in early 2006. It is probably difficult for people in many parts of the country to understand that this price range could be considered average, but that was the reality at the height of the market. Let us also assume that you bought responsibly with a 20% down payment of $120,000 (now that is no small chunk of change) leaving you with a mortgage loan of $480,000. The new agency jumbo loans should be available to you in order to refinance your adjustable loan to a fixed rate. Let us also assume that after almost two years, your home is now worth (on paper) only $540,000, a 10% loss from the previous highs due to declining market value. Under this new law, the bank is going to further reduce this value by 5%, since your home is in an area that has been identified as "declining". So, the new calculated value of your home is $513,000. Since you owe $480,000 this means the new loan would be a 93% loan-to-value (value of the loan as compared to the value of the home). You have just been DECLINED as the new agency jumbo will not allow you to finance greater than 90%. No one is taking into consideration the $120,000 cold hard cash that you worked so hard to save and put down on the property. Where is that money now? Gone!

This example is extremely conservative as most areas have declined more than 10% and most people have minimal equity by today's standards if not being totally upside-down on value. What good is this new bill if no one can benefit from it? How is this helping the economy recover? It isn't. Our inability to obtain loans to assist with the purchase and refinance of homes has caused values to slip even further. Our home prices are in a freefall due to the high amount of foreclosures and subsequent bargain basement pricing. Faulty implementation of legislation is further exacerbating an already critical situation.

A Fatal Blow:

As if the value issues of our homes were not enough to keep us from refinancing, the new credit criteria established by Fannie and Freddie has severely limited our lending options. The over-tightening of the credit underwriting standards has eliminated most of us from eligibility in the mortgage market. It would seem that the only individuals who are eligible are those who don't really need the loans. Lots of good that does to fix the economy and solve the lending crisis!

The Feds (thanks Ben) have identified "stated income" loans as being the major culprit in our foreclosure difficulties. May I *state* that virtually all loans in the past few years have been written as "stated income" loans because of the simplicity of the documentation, and not because all borrowers could not verify their income. Why would anybody want to produce two years of tax returns, 60 days of bank statements, retirement accounts, paystubs, W-2's and on and on depending on a borrower's circumstances, when they could obtain the same financing while not providing anything? We didn't make up these rules, the banks did. Not to mention, and I will get into this further in a later chapter, we are using outdated and ineffective methods of verifying income that came straight out of the 1960's. The era of blue-collar salary workers (we shipped all of those jobs overseas), does not compare to the era of the self-employed entrepreneurs. Without updating our methods of documenting income, we have become prejudiced to the self-employed. Stated income loans have been around for many years and only recently have there been abuses because of loosey- goosey underwriting standards. If we were to return to the sane and common sense underwriting that prevailed prior to the 2000's, we would at least give more borrowers a chance to redo their mortgage loans and reduce the risk to our economy. **The answer is not irresponsible tightening, but responsible lending**.

Basically, all loans today are being underwritten by Fannie Mae and Freddie Mac's guidelines that were imposed after H.R. 5140. (How to not loan any money and price gouge at every juncture possible.) Since we have a limited amount of players in this market, the remaining ones get to dictate the rules of the game. Want to hear how stupid these rules are? Here we go:

Jeff and Susie refinanced their home loan in 2006 in order to take out an additional $50,000 in cash and buy a new SUV that they have always wanted. They are now refinancing in order to get a fixed rate since their current loan is adjustable. This loan is categorized by our industry as a "rate and term" refinance and is eligible for the best of terms. It is actually priced the same as if they were purchasing the home.

Now, let us consider their neighbors, Tom & Liz. They too want to fix their loan and they too, go for a refinance. Tom & Liz still have the same loan on their property that they purchased the home with in 2004. However, in 2005, they took out a home equity line of credit to remodel their kitchen. They haven't used the equity line since 2005 and have been faithfully paying it down. Their loan is considered a "cash out" loan and is subject to worse pricing and restrictions on loan-to-value. WHY?

Because, Fannie and Freddie say so! Both of the above examples are exactly the same, except that borrower number two took out an equity line instead of refinancing their first trust deed. The first set of borrowers actually took cash out of their home for a luxury purchase. Borrower number two put more value into their home through their second trust deed loan. Under the new Fannie and Freddie guidelines, paying off any junior financing is punishable by higher prices and lower loan-to-value standards. In many cases, borrowers like the ones outlined here are being declined or paying very high rates for taking out a line of credit. This is outrageous.

We are being *punished* for what they were *pushing* less than two years ago. Every lender was peddling HELOCs (Home Equity Lines Of Credit) like they were the best things since mother's milk. For a while, they were even offering these credit lines at 125% of our home's value. Most of these HELOCs were free of charge and a great income producer to both the bank and the loan officer who got paid extra by the bank to offer them to every client. The banks loved these credit cards attached to the homes. Even if your borrower had a 20% down payment when they were purchasing a home, they were encouraged to only put 10% down and keep the rest. The 10% equity line allowed these borrowers to avoid having to pay a premium normally associated with 90% financing. The free and easy money that the banks wanted us to have is now costing us dearly. During the time when Greenspan had the interest rates so flat, these loans tied to prime were cheaper than first trust deed loans. I know of people who paid off their stable fixed rate mortgages in favor of these highly adjustable HELOCS, because the interest rates were in the 3's. We are being unfairly punished for the sins of Wall Street and our government is blinded to their corrupt deeds. Did money talk? Loud and clear!

Another Government Solution: Hopenow.com

Our government is currently sponsoring (via our tax dollars) phone help lines to assist the many homeowners who are in default and/or in jeopardy of losing their homes to foreclosure. I decided to call this agency, at 1-888-995-HOPE, masquerading as a potential client to determine what assistance they could offer. After all, if this credit crisis does not abate, I may be joining the thousands of my associates who have defaulted on their mortgage loans due to loss of income. After being routed to Consumer Credit Counseling Service, I was told to call back later as they were currently too busy to take my call. I am so glad this was not a suicide prevention hotline.

I am familiar with this type of agency and how they do business. Our paths often cross in my line of work. The counseling may be free but someone is paying for this service. They are in the business of *selling* credit negotiation. Why is this hotline being so highly publicized by our government on all of their web sites? Big money is now being made in the *avoid foreclosure* business. Don't let the term *not for profit* fool you. There is no such thing as non-profit, other than how they are taxed, or should I say NOT taxed. These organizations are also eligible for massive government grants, donations, and other free money. Gee, didn't the new law that was just passed have a few billion in there for this cause? Hmmm. The media has reported as of April '09 that this agency has only been successful in modifying one mortgage loan. You could have paid off many of the defaulted mortgage loans with the money we have paid this organization to date.

If you choose to forego this "hope" route and put in a direct call to your lender, it is my understanding, from many of my colleagues that lender assistance can only be given after a mortgagor has defaulted on at least two payments. I am also told that many people seeking help are opting to go into default in order to get some sort of mortgage relief. A little "Catch 22", don't you think? In either case, your credit history will be destroyed by this action. Given five or so years into the future, there may be a big forgiveness factor for people who defaulted during this time period in our history. That is, if we are out of this mess in five years. Could encouraging people to default on payments in order to get help be adding to our foreclosure woes and maybe skewing the numbers?

Loan Modifications and the Hunt for Your Note Holder

Companies are springing up everywhere offering to assist you in getting a loan modification. They want cash up front and use of your credit card is an acceptable form of payment. Borrowers, frustrated by trying to work out a plan with their lenders are turning to these new companies in droves. Remember all the subprime hucksters that lost their jobs – they found a home in these companies. It doesn't matter if they are successful or not because they have your cash in advance. There seems to be a major problem in getting a loan modification despite the billions that have been allocated to this problem. Seems nobody is able to find the original note holder(s) of these mortgage loans. As I explained in an earlier chapter, banks don't *own* your loan, they just service them. It is up to the owner of the mortgage note to grant approval to the modification. It is being reported that the CDO (collateralized debt obligation) packages designed by Wall Street for trading of various loan instruments may have contained parts of loans and not the loan in its entirety. It would appear that loans have been parceled out to multiple investors and therefore the hunt for the actual owners of these notes has become quite difficult. Given the magnitude of the problems that we are facing, I am questioning in my mind just how many parts of the loans were sold. Did they sell more than 100%? It would explain why they are calling them toxic mortgages. This is a question that we may never know the answer to.

H.R. 3221 – Housing and Economic Recovery Act of 2008

As if we weren't in enough trouble already, here comes the new legislation. If you go to govtrack.us, you can read the summary of this bill that was passed on 7/30/2008. It's another Nancy Pelosi sponsored bill, with multiple names and multiple agendas. I tried to read the actual bill itself, but a whole group of attorneys probably couldn't interpret the real impact of this bill as it will be up for interpretation for many years to come. It certainly has abolished one governmental agency and replaced it with another, with much stronger teeth. It has made the role of government brutally strong in our lending market, and it would seem to put the last nail in the coffin on several lending issues.

This bill gave the government the ability to take over the operations of Fannie Mae and Freddie Mac. Do you think our Washington Bureaucrats know more about the lending industry than these two agencies do? These agencies have certainly faltered a lot over the past few years as their greedy CEOs took too much money from the profits of easy lending. There definitely was a lack of oversight as there seemed to be nobody guarding the hen house. However, this foreclosure fiasco is not just the result of Fannie Mae and Freddie Mac lending policies. We are suffering because Wall Street designed bad loans and triggered a housing bubble to explode, causing all of us to become casualties. I remember when Fannie and Freddie had prudent lending policies. Wasn't it Washington bureaucrats who insisted that they provide loans to individuals, credit worthy or not, so that everyone could be a homeowner? News alert: Not everyone is responsible enough for home ownership. Case in point – our current crisis. As I will address in future chapters, the changes in Fannie Mae and Freddie Mac lending policies since they have been under the conservatorship of the US Government is enough to send us into the next Great Depression.

H.R. 3221 allows the government to go into partnership with us on our homes. If we take a cut in our mortgage loan, due to renegotiation, we get to share our future profits with our government. Does that mean that the house that I overpaid for and that is now worth a fraction of its original value, when and if it does recapture its original value, is now partly the government's profit? Sorry, I'll take a walk first. We need a better option than this one.

This bill requires the mortgagee to document and verify the mortgagor income. Is it okay if we use the income we had before this crisis? Those of us who have seen our income reduced to almost nothing are no longer even eligible to refinance our own homes!

Just like the previous bill, H.R.3221 also allows for higher lending limits through Fannie Mae and Freddie Mac. This bill will allow the agencies to increase their loan amounts up to a lending limit of 115% of the area's median house prices. Wait a minute….. the previous bill allowed us to loan up to 125% of median house prices and now we can only go up to 115%? Where is the rationale? As I showed by the earlier example, it doesn't work at 125%, so it won't work at 115%. Also, at what juncture do we calculate our median house price? Do we use today's "nothing is selling and therefore nothing has value", prices? I guess we won't be raising the lending limits at all, will we? With home prices continuing to drop, this bill will not provide the resources for financing of larger loans that are desperately needed to purchase properties out of foreclosure. There will be no recovery and we will only see our property values continue to drop. More banks will fail. The whole problem is self-feeding. Way to go, Washington!

The problem we have here is that a group of elected officials who don't know beans about the lending industry have passed bills into law that will deliver the death blow to the already barely breathing housing market.

High Unemployment Numbers

According to the Bureau of Labor Statistics, as of May 2009, unemployment is at a rate of 8.9% nationally. Ouch! They are reporting that 13.7 million people are out of work. These numbers are based on people who file for unemployment benefits. I believe these numbers to be vastly understated as many of my colleagues in the mortgage and housing industry are self-employed. We do not get pink slips. We do not file for unemployment. However, we are nevertheless without income or very little income. Realtors don't get salaries. Appraisers are usually self- employed. Most loan brokers own their own businesses. Most loan agents work on commission. How about all of the other self-employed individuals, who have seen their income diminished or disappear due to this recession, is anyone adding up these numbers? President Obama has just informed the American people that we will probably see unemployment over 10%…..isn't that depression territory?

Resuscitation Plan Needed

So there you have it. The story has been told. You know who did it, how they did it and even why they did it. But understanding the story is not going to solve the crisis. Our current recession began when the housing bubble burst. In order to fix the economy, we must first fix the housing issue and that means fix the lending dilemma. We must solve our problems before the recession we are experiencing grows into a depression (that is – if we aren't already in a depression). The next section of this book offers a complete and thorough evaluation of the problems we are facing with our lending standards and how to fix it.

Bring in the paddles and let's resuscitate the dying patient.

The Secret

How to Fix It!

What They Don't Want You to Know

__Introduction to Section II__

Sub-"Crime" Mortgage Crisis

We the American people have been the victims of a crime – the subprime lending tragedy. The trauma resulting from this crime has been sufficient to bring the United States economy into a major recession and if not soon healed, could result in depression. The impact of this crime(s) is being felt on a global level as the entire world's economic stability is uncertain.

The Merriam-Webster dictionary defines the word crime as follows:

1: an act or the commission of an act that is forbidden or the omission of a duty that is commanded by a public law and that makes the offender liable to punishment by that law; _especially_: a gross violation of law**2:** a grave offense especially against morality**3:** criminal activity <efforts to fight _crime_>**4:** something reprehensible, foolish, or disgraceful <it's a _crime_ to waste good food>

__These Crimes against Society Include:__

1. Failure on the part of our government to regulate the activities of Wall Street investment firms and U.S. banks.
2. Failure of all lending institutions to uphold a standard of underwriting for the borrowing population.
3. Foolishly granting loans to unqualified individuals.
4. Valuing money over morals.
5. Reprehensible compensation of corporate executive officers.
6. Illegal activity leading to the collapse of century-old institutions.
7. Disgraceful – you name it and they did it.

Throughout the first section of this book we have identified the participants in this criminal activity. The list of conspirators stretches all the way from Washington, D.C. to Main Street, America. The verdict has been read and delivered:

GUILTY! GUILTY! GUILTY!

Punishment is in the process of being delivered. Freedom has been lost. Unfortunately, the crimes are continuing to happen. Only the activities have changed:

The New Crimes Against Society Include:

1. Over-regulation on the part of Washington against all of our financial institutions.
2. Government seizure of publically traded companies.
3. Restrictive lending practices that discriminate against even the creditworthy.
4. Failure to provide adequate financing for the borrowing public.
5. Rape and pillage fees by Fannie/Freddie that are making financing too expensive for most.
6. Inability to modify current abusive loan instruments due to failure to find original note holders.
7. Unjust closing of our current credit lines and credit cards by the banks without cause, further punishing the borrowing public for sins they didn't commit.
8. Damaging legislation that continues to penalize the wrong people.

It is a CRIME what they have done to us.

It is a CRIME what they are doing to us.

But interestingly, the term CRIME is also an acronym for what needs to be evaluated in order to fix the lending crisis.

CRedit, Income , Money and Equity

In this section of the book I will look at CRIME in a whole different way. I will reveal and share insider **SECRETS** that have/are being used in the granting *or not* granting of mortgage loans. I will detail what responsible lending practices were prior to the "anything goes" era of the past few years and what needs to be reinstated for our future lending success. I will attempt to share the "insider" information on all aspects of the mortgage lending industry, from understanding the fallacy of the credit scoring system to the reason we need those "liar" loans back. You will get to see actual rate sheets that lenders *forbid* wholesale brokers from sharing with their clients, and you will be outraged by the recent pricing additions imposed by Fannie Mae and Freddie Mac that are making mortgages much less affordable, despite lower interest rates. Our legislators in Washington obviously don't understand the mortgage lending industry as evidenced by the many faulty bills they keep passing and the rhetoric we are constantly hearing.

Our current foreclosure statistics are evidence enough that people need to understand more about the various mortgage products and procedures so they don't ever fall into the *"I didn't know"* trap again. Responsible underwriting practices must be reinstated without placing limits on common sense. We cannot continue to swing the pendulum from one extreme of *"lending to everyone"* and then watch them stop *"lending to anyone"*.

It is my sincere desire that the information presented here will serve to light the way back to honesty, once again.

7

The Gatekeepers or Crime Watchers

The Underwriting Function-The Art of Saying Yes or No

The American dream of home ownership for many has become a nightmare because the gatekeepers, who were supposed to say NO, said YES. Home ownership is not a right of citizenship; it is an earned responsibility. Despite the fact that everyone wants to own a home, it should be a planned event. How convenient the designers of easy credit have made it for us. Credit cards allow us to take immediate possession of any impulsive desire. Car dealerships allow us to drive off the lot with no down payment on the vehicle that they may have talked us into buying. We seldom have the discipline of saving and working towards something. If we want it, we want it now. After all, tomorrow we may want something different.

Defining Home Ownership

According to the US Census, 30% of homeowners actually do own their own home. The rest of us are _mortgagors_. This means that we own our property jointly with a mortgage holder until the encumbrance is paid off. It also means:

- ✓ If the furnace quits, you might freeze if you cannot fix it.
- ✓ If the air conditioner breaks down, you may be hot under the collar.
- ✓ If the roof caves in, it's a real headache and a major expense.
- ✓ If the plumbing doesn't work, it's a stinky problem until it can be resolved.
- ✓ If the house falls apart, you do too and so does your bank account.

It absolutely means:

- ✓ Expect annual visits from the tax man with property bill and assessments in hand.

- ✓ Better have a piece of the rock (insurance) to stand on, should a catastrophe hit – lest we forget hurricanes, "Ike" and "Katrina", the annual fire hazards of southern California, the tornadoes of the Midwest, the ice-storms of the frigid north and so many other unexpected events over which we have no control.

- ✓ **If you stop paying your mortgage, your home ownership rights end.**

Home ownership carries with it a great responsibility. There is no landlord to call when something goes wrong. For many of us, owning a home will be the largest financial decision we will ever make and therefore it should be done with planning and preparation. We must know how much we can afford to spend each month for this obligation and have a necessary emergency fund for those things we cannot possibly anticipate but will inevitably happen. The "Money Pit" was a movie a few years ago that spoofed the hazards of owning a home when everything possible started to go wrong. If you own a home, it is a guarantee that things will need to be repaired, replaced and eventually updated.

The gatekeepers of our mortgage community have done a grievous disservice to many of our citizens who were allowed to purchase homes prematurely and without any of the safeguards that needed to be in place. Talk to these victims now. Losing a home is more difficult than being told "NO" up front. ***Just say No"*, is not for kids only**. Sometimes adults need to hear No as well.

Who Are the Gatekeepers?

Underwriters are the individuals in a financial institution who shoulder the responsibility for making judgments regarding the people who wish to acquire a mortgage loan. These underwriters are normally trained in the art of decision making, or at least they used to be. Their decisions, however, are based on the guidelines provided to them by the lending institutions that employ them. The lending institutions usually follow the guidelines of the secondary markets who will eventually buy the loans. Traditionally, Fannie and Freddie have been the rule makers and their guidelines have been used as industry standards, even if they were not the purchaser of the loan. Wall Street financiers caused us to abandon all reasonable rules in the past few years as they offered the lending institutions a blank check to purchase anything and everything that was securitized by a mortgage note. Our Gatekeepers fell asleep at the wheel and let these thieves drive the get-away vehicles. Didn't they expect a "CRASH"?

Additionally, computer software programs provided by the lending giants Fannie and Freddie have been designed to take the human element out of the decision-making role. After all, humans are corruptible! As long as the computer approves the scenario, then the lender is blameless. Do you think we human beings can't figure out how to input the *right* scenario?

The Way It Was

In the George Bailey (It's a Wonderful Life) era, bankers and savings & loan officers often knew the people in their communities and were willing to take a risk based on information known to them. As communities became larger and the banker didn't always know the people personally, they formed loan committees to evaluate applications for credit. Many community banks still use loan committees, very successfully, as they evaluate who they will lend their dollars to. Often these loan committees are made up of board members who are personally liable for the bank's decision making. If this personal liability had been in place over the last several years, I'm quite sure there would have been more diligence as to who was extended credit and who wasn't. The CEOs and other top executives of major corporations and banks do not seem to have any personal liability for their decision making. These top dogs are still garnering huge bonus checks even as the taxpayers of America are feeding them billions of dollars in **TARP** (**T**roubled **A**sset **R**elief **P**rogram) funds. If we would **TARP** (**T**ake **A**way **R**idiculous **P**ay) from these individuals and start demanding pay for performance, then our dollars would be better spent. After all, these are publically traded companies, not private enterprises.

The Art of Decision Making

Every loan request should tell a story and it is up to the underwriter in a financial institution to listen to the story and evaluate each scenario based on prudent guidelines before making a decision. These guidelines are for the protection of the institution and the person applying for the loan. The seriousness of this decision-making process cannot be overemphasized as we are talking about people's lives. Behind the paperwork are real flesh and blood human beings who need someone to be responsible on their behalf. The banks are taking peoples' hopes and dreams, their children's futures, and their financial security into their hands every time *decisions* are handed down about them. The decision making of the past few years has been more like "Fantasy Island" with no paperwork to support the story and it has brought about "Truth and Consequences" that even Tattoo can't fathom. We must restore common sense guidelines to the underwriting process once again. Notice I said guidelines and not rules. Too many rules are just as damaging as no rules. They restrict an underwriter from effectively judging the creditworthiness of a loan applicant and can result in the inability to grant financing to individuals just because they don't *fit the rule*.

The 4 Basics of Credit Worthiness:

In chapter 4, I briefly touched on the four areas of underwriting criteria that have been the benchmark for mortgage lending for many years. By evaluating "**ALL**" of these four areas of a person's life and story, with supportive data, an informed decision can be made regarding their creditworthiness for any mortgage loan request.

- ✓ **CR**edit History – defines a person's desire to repay
- ✓ **I**ncome Verification – defines a person's ability to repay
- ✓ **M**oney or Reserves – defines a person's ability to have time to repay
- ✓ **E**quity – defines a person's motivation to repay

Although there are four separate areas to be investigated, they cannot be treated separately, as they must be evaluated collectively. Together, these four things tell the full story of a person's desire, ability, time and motivation to repay any loan request. When even one of these areas is totally overlooked, a high-risk lending scenario can result.

What is High-Risk Lending?

1. **Little or no equity in the property:** The highest risk factor of default in any real estate transaction is when an individual has minimal equity or investment in the property. Equity defines your motivation to repay a mortgage loan. No equity –No motivation. The reason we have so many foreclosures today is that people were allowed to purchase property with no money down. This is a fatal flaw. If you do not have cold hard cash in a property, you have minimal motivation to keep up the payments when times are rough. Conversely, when a person has significant equity in their property, it is almost a guarantee that they will do everything in their power to keep it.

2. **No cash reserves:** The second risk factor in a real estate secured loan is when the

person has no safety net. Unemployment is causing many people to default on their mortgage payments because they have no money in the bank to carry them until they get their next job. Money in the bank buys time. Your emergency fund is crucial because life happens. As I will show in a later chapter, Fannie doesn't care if you have any cash in the bank these days. Very unwise.

3. **<u>Unstable Income</u>:** The third risk factor in evaluating a person for a mortgage is when they have a history of income that is not stable. People that bounce from job to job may be demonstrating no long-term commitment to themselves or their employers. Others become dependent on overtime earnings that may disappear very quickly. A person's ability to repay a loan is dependent on their ability to produce steady income. This risk factor is obviously offset if the person has significant cash reserves.

4. **<u>Poor Credit History</u>:** Lenders today seem to put our credit score at the top of the list for evaluating a mortgage loan request when it really is the least significant of the four. However, a person's credit history (not score) is important to show how seriously they take their debt responsibilities. Providing a person has equity in their property, cash in the bank and income to supply the funds for repayment, timeliness of payment is a servicing issue more than a risk factor.

The balancing of these four areas of a person's history is what underwriting should be all about. I will address each one of these four areas separately in the chapters to follow. You will see the importance of each area in the decision making process. Perhaps the mortgage lenders, or who is left of them, need to relearn what true gatekeeper responsibilities are all about. Fannie and Freddie need to dust off their old underwriting manuals and go back to guidelines that work. The idiotic new rules of real estate lending are not working and will further send our economy into a nosedive. Now that our government is intimately involved in real estate lending perhaps the members of our legislative bodies need to be informed as to what constitutes credible lending standards. Once educated they can stop passing laws regarding underwriting criteria that restrict the industry from exercising good judgment.

Two key solutions have been outlined in this chapter. The first solution is to restore underwriting into the hands of qualified and trained human underwriters. Give them the ability to weigh the pros and cons of a loan applicant and make an informed decision as to a person's creditworthiness. The second solution is to get rid of the hard and fast rules in favor of responsible guidelines. Stop denying credit to worthy individuals who don't necessarily fit into the neat and tidy box that the current restrictive rules have outlined. For example, many people have a collection account they are unaware of that lowers their credit score to a level not currently acceptable. A trained underwriter can evaluate and disregard a one-time occurrence that is inconsistent with overall credit history. Another example would be an individual who derives income from unconventional sources and can demonstrate their ability to repay the loan with their reserves. Throughout the next chapters I will give multiple examples that show the inequality of our current rules and why they need to be changed. We need the human touch to be restored.

In the first section of this book I refer to the overpaid bank representatives whose job it is to solicit loan applications from brokers. It was not uncommon for many of these reps during the housing boom to earn up to a half million dollars a year, at least here in the southern California area. The individuals who serve as the gatekeepers of our lending institutions only earn in the $30,000 - $60,000 a year range. Sometimes you get what you pay for. Maybe if the banks start paying for quality instead of quantity of loans, we will not have to repeat the mistakes of the past few years.

In following chapters, I will use real life stories that I have personally encountered because this is about real people and their lives and why we need to make the changes to our current underwriting rules. I have changed the names of the innocent to protect their privacy. In all cases, the names of the guilty have been changed to shield them from further embarrassment.

We need our Crime Watchers (underwriters) to be Crime Stoppers.

8

<u>Score This!</u>

<u>*Underwriting Credit History - the Desire to Repay*</u>

Our financial history can be summed up by a three digit number – our credit score. Many businesses are capitalizing on this as they invite you to check out your FREE credit score (for a fee of course). It says *for free* but this is only if you sign up for their monthly service. Congress, in order to *protect* our rights, has mandated that each person is *entitled* to a *free* credit report, once a year. This is to assist you and me in knowing what is being reported by the bureaus and to make sure that the information is correct. I decided to apply for this *free* credit report that I am *entitled* to and was shocked at the procedures that I had to go through to get it. In order to determine that I was who I said I was, I had to put in a credit card number that would identify me to the bureau....and then another credit card number. When they asked for a third credit card or other reference I almost gave up. I did get my report...and guess what? No score. If you want to know what your score is, you have to pay for it. By then, they already had my credit card numbers so all I had to do was say *yes*. I guess Congress wasn't specific enough or doesn't care if you know your score. Is this just a ploy to get you to sign up for the monthly fee-based service to inform you every time your score changes? And I'm protected **HOW**????

When I started in the mortgage industry as an underwriter, there was no scoring on the credit reports. Credit scoring came into existence in1995. Prior to this I was the one trained to review a person's credit history and make a determination as to their worthiness for the requested loan. A review of a person's credit report can be very revealing and interesting. It often tells us if the person likes to shop at Saks or Mervyns; if they drive a Beamer or a Nissan; if they use a lot of credit or just a little. It also shows, for the previous seven years, any late payments that were made and when they occurred. The report tells us if there have been any collections, judgments, tax liens or a bankruptcy in the last ten years. Your credit report lists every time you even inquire about getting a new loan. I can always tell when someone is out shopping for that new car.

Where Did Credit Scoring Come From?

There are three major bureaus that creditors report to: Experian, Equifax and Trans Union. Each of these three bureaus generates a different credit score from their software model. FICO is the best known of these three scores and is an acronym which stands for Fair Isaac Corporation, who first developed the scoring system. Fannie and Freddie "bought" (or were paid to use) this scoring system in 1995 and it has been **enforced** ever since. This is not a *free service*. Money is generated every time a score is issued. So what are we as a society getting for our money? After all, it is we who ultimately pay for this service. Recently the credit scoring systems underwent a change in the evaluation of scores and most people saw their credit scores improve. Did their credit history improve? Is this scoring system really evaluating risk in the lending community?

Scores range from a low of 300 to a high of 850. It was generally accepted that a score above 680 was considered a good score while one over 700 was great. A bad score was under 620. That was before they changed the scoring model, and now a score of over 740 is needed if you don't want to pay through the nose for your next mortgage loan. Yes, our mortgage loans are now being priced based on our credit scores. A low score can result in thousands of dollars of additional fees to the bank or significantly higher interest rates, or both. In a later chapter on interest rates I will show the actual pricing charts and what the cost is to you and me, but for now, it is important for you to understand more about what credit scoring really is.

Credit scores change every time something new is reported to the bureaus. If you happen to be someone who charges a lot and then pays it off at the end of the month, you better hope that the day they run your credit is after the payment has been received and recorded by the creditor who is reporting you. The score is but a snapshot of the day the report is run. The following examples will illustrate why I believe this to be a flawed system and why we need to petition our political leaders to have this defective system changed.

Several years ago, a 73 year-old gentleman contacted our company in regards to refinancing his home so he could help his son buy a home. His house was worth over $400,000 and it was debt-free. We assured him that this shouldn't be a problem. Upon receiving an application, the first step in evaluating a new client is to run a credit report; unbelievably, he was unknown to the bureaus. No credit score at all. No credit history at all. It was as if he didn't exist. The credit report only reflects activity that has happened in the past seven years (ten for legal items). This man had not borrowed any money in years, and despite living a very financially solid life, owning his home free and clear, and with no other indebtedness, he would not be able to get a break in today's FICO driven credit world. **Credit scoring discriminates against the individuals, especially the elderly who don't use credit anymore or those who deal on a "cash only" basis.**

I received a loan application from Ted and Jennifer as they wanted to refinance their home loan. They had been shopping online for the very best loan that they could get, but the whole process was just too overwhelming. Ted was a bit of a computer geek and thought he was being responsible by checking out every lender he could find. Upon running their credit report, I discovered that their scores had dropped to an average of 562. There was no "bad" credit being reported, but the sheer volume of inquiries into their credit history had plummeted their scores to the point where there was nothing we could do for them until their scores improved. Chalk this one up to ignorance – who knew shopping for a good loan was a bad thing? **Credit scoring unfairly punishes an individual who is shopping for good credit terms. Multiple credit inquiries do not mean multiple loans.**

Ben was ready to refinance his home loan and take out a little cash. Upon running his credit report we discovered an unpaid collection for $24 that had been placed against him. Ben was outraged, as he had always paid all of his bills on time and was someone who prided himself on having a perfect credit history. He was sure that this had to be an error, as he knew nothing about it. I gave him the information from the credit reporting bureau in order for him to track down what this unpaid charge was from. He called back to report that it was a small amount that the insurance company had not paid when his son was born. He never received a bill from the hospital. No collection agency had made any contact with him. They simply put him into collection knowing that it would show up on his credit report. This unscrupulous action by the collection agency plunged Ben's FICO score to 699, a 60 point drop. Want to know how much that $24 will cost him in penalty on his refinance? How about $6,255…..OUCH!!! (see chapter 13 for more details)

Unpaid collection accounts **frequently** appear on many peoples' credit reports without their knowledge. Collection agencies often purchase the entire amount of unpaid debts (collectibles) from hospitals, doctor's offices, dental offices, etc., for a fraction of the total amount due. If a debt is small, the agency does not pursue the debtor as it is not cost effective. They simply place a collection against the person and at some point in the future the person discovers this debt and contacts them. This is a racket, and should be illegal (and maybe is) because the clock is running. No reason to pursue someone for $24 if you can wait for it to grow with compounding interest. The longer it goes, the higher the debt repayment. I have had many clients contact the originator of the bill, only to discover that they were powerless to waive or reduce the charges, as they no longer *own* this debt. Often the provider of services had no intention of even asking their client to pay a pittance that may have resulted from the insurance company not paying the full amount charged or overcharged. Too late; they sold you as bait for the sharks. Once the collection agency sinks their teeth into you, they are not letting go until they have their pound of flesh. I have told many a client to just pay it as an investment into their good credit history. You can't win…most of these agencies are owned by attorneys. How sad that we are rewarding the thieves and punishing the innocent. How much in interest rate are we charging the client for an unpaid collection that they knew nothing about? Do you think the lender is going to waive this FICO addition to the mortgage pricing? They can't, it is a secondary marketing charge. It comes from Fannie Mae and Freddie Mac (our own government run institutions) who insist that we use this flawed scoring system. **Credit scoring unfairly punishes the credit-worthy for items on their credit report that they have no knowledge of, that they do not owe, and that are not even their responsibility.**

Debbie was involved in a serious auto accident and was in a drug induced coma for over 3 months due to the extensiveness of her injuries. It took a long time for her to fully recuperate and get back to work. Her medical bills were piling up and it would take time for the insurance company to settle with the various providers of her services. Her husband John had never run the household prior to her accident. He had never been responsible for feeding the kids, handling the schooling issues and he had never paid the bills. He was so preoccupied with her condition that he spent all of his extra time by her bedside in the hospital. Needless to say, their credit scores took a dive. John came to see us in order to obtain a refinance loan that would help him get through the rough times ahead. They had abundant equity in their home, and prior to the accident, their credit history was perfect. In the days before the use of credit scoring, we as human beings could see a change in credit patterns that was the result of an unexpected event. We could document what had happened and not penalize the client further. John and Debbie got the much needed cash, but it was not cheap. Talk about kicking you when you are down. **Credit scoring does not allow for human intervention when emergencies happen beyond**

our control and cause us to need our credit histories the most. Credit Scoring is INHUMANE!

Margaret had four separate credit cards with balances. One card with $1200 on it was for the computer she had purchased 12 months earlier. Another credit card carried the $2200 that she had spent on her recent trip to Hawaii. She still had an $800 balance on an American Express card that was used for business. And she owed $500 to Nordstroms on a new credit card that she had opened to take advantage of a 20% discount on her initial purchases. In total she owed $4700. Her credit score was 760. A credit card offer arrived promising "0" interest for the next 12 months and she quickly took advantage of this offer. Although Margaret had the cash to pay off all of these cards, the idea of earning interest on her savings and not having to pay interest on this new credit card appealed to her. She had always been very conscientious with her credit and decided once the four balances were transferred that she would close these other credit cards and only keep the new one. This was a big mistake. Her credit score dropped to 657. Why? Her new credit card available balance was for $5000 and she now owed $4700 on it. Closing her other credit cards signaled the computer scoring system that she did not have sufficient credit available. The computer does not know how much cash that Margaret has. It does not compute that she still owes the same amount as before. Your credit score will fall off the cliff any time you charge close to the maximum available balance on a credit account. Watch out for those low balance cards – they will punish you. **Credit scoring rewards a person for having a lot of open credit, and punishes someone who has too little.**

Bill had a dispute with a credit merchant over a charge on his account for a late fee that was in error. When he called the servicing department they agreed to remove the charge and that was the last time he thought about it. He had paid the account in full and it was not until a year later that he discovered this account was being reported in excess of 120 days late. His credit score was tanked, and he was livid. The late charge kept rolling and it looked like he was late for many months when in fact he didn't owe anything. It was the erroneous late charge not being removed from his account that caused a problem. This one account was inconsistent with the rest of his perfect credit history, but the scoring system does not seem to recognize this. I can remember when everybody used to have at least one late payment showing from a major retailer who obviously had an ineffective servicing department. Maybe they just wanted to collect late fees. After them, it was a major credit card company who continued this incorrect reporting. I won't say who it is, but what's in your wallet? In today's credit scoring system, these erroneous late payments cost the borrower greatly. **Credit scoring does not recognize a mistake on the part of the merchant reporting it.**

Linda applied for a mortgage loan to pay off over $50,000 in credit card debt. This was not the first time that she had done this. In fact, she seemed to need to refinance every two years in order to pay off all of the credit that she continuously amassed. She admitted to me she had a problem, but thankfully her home had continued to appreciate faster than her spending habits. Linda had a desirable credit score of 750 since she knew the magic secret; never let the unpaid balance on the credit card exceed 50% of the available balance. She had many credit card accounts and when one card got too close to that 50% mark, she would start using another one. I cautioned her that a day may come when she could no longer afford to do this, but habits are hard to break. I wonder if Linda still has her house! **Credit scoring REWARDS heavy credit users as long as they know how to manipulate their score.**

A person's **desire to repay** their debts is evidenced by the manner in which they handle their credit responsibilities. It used to be the underwriter's job to review a person's credit history to determine how they handled repayment of their debts; now a score is supposed to tell the tale. As shown by multiple examples, the scores do not always reflect a reliable story. Are thirty day late payments commonplace or a one-time isolated occurrence? Is all the derogatory information centered around one time period, or does it span several years? Does the person have one unknown collection account or multiple accounts that have gone into arrears? I had a client who at one time had twenty or so collection accounts. These unpaid amounts were all very small and could easily have been paid at the time incurred. He stated that he had an issue on each of them and didn't feel that he owed the money. He had refused to pay these accounts by stating that "it was the principle of the thing". Yeah, well principle this, – you are not a good credit risk. There are many people who will pay their bills but not always on time. They don't seem to mind the horrific late fees added to their unpaid balances, stating that at least they paid it. FYI, a creditor does not report (or is not supposed to report) a late payment unless the account has gone a full 30 days without a payment. Many people are late, missing their due date, but do not "skip" payments. It is the skipping of payments that becomes a problem. However, just because someone misses a payment here or there is not sufficient reason to decline them from financing. Unfortunately, today it means that their interest rate will be sky high.

Again, this is where our lenders must look at the entire picture of a borrower and not just a number. Can this person afford the debts that they have currently? Are they an excessive credit user? How come there are four open car loans on this person's credit report? Was bankruptcy in your history and now potentially in your future? This individual has a strong income and tons of cash, so why can't they pay their bills on time? It is obvious that during this one time period a family had several late payments that were inconsistent with the rest of their credit history; what happened? The answer to these questions can help an underwriter to decide if someone is taking their credit seriously or not. For example, I have seen individuals who easily co-sign for others, especially their kids, jeopardizing their own credit history. Co-signing is never a good idea unless you have payment control. Four open car loans can be the result of co-signing or it could also be business debt reported on an individual's personal credit. In the latter case, it is not a reflection of personal debt if you can prove that it is paid through a business account. It is not uncommon for people to use their own credit cards for employer-related business expenses, especially those involved with travel and entertainment. They may file an expense report and get reimbursed monthly from their employer. If this happens to be an especially expensive month, your personal credit score may dive to the depths until the employer pays you back.

Underwriting criteria was always intended to be a guideline, not hard and fast rules. Again I want to stress that human underwriters should review a person's request for credit with documentation to show the **whole story** and then make an informed decision whether or not to grant the loan. We have just seen the cataclysmic results of extending credit without guidelines to follow. Now we are seeing no credit being extended because of restrictive lending practices where all decisions are being made by a computer software program. A number is not how we should be judging or pricing loans. A score should only be used (if at all) as a "guideline". Here is one person who believes we need to rethink this whole scoring system and teach underwriters how to evaluate a person's credit worthiness by all the facts – *not just the three digit number!*

Credit scores can be manipulated if you know what the risk factors are. They are not a true reflection of a person's creditworthiness as outlined by the examples shown above. People with money can pay companies to "fix" their credit score. In fact, this is a huge business. Just look at the many companies out there who offer to "fix" your score for a fee. How reliable is that? The whole system of scoring discriminates against borrowers and falsely assumes risk where no risk exists. Likewise, many people have good scores who are very high risk borrowers. We are paying dearly for this mismanagement tool that has cost homeowners in both rate and fee. It takes a human being looking at an entire picture to determine credit worthiness. The credit bureaus don't have access to our income data (at least, not yet) to determine if a person can even afford the debt they are carrying. The computer model doesn't seem to know when a person is pyramiding debt and in risk of bankruptcy. Pyramiding debt is where you pay off one credit card with another until you run out of time and space to do so. The credit scoring system cannot distinguish between a credit flake and a person who has had a one-time occurrence where they were unable to pay their bills on time due to illness, death or other traumatic event. Do we have to penalize a person unfairly when life has penalized them enough? I have processed and underwritten thousands of loans over the years and I believe the entire scoring system to be seriously unsound – and we are pricing loans using this flawed system? **Are these numbers being manipulated and then turned into "gold" by the fee income that they generate to the very sources who determine that we must use this faulty and inconsistent scoring system?**

To make matters even worse, insurance companies, landlords and employers are now using this imperfect system to determine your worthiness for insurance coverage, a place to live, and even whether or not you get a job. And, to compound an already difficult situation, banks are now aggressively closing credit lines, reducing credit card limits, raising interest rates, and doing all of the things that devastate our good credit history; sending our credit scores lower. This is happening despite good payment records and long-term relationships. The effects of low interest rates are being negated by the very acts of the banks that are still standing. How long until nobody has a credit score worthy of lending on?

Washington, please take *score* and look at this one.

9

Liar, Liar

Underwriting Income: Ability to Repay

"Liar, Liar, pants on fire, hanging on a telephone wire." If you are old enough, you probably sang this little rhyme as a child. Liar loans are now synonymous with the defaulted loans of the past few years. Stated income loans, now called "Liar Loans" became the norm as Wall Street established loans with non-existent underwriting standards.

Documenting income is crucial to the establishment of how much mortgage a person is able to successfully carry. Years ago, it was determined that if a person were to allocate no more than 25% of their **gross** income towards their housing expense, then they should be able to live comfortably on the remaining 75%. In addition, no more than 33% of **gross** income was to be attributable to housing expense plus all other credit indebtedness. Just to clarify –**gross** income is the money that you are paid *before* they deduct the federal tax, the state tax, the FICA tax for Medicare and social security, the health insurance premiums, and all the many little extras that are taken out of your paycheck before you actually see any cash in your hand. Don't you think it is *gross* what you have left after they raid your earnings?

Fixed versus Discretionary Expenses:

The lending community has separated your expenses into two basic categories, fixed or discretionary. Your fixed expenses include your housing and total obligated debts. Your housing expense is the combination of principal and interest on the mortgage loan, insurance and taxes on the property, and any associated costs, such as homeowner dues. Your other fixed expenses are the items that appear on your credit report that you have already committed yourself to paying. These may include a car loan, school loans, installment loans, and any credit card debt. Also included in these fixed expenses are amounts that you are required by law to pay for child support, alimony or any other court ordered items. The rest of your expenses are deemed discretionary.

What does the Lender Consider Discretionary Expenses?

✓ Food

✓ Insurance: for life, health and autos

✓ Medical expenses, dental expenses and pharmaceuticals

✓ Utilities such as electric, gas, water, sewage, cable, phone, internet

✓ Entertainment of all kinds including any vacations

✓ Clothing and shoes

✓ Health and beauty

✓ Repairs of every nature

✓ Vehicle expenses of gas, oil, parking, and replacement

✓ Kid activities including child care, music lessons, sports

✓ Education

✓ Charity

✓ Taxes

Unfortunately, last I heard, Uncle Sam does not deem his "cut" as discretionary. I personally don't think that food is either. The items listed as discretionary are not used in the evaluation of a mortgage loan applicant, as lenders are only concerned with your fixed expenses. These other expenses, though, can certainly be a very significant part of your budget.

Qualifying Ratios

Your FICO score is not the only number that the lender is evaluating in qualifying you for a mortgage loan. You must also pass the test of qualifying ratios. The ratio of your housing expense versus your gross income is your *Housing Ratio*, whereas *Total Debt Ratio* is your housing plus all other committed debt. By using ratios, theoretically a lender can determine if a person is applying for too much mortgage or if they are carrying too much debt, based on their current income level. Depending on how much indebtedness a person has can determine how much mortgage they can afford. Monthly payments for credit cards, auto loans, school loans and other installment debts are factored into how much of a person's income is already committed. These payments will limit what a borrower can (statistically) afford to pay for housing expense. Since housing has become more costly, lenders have allowed a greater percentage of gross income to be allocated to this major expense. It is not uncommon, although not necessarily wise, to see lenders allowing up to 50% and more of a person's gross income to be dedicated to their housing expense. The decision as to what ratio is acceptable has already been programmed into the software of the computer underwriting systems and will unerringly issue approval or declines based on the information fed to it.

Who Decides on "Acceptable" Ratios?

As discussed throughout the first section of this book, we know that the rules of mortgage lending are determined by the secondary markets that will eventually purchase these loans. Primarily, it is now Fannie and Freddie who set the criteria for what a direct lender is allowed to approve. Desktop Underwriter (DU) is the computer software program of Fannie Mae and Loan Prospector (LP) is the system used by Freddie Mac. All loans must pass this automated system of underwriting to be eligible for purchase by these entities. This non-biased program will deliver a verdict of approve or refer (can't use the term decline) based on the information that it is provided. There are several problems with this non-reasoning, inhuman, approach to underwriting loans. One major problem is – who decides how much income a person really has at their disposal? Isn't the computer software system only as reliable as the data that it is fed? Garbage in means garbage out!

Martha is a first year teacher making $36,000 per year. Can she afford to dedicate as much as 50% or $18,000 toward her housing expense, leaving herself only $18,000 for everything else? Those discretionary expenses, especially payroll taxes, really add up.

Larry earns $75,000 per year and maybe could afford $37,500 toward his housing expense. After all, he would have more money left over than Martha even earns.

Hard and fast RULES seldom work because there are so many variables. How many people does Larry support on his income? Does the underwriting software program understand that Larry pays over $500 per month commuting and parking expenses out of his salary? The acceptable income ratios are hard to pre-set into a software model when life has so many variables.

Mark is a Navy sailor who spends a great deal of time deployed under the services of our government. Some of these deployments last at least six months and can be very trying on the family. His wife Susan used to work as a transcriptionist for a large medical office but whenever Mark was out to sea, she had difficulty keeping reliable childcare for their three kids. After an especially trying time, Mark and Susan decided that it was better for her to stay home, even though they desperately needed her income. After only three months unemployed, Susan got the idea that she could work from home as a medical transcriptionist and still be on-site to provide stable care for her children. Since she had many contacts in the medical community, it didn't take her long to get a few clients. The doctors paid her as an independent contractor and she became self-employed. Within the first few months she was actually earning more money from home than she was while working on salary. Mark and Susan wanted to refinance their home loan in order to lower their interest rate. They have been declined.

WHY?: **Income from self-employment earnings can only used when documentable by two complete years of tax returns.** Can we not take into consideration that Susan has over five years experience in her field? Does it not matter that she earns more money now than before? Is no one taking into account that she no longer has the many expenses associated with working outside of the home, especially child care costs?

Jim just lost his good paying job in the pharmaceutical industry due to the recent recession and thankfully got a significant severance package. His wife Lisa is employed but her earnings are not as strong as Jim's. They know however, they can survive a long time until Jim finds another job because they have plenty of money in savings. There is no reason for him to panic and just take the first offer that comes his way. He has the ability to be selective and wait for the right opportunity. They want to refinance their mortgage to take advantage of the lower rates and help them cut their overhead further. Despite a great credit history, good equity in their property and a large savings account, they were declined because Lisa's income alone is not sufficient to qualify them for their mortgage loan.

WHY?: **Severance packages are not deemed as ongoing income and cannot be used as stable income.** Jim's severance pay was equal to nine months of his former salary. He also had sufficient cash in the bank that would equal 36 more months of his previous salary. In fact, Jim would only have needed to earn $10,000 per year to qualify for the requested loan. Based on those earnings, he would be able to carry the mortgage for an additional ten years. Where are the logic and the reasoning skills?

William is a builder of custom homes. He has a long history of stable earnings but the past two years have been very slow due to the downturn in the economy. He owns his home free and clear, and wants to take out some cash to carry him for the next year or so, until the market picks up. William could sell some of his properties but at current prices he would be practically giving them away. He just wants to utilize some of the equity in his home to carry him through. Much of his taxable earnings come in the form of capital gains, but the past year there was none to report. Say Nil to Bill.

<u>WHY?</u>: **Capital gains earnings can only be used if you can show a consistent three year history.** If you don't sell – you don't have any capital gains to report. These earnings are only taxable the year they occur. Same thing is true with stock options. Most people weren't selling in 2008 – who wanted to take the beating?

Most of us have seen our income pummeled in the past two years due to the very actions of those who now call the shots. They are turning us down when we need help the most. Susan is actually making more money than before, but not from the conventional "salary" route. Jim has staying power because he was wise enough to squirrel away money when times were good. William could sell off assets if the worst came, but why should he? Where is the common sense? All of these people are solid credit risks and have lived financially responsible lives. Does their past history not count for anything?

Unless you get all of your income from a salary, it is up to the discretion of the underwriter as to how much income they will use in your "qualifying ratios" or if they will even use your income at all. Underwriters are usually salary workers who fear for their jobs in this time of uncertainty. They are not going to stick their neck on the chopping block for Susan, Jim or William. Lenders fear that the secondary market will reject a loan if it does not meet the very narrow definition of what constitutes income. None of these people would have had any difficulty getting a loan before. However, our legislators, in an attempt to correct the horrible violations of the past several years, have now committed a more heinous offense by legislating that income must be verified. The problem is, by what standard? They don't know enough about the lending industry to make such a rigid law. This law has now totally banned "stated" income loans. **Where is OUR bail-out?**

Previously, the requirement for obtaining a stated income loan, before the "anything goes" era, was to document that the borrower was strong in three of the four underwriting areas. To utilize stated income you must have had an impeccable credit history with credit scores over the 680 mark (today, since they have changed the scoring method, it would probably be over 720), have significant cash in the bank, and have at least 20% or more equity in the property. **In other words, be able to demonstrate your creditworthiness by your past history.** The stated income loans, using the strengths of equity, money and credit history, are not the source of the foreclosures that we are now experiencing and yet people who cannot document their income by today's ridiculous standards are being punished and unable to purchase or refinance homes. People who previously obtained their adjustable rate mortgage loans using "stated income" are going to need to find longer term stable mortgages. What will be the fall-out when they are declined for refinancing?

Another client, Diane, has been in the same long-term relationship with her boyfriend, Ken, for over 25 years, but they have never married. They bought a home together over 12 years ago with the down payment assistance of Diane's mother, who also lived in the home but has since died. Diane and her mother Emma took title alone so that the property would pass someday to Diane's daughter. She wants to refinance the loan to a 30 year fixed since her current adjustable loan is due to reset in November. The home appraises (even in this market) for $750,000. The loan needed is $380,000 which is only a 51% LTV (loan-to-value). Diane has a decent job that pays an average income, but it is not sufficient to qualify for this mortgage loan. The bulk of the resources for paying the housing expense come from Ken's paycheck. Diane has a credit score of 780, and has around $50,000 in savings. There has never been one late payment in all of the twelve years that they have owned this home. Because of H.R.3221, she cannot qualify for this loan without the income from Ken, and since he is not a spouse, his income cannot be considered unless he goes on title. **Shouldn't Diane be able to refinance her current loan in order to stabilize her interest rate? Do you think she will walk away from her home with 50% equity in her property?**

I will be the first to agree that many of the loans done in recent years had little basis in reality. **They weren't "liar loans" because people could prove their creditworthiness; they were "liar loans" because they couldn't.** Stated income loans are now tarnished with the abuses of the Wall Street gang. I am not advocating that we go back and repeat the sins of the past. There is a significant difference in evaluating a person's creditworthiness by looking at their equity, credit history and liquidity, versus the no-documentation loans where everything was allowed. I could fill this book with many stories from my own experiences with clients that need the option of being able to have a stated income loan and that are very good credit risks. **These people need stated income loans due**

to their inability to verify income high enough by antiquated standards in order to qualify for the loan that they have been paying on faithfully for years.

Income in the 21ˢᵗ century is quite different than what it once was. Many people have cash flows that are significant, but out of the ordinary. Multi-family living arrangements, side jobs, family support, outside consulting, part-time employment when needed, renting out that extra room on occasion, exercising stock options, etc. are all many avenues of cash flow that are not necessarily documentable as stable or ongoing income by the narrow guidelines of Fannie and Freddie. **We can't always PROVE, to the documentation levels they are now requiring, all of the resources we have available to us as "cash flow".** How can we prove that mom is there to help whenever needed? I have a client who receives a non-taxable gift from mom each year of $10,000 as do his wife and kids. We allow this transfer of money from parent to child without tax consequences and yet this money cannot be used as income, as there is no way to provide proof of its ongoing nature. In today's economy, who can be certain that they will still have their job tomorrow, and yet this wage earner income is deemed ongoing.

The use of computers has allowed many employees to become telecommuters and set up self-employment earnings where salaries used to be. Working from home has opened up a whole new world of income where an employee elects to be paid as an independent contractor instead of punching a time clock and wasting time commuting to and from an office. Many companies have contract employees stationed all around the country (and world) as they no longer have a need for physical offices. This new work environment has opened up many tax advantages for the "at home" worker who can now write off an office in the home, equipment and a vast assortment of other deductions. Also, a person working from home is no longer paying the gas, oil, and maintenance on a vehicle, an expense normally associated with working. No more parking fees. They don't necessarily need the very high cost of child care since they are working from home. Maybe mom and dad work different time periods to accommodate this. They certainly don't need an extensive wardrobe, saving them hundreds, if not thousands of dollars especially in this designer-crazed world. **Are all of these work-related costs taken into consideration when we qualify a salary person as opposed to a non-employee status person?** These people have lessened their discretionary expenses significantly by working from home.

Accountants and tax preparers can often be hazardous to your ability to get loans, when they are paid to find every conceivable deduction in order to save their clients money. The really good ones are very skilled at hiding income from the IRS while making our job as underwriters impossible. I once reviewed a loan for a gentleman who owned such vast holdings that his financial statement was an inch thick. His tax returns showed losses for that year, and yet he still received huge government incentives in the form of tax credits, despite his losses. ???. His team of accountants was doing a very good job for him but he probably wouldn't qualify for a loan either.

When a salary person loses their job, chances are they are going to be without income until they find another job. In this current recession that may take some time. Self-employed individuals can't lose their job - they *are* the job. When they find their work slowing down or stopping, their ingenuity and risk taking skills often come into play and they will find a way to survive until money flows again. This is the nature of the entrepreneur. Many of these self-employed people are finding themselves being declined for loans because they have had less earnings to report over the past tax year. Yeah, no kidding! **We have taken the decision making away from individuals who might judge someone's ability to repay and replaced it with hard and fast rules of lending.** No longer do we have *people* looking at *people* and deciding what makes sense. Very often, people with non-traditional income sources can show the cash flows that they derive or at least show that they have the ability to hang on during an income interruption. The same cannot always be said for the wage earner. **Our current industry standard is to extend credit to people who bring home paychecks with no regard to cash in the bank or equity in their property**. The lenders would rather give Joe the wage earner a 95% loan, even though he has no cash in the bank to carry him if his job is terminated, than to give Sam the millionaire a 50% loan because he can't show you (to your satisfaction) how he makes his vast earnings. We survived many years under stated income scenarios without massive defaults from these borrowers. **We just need to return to the old underwriting standards, prior to 2000, before the invasion from Wall Street.**

Obviously everybody doesn't need a stated income loan. Most people can show, to the satisfaction of the lender, how they intend to repay the loan that they are requesting. This chapter is not written to state what is obvious. It is written to address the individuals who currently are being denied credit and can demonstrate through other means that they have the ***ability to repay the loan***, but not necessarily through the limited definitions that we are now using.

Just to clarify, I am not advocating that everyone who applies for a loan should get one. Some people should be denied a loan when there is no evidence of the ability to repay the requested loan. When innocent (and the sometimes, not so innocent) individuals want to purchase homes without so much as a nickel for a down payment, questions should be asked, like: "If you can't save any money now when you are paying rent, what makes you think you can afford the responsibilities of home ownership?" Or…"If you would make an effort to pay off your existing debt and free up some of your cash flow, then you would be able to afford more of a house than you are currently able to purchase." Or…"Didn't you just take money out of your home last year and where did that money go?" Or…"If you took your financial responsibilities more seriously and paid your bills on time then your credit history would not be in such bad shape and you could afford a lower interest rate"… or… or… or. This is logical, common sense reasoning that has been lost in our industry.

Underwriting income and what constitutes stable, ongoing cash flow is the most contentious of all the underwriting criteria as there are so many variables. Understanding a person's ability to repay a mortgage loan involves more than just looking at paystubs and tax returns. It is the art of looking at the whole person, in their entirety, including how they have handled their credit in the past, how much money they have in the bank (or other assets) and what equity position they have in the proposed property or current home. The art of decision-making is about assessing risk and determining if the requestor of a loan is going to repay this loan and how. Lending money should be about helping people, not burying them and certainly not denying them when they are able to demonstrate their ability to handle the financing that they are requesting.

Washington, give us back our stated income loans and more flexibility in the underwriting of income!

10

A Cushion Between a Rock and a Hard Place

Underwriting Money/Reserves – Time to Repay

Have you recently checked the contents of your economic "survival kit" in case of an emergency? If you suffered an income interruption, how long could you survive -a week, a month, or no time at all? Brink living, or living on the brink of disaster is living from paycheck to paycheck with no cushion between the rock and the hard place. How tight are your living quarters? Big money is being made by the "Cash until Payday" shops as people flock in to get advances on money they haven't even earned yet.

A part of the underwriting decision is evaluating how much money a person has left after a real estate transaction is completed. Most lenders will require that you have a minimum of three months worth of housing payments set aside to show ample reserves. For example, if your total housing payment, including principal, interest, taxes and insurance is $2,000 per month, then guidelines say that you should have at least $6,000 in the bank after purchasing a home or refinancing a mortgage. In my opinion, you should have a minimum of three months worth of GROSS earnings tucked away as a safety net for unforeseen emergencies. This is a minimal amount that everyone should have, and much more if possible.

The amount of money that a person has in the bank or other investment vehicle tells a lot about them financially. When a person typically spends all of their earnings each and every month, then the following assumptions can usually be made:

- ✓ They are living above their means and need to find areas of their spending that should be reduced
- ✓ They lack discipline in their spending habits

✓ They are totally unprepared for any emergencies that may arise

✓ They are a high risk borrower

Contrary to that, when a person has a large amount of available liquid assets they are showing tremendous discipline and are therefore a low risk borrower. This statement is of course qualified by the amount of reserves the person has versus the amount of money they are borrowing and the amount that they earn.

Bruce worked for his employer for over thirty years and was eligible for retirement. Instead of drawing a pension, he elected to take a lump sum distribution from his employer. I have seen many of my clients do this over the years, including one former airline pilot who took his lump sum distribution shortly before the airlines that he had worked for went bankrupt. Now that truly was a golden parachute. Bruce, in addition to this lump sum distribution, also had a large amount of stock options with various maturity dates, guaranteeing him continued income into the future. His total cash assets exceeded a million dollars; however, he had no history of earnings from this cash and so in order to compute his ongoing income, the lender allowed a modest amount of 3% interest to be usable as ongoing monthly income.

$1,000,000 x 3% = $30,000 per yr or $2,500 per month. In today's real estate market this didn't qualify Bruce to buy a pup tent. Bruce was purchasing a new home for $500,000. His former home netted him over $200,000 in cash that he was putting down on the new home. His loan request was for a $300,000 mortgage. Bruce had excellent credit, over a million in the bank, a large equity stake in his property and was declined. WHY? Not enough income.

Lenders often punish people who elect to borrow an amount of money that they already have in reserves. They could clearly use their own funds for the transaction but this causes them to lose out on the tax deductions of a mortgage loan. Also, most borrowers in this category want their funds working for them. The theory of many lenders is that Bruce could end up spending this money and not have it as a source of income. That is like saying you cannot loan to anyone with a job because they might get fired. None of us have any guarantees of what tomorrow may bring, but I'll put my money on the person with cash in the bank every time.

It has been my experience in dealing with people that those individuals with a large amount of reserves do not see those funds as disposable cash, but as security for the future. They are usually always adding to those funds in order to build them into greater amounts. Money in the bank is a lifestyle choice. They choose to live beneath their earning capability. While their peers may be out buying the latest model vehicle, these people are content to drive a paid-for and often out-of-date one. Am I stereotyping? This is just an observation from thirty years of experience.

There are several families that I have encountered over the years where the parents assist the grown children in getting into their first homes. It is not uncommon to see a family business that is the source of a financial safety net for multiple family members, even though the actual cash may not be in the name of the participant in the transaction. Knowing that a borrower has a strong family behind them can help in the weighing of the loan decision, especially where money for the down payment comes from the parents. It is doubtful when someone gives you a large down payment that they are not going to be there should you need help with ongoing payments. An example of this type of support is illustrated by the Douglas family. The father, Dr. D, is a practicing physician and hopes that someday his son Josh will go into private practice with him. While Josh was still in medical school, he wanted to purchase a condominium where he could reside when he was home from school and after he graduated. Since he was still in college, he was not yet producing income. Dad lent his significant financial strength to the deal and we closed it, knowing that this loan was a good risk. Don't forget that each loan tells a story. This story is of a loving, caring, responsible family who will be there for each other through good times and bad.

Sometimes the stories aren't happy ones. Another client, Fred, had a huge income as a stock broker. We helped Fred and his wife Susan, buy their first home and we watched as it appreciated significantly. Fred asked us to help him refinance a couple of years later in order to take out cash for a major remodel. It was interesting to note that Fred basically had no money in the bank despite his very large paychecks and that he needed to borrow to do the improvements. He came back to refinance frequently as his need for cash continued. First, it was the remodel, and then to buy a boat, and later for a vacation home down payment. He could not survive on what most people would consider a very generous income. He continued to mount his debt higher as his desire for a lavish lifestyle continued. The day came when we could no longer help Fred refinance his home. We felt that he had escalated his debt to a point where he could be insolvent and a high credit risk. He went to someone else and continued to borrow on a subprime basis. It ended with him losing his home, his wife and his job. Fred was a well qualified applicant on most of the loan transactions because he made a lot of money, but he always lacked in the category of reserves, and he lacked control of his spending habits. Money in the bank is a reflection of a disciplined financial life.

In the era of "no documentation" loans, reserves were not an issue. We allowed people to borrow 100% of the value of their new home with no consideration as to how they could handle an unexpected financial event. As previously stated, home ownership is a guarantee of an eventual emergency. I am surprised that current lending policies are only concerned with documenting income and the almighty credit scores. Documentation is not being requested on this very important aspect of lending. I am told by several lenders that Fannie Mae is not requiring the documentation of any liquid assets. When we input a loan into the DU system of Fannie Mae to be computer underwritten, the bank statements will only be requested if we disclose that they even have any cash. If we do not put it on the application, we don't have to verify it. How sound is that lending practice? It is like painting a portrait without a head. The amount of reserves includes all cash in the bank, stocks, retirement funds, cash value of life insurance policies and any other liquid assets that attest to the overall strength of the client. The fact that a person has cash in the bank (of any sizeable amount) can offset the possible weaker factors such as higher ratios. It demonstrates discipline and preparedness for emergencies.

For example, I am currently processing a loan for a semi-retired couple who wish to secure a long-term, low rate fixed mortgage. Their home price has dropped and to pay off their current financing and without having to pay mortgage insurance they are bringing in a sizeable amount of cash to pay down the balance of their loan. This in and of itself is proof of their creditworthiness. After this cash infusion they still have several hundred thousand dollars in liquid assets as part of their investment portfolio. Their reportable earnings are such that their income-to-debt ratio is quite high. A sizeable monthly installment loan payment on a recreational vehicle is to blame for this high ratio. They could pay-off this loan at any time from their vast resources; however, this is not a consideration in today's computer driven underwriting scheme. If the numbers don't say what the computer model wants, they are denied......where is the common sense? Other people with no cash in the bank are being approved and don't have a fraction of the creditworthiness of this couple.

Cash reserves buy time. Time needed to find a new job after a company has downsized and/or not having to settle for the first job that comes along. Time to mend from an illness. Time to spend with a loved one who won't be here forever. TIME....... How much does time cost?

Do you have a sizeable cushion between your rock and the hard place?

The current lending trend set forth by Fannie Mae is to grant loans based on a person having a job and a high credit score. As I've shown in a previous chapter, credit scores mean nothing. Having a job can also mean nothing if you lose it. The current underwriting guidelines of Fannie tend to disregard the person's cash in the bank altogether. It is not even necessary to put it on an application, other than to provide proof of down payment funds in a purchase transaction. This omission is a blatant disregard for the importance of one of the highest risk factors of people going into default. They have no cash. The industry is also not using good judgment in denying loans to borrowers who have demonstrated a very prudent lifestyle by the cash they have amassed. Let's restore balanced underwriting once again. In an attempt to not discriminate against the poor, we are discriminating against the truly creditworthy individuals.

Hasn't cash always been KING?

11

Home Sweet Home

Underwriting Equity- the Motivation to Repay

Be it ever so humble, there is no place like home. Your home is your castle. Home is where the heart is. Oh, how we love our homes! Childhood memories often take us back to the home where we grew up. It is about the good times around our kitchen tables, the warmth of our beds, the sharing of our lives with the people that we love. It is the place where we celebrate our holidays with our families, our years in school, our first jobs, and our neighborhood friends. If you really focus on those years, you can often even smell the very aroma that is associated with the feelings. Home is where the heart is. What value do you put on your home?

For many individuals, who do not need or intend to sell their homes, value is inconsequential and often immeasurable in terms of dollars. How many of our closets hide the growth charts of our children? What would you take in return for the many years of memories that you and your family have amassed in your home? How much pride do you feel when you see the tree house in the backyard that you and your son built? Can you remember the first time that you took the training wheels off of your daughter's bicycle and watched her maneuver down the street on her own? Look at the swing on the porch and remember all of the family problems that were solved there. Memories can't be bought with a price.

There are people today who own homes, with little or no vested interest in the brick and mortar that houses them. They purchased the house with little or no down payment and now, with an economic downturn, are willing to just walk away without a fight. Nothing vested, nothing gained. There are other people, who put large down payments of hard earned and saved dollars into their properties, only to be informed that their homes have no equity value.

Juan purchased his home in the Temecula area of Southern California in 2004, before the height of the market. He paid $450,000 for a brand new three bedroom bungalow style home. Juan had a sizeable down payment of $250,000 and only needed a mortgage loan for $200,000. A couple of months ago, Juan contacted us to refinance his mortgage into a lower fixed-rate loan. His existing rate was 5.875% but current rates were at least one percent lower. The appraiser that we contacted told us that it would be impossible for him to value the property over $235,000 based on the current distressed sales in the area. Temecula is in Riverside County, an area especially hard hit by foreclosures as it was the site of many 100% financed homes and sub-prime loans. In order to refinance into a better rate, Juan would have to pay for mortgage insurance as his home would now be an 86% LTV loan and deemed a high risk. Plus, with all the additions to pricing at that high of an LTV, he wouldn't get the rate that would make sense for him to refinance. Bottom line here; his ending monthly payments would go up and not down..... HOW UNFAIR!!!!! What happened to the $250,000 that he put into the property? Can that not be counted towards his "equity" in his home? Remember, Juan is not looking to take cash out of his home, but only to better his loan with a lesser rate. Is this not discrimination?

Fannie Mae has just announced they will refinance loans currently owned by them with lesser regard to current value, even up to 105% of current prices without needing mortgage insurance.(if the original loan amount was under 80% LTV) This is a definite step in the right direction. Unfortunately, Juan's current loan is not serviced by Fannie Mae so he is out of luck. If a person can show, by reason of the original closing documents, they have invested cold hard cash into their property, why can't this be used as equity? I'll guarantee you nobody is going to take a walk from their property when they have invested even as little as 10%, at least not without a fight.

Lucy is one of those individuals whose home really is her castle. She is constantly upgrading, remodeling and improving on her home as money permits. Being very handy and having a husband who is as well, they do most of the work themselves and only have to pay for supplies. This investment into their home is called sweat equity, and it is an emotional investment. Their home shows the pride of ownership from years of hard work and love. They have made their home into one of the nicest in an area of mostly modest homes, but they haven't seen their value increase as much as if their home were in another neighborhood. This has never mattered very much to them as they know all of their neighbors and never intend to move out of that home. It is the place where they want to retire some day. Are they motivated to keep their home – you bet!

Today, placing a dollar value on our homes is very difficult, in fact, almost impossible. While it is true that there is no monetary price tag that can be placed on the memories of our lives, houses must have a monetary valuation. The county establishes a value on your house in order to assess your property tax. If you want to sell your home, then the free market system establishes a price. For the purpose of mortgaging a home, a value must be determined.

The market value of your house is the price for which it will sell in a competitive and open market when a buyer and a seller are equally motivated to complete a sale. The problem today is we don't have a competitive market. Homes are not selling unless they are priced at bargain basement levels. Many of the buyers today are investment conscious and seeking to profit on the many foreclosed properties that are available. There is such a surplus of properties on the market, many of them severely distressed, that it will be a buyer's market until this excess is eliminated. Also, financing is very limited and not available to the many who would seek to capitalize on this current fire sale of properties. So how do we value properties in this current economic climate?

The Appraisal Process

Appraisal reports, completed by licensed and trained appraisers, are what lenders depend on to establish the security or collateral value for the property that they are mortgaging. Traditionally, there have been three methods of establishing a property's value:

Cost Approach: The cost approach computes the replacement cost of the subject property in the current marketplace. This section of the appraisal has rarely been used in the past few years, as the market value of property has determined its price. In evaluating a property by cost approach, you first determine the value of the underlying land at its highest and best use. You then estimate how much money it would cost on a square footage basis to rebuild the home, taking into consideration its amenities. For example, a highly upgraded home would have a higher per square footage cost to rebuild than one that is not upgraded. Additional structures on the property are considered, like garages or gazebos. A pool and hardscape (permanent outside fixtures, like retaining walls or patios) are added values. The property is then depreciated, based on actual age and condition of the improvements. If a property has been recently rehabilitated or remodeled, then it is considered like-new, even if the actual age of the property is older. Basically, you are establishing a value that would insure the property in the event of total destruction by fire, flood or other calamity.

Market Approach: The market approach to value compares the subject property with similar properties in the area that have recently sold. Generally, all sales of similar properties must be within the previous six months and be within a one-mile radius. Due to declining market conditions, lenders are now requiring appraisers to use only the most current 90 days of sales data, a very difficult task when nothing is selling. These are lender guidelines, but are not always practical. Even in an active market, an appraiser must often go to a wider area of search or a longer sales period due to a property's uniqueness. For example, if a property being appraised is a 1500 square foot home, in an area of predominantly larger homes, then it would not be appropriate to use the sale of a 3000 square foot home as a comparable, even if it was next door. The market approach to pricing has always been the leading indicator of value.

Income Approach: The income approach estimates the value of property based on the income that the subject property would produce as a rental or leased property. This approach is commonly used with units and commercial property, but is seldom given any credence in the single family residential marketplace.

How do you appraise the market value of a piece of property when nothing is selling? As long as there are so many limitations on mortgage loans, then nothing will sell. The current value of our homes is being established by the sales of distressed and foreclosed properties that are being gobbled up by investors for a mere fraction of their worth. Builders cannot even build new homes for the low price tags of the current foreclosed properties.

"Buy and Bail" is a new term for individuals who are trying to quickly buy houses at absurdly low prices with the intention of bailing on their current over-mortgaged homes. This is happening with alarming frequency and lenders are now becoming aware of this practice. You can't really blame people for trying to better themselves, knowing that they will be unable to sell their current homes for a price high enough to even pay off the existing mortgage. If they allow their property to be taken back by the lender in a foreclosure, then it could be many years before they are deemed credit-worthy enough to purchase another home. Who wants to own a piece of property that may not recover in value for many years to come? How long will it take until our homes are worth what our mortgages are? We must try and stop this practice of "buy and bail" and others like it, or we will continue to see our home prices erode even further.

Local and State Fallout from Low Property Valuations

Many people are petitioning their local county assessor's office to reduce their current property tax liability. They are able to effectively prove through today's market sales data that their homes are no longer worth the assessed value they are being taxed on. Companies are even springing up, offering to fight the tax man on behalf of the homeowner, for a fee of course. Amazing how quickly people find ways to profit at other people's expense. As more people obtain relief from tax liabilities, the more local revenues will drop. Add to this the area foreclosures, and that means even less revenue. How long will it be before our city, county and state governments don't have the funds to provide the services needed for our education and safety? California, which ranks within the top ten economies of the world, has already experienced a short-fall in revenue to the point of having to pink slip many teachers in our schools. This year, my granddaughters are being driven to school by their mother, as the bus service was suspended due to lack of funds. Who will pay for our teachers to continue to educate our children? How many firefighters can we afford to lose before we have a catastrophe? Here in San Diego in October of 2007, we experienced one of the worst fire seasons ever. As it was, we needed additional fire support from outside of the state. We can't afford to lose any of these needed tax dollar supported services. What happens if we can't afford to pay all of our police officers? Who will protect us? During times of deep economic hardships, we often see a rise in criminal activity. Will we be declaring martial law?

The systemic risk to our U.S. economy is based on the underlying value of the properties that secure our mortgage loans, particularly the ones that are being referred to as "toxic". We can no longer devalue our properties to the point of the current economic market conditions. We must have a measuring stick capable of establishing a value for these properties until such time as we can eliminate the surplus of homes. Once a value is established, then we can open up the lending channels again. When lending is re-established, then purchasing power will return.

Take Note Washington: Here's a Solution that will Work.

Base current home values on the "Cost Approach" of the homes, until market values can be re-established. We must create a floor under the free-falling home prices before we can ever hope to recover from this housing crisis. A new ground-zero must be set in place. A house should be worth no less than the cost to rebuild it.

Our banking system must have a credible way of evaluating the underlying assets of their lending portfolios. I believe that many of the current bank failures could have been avoided if the prices of the homes securing their total mortgage loans were not so devalued. The actual percentage of bad loans is very small compared to the performing loans. On the Federal Reserve website, the statistical data for charge-off and delinquent loans is at an all-time high of 6.14% as of 4th quarter of 2008. That means that 94% of real estate secured loans, which includes all types of residential and commercial loans, are not in default and are paying on time. Why are banks forced to write down property valuations of a portfolio where 94% of these loans will actually perform? Why not re-establish home prices for what it would cost to rebuild them, as truly that will be the future cost once this crisis has been averted. Time heals all wounds. We just need time.

Lending cannot be restored until we have a viable way to appraise properties that are not in distress. Appraisers are trained to provide valuation using a cost approach. This has always been an acceptable assessment procedure for insuring our homes. Why not use this approach for lending so people can refinance their existing mortgages without being penalized by those homes that are in default. The majority of homeowners will faithfully pay their mortgages, especially when they do not feel hopeless and can see their home equity in terms of real dollars. They should be able to refinance existing loans based on realistic appraised values that are not just reflective of deeply discounted properties.

The temporary appraisal by cost approach will give the markets time to recapture their value, while not destroying our economy. It may take a while for our market approach to value to be re-instituted as the excess inventory of unsold homes works its way out of the system. Once this happens, we can then restore a valuation that is based on market sales. In the meantime, the cost approach can restore hope and confidence in our homes, our banking systems, and our government. Just Do It!

Newest Lending Nightmare

The latest disaster facing the lending markets today is the new HVCC provision enforced by Fannie and Freddie as of 5/1/09 and now fully implemented by all mortgage lenders. The HVCC (pronounced Havoc) is the Home Value Code of Conduct (a copy of this document is in the supplemental section of this book) and mandates that all appraisals must be ordered by non-interested management companies who contract out appraisal services to independent appraisers. What does that mean? No longer can we as mortgage brokers order the appraisal direct with our local and trusted appraiser. We must order the appraisal through the bank who will then order thru a centralized management company who will then order through a local appraiser. Sound confusing? It is. One of the difficulties facing the industry today, as previously mentioned, is the lack of "normal" sales data that is not just reflective of foreclosure, short sales or purely distressed sales. Obviously, these distressed sales bring the value of all properties down because not only are they sold for pennies on the valuation dollars, but they are often in disrepair condition as people who can't afford to pay their mortgage certainly aren't going to spend dollars to upkeep the property. Appraisers must work extra hard these days in order to search out sales data that is not just reflective of these distressed sales and to establish the lendable value of the homes for people who want to refinance and take advantage of the lower rates. If you send out totally disinterested appraisers who will get paid whether or not the client is going to be able to use the report, then how hard are they going to search and get the comparable sales, in order to make a transaction work? The borrower or the broker is going to pay for this report whether or not it has any merit.

When a loan officer requests *our* appraiser to do an appraisal report, they know the value that we need in order to make a deal work. If *our* appraiser cannot get that value, they will generally call and let us know so the client doesn't have to go to the expense of an appraisal, which often costs around $350 or more. Any appraiser that I have ever worked with is not in the business of making up values just to satisfy the client. They have their license to protect. Maybe we just aren't big enough to have that kind of influence. The HVCC states that appraisers cannot know what your loan amount is or what value you need on the report. This means that with the current low property values, most of these appraisal reports will generate fee income for the appraiser and the company that they work for. It will not save the little guy the $350 that he must pay to validate that his home is not worth enough to refinance. Brokers will be on the hook for the fees associated with these non-usable reports. Maybe the homeowner can use these reports to get their property taxes lowered, but it is certainly not going to assist us in helping homeowners refinance bad loans into good loans or lower rates on existing mortgages.

Our appraisers are willing to check, periodically, to see if sales data has changed enough for them to be able to give an appraised value high enough to assist us with helping our client to achieve a better loan. Do you think we will pay $350 each time for this information? We can check through our local realtor to provide updated sales data but we cannot furnish this information to the appraisal management company (because the HVCC says we can't), and thus we have no idea if we are just throwing money we don't have away. What bonehead wrote this #^$$%&* code?

The banks, the originator of many of the abuses we are currently trying to safeguard against, are now going to be in control of this appraisal process as THEY get to pick which management companies they are going to work with. And, by the way, they aren't willing to use the appraisals ordered by other banks' management companies….Hmmm. Countrywide, now Bank of America is ordering all of their appraisals through a company called Landsafe. Landsafe is a very large company that does credit reports, appraisals, flood certifications and various other services to the lending community. Landsafe is a wholly-owned subsidiary of Countrywide. No code of conduct issues here!!!!! That means they win, whether or not they get a loan out of this or not. The fee income generated here is massive as the appraiser is only getting a dribble for his participation in this farce. Several appraisers that I know can't get on the list of these management companies who have all of the appraisers they need. These veteran appraisers are now joining the ranks of the unemployed, but don't look for them on the recent statistics. Self employed people without the ability to produce income; just means poor. Andrew Cuomo, the attorney general of New York is responsible for destroying an entire industry through the HVCC that he bullied Fannie and Freddie into adopting.

So let's get this straight – our client, the homeowner, who comes to us because we have years of trust built up, is asking us to help them refinance their loan. Under normal circumstances, we pick up the phone or email our appraiser and ask for comparable sales data. They let us know, yea or nay, as to whether this is a do-able deal – right now. They may even say there are pending sales that could support it if we wait to see if these sales close. This is a valuable service to us as a lending professional and to our client the homeowner. We certainly don't want to charge them for a service that we cannot provide. Now, we must order an appraisal from Lender One and pay for it, when previously a phone call would have given us the pertinent information. If the appraisal does not support the value, but our local real estate data would indicate that there are sales to support it, we cannot provide the appraiser with this information. Handcuffs anyone? So, we go to lender number two – another $350. Here is another example of an over correction that has gone really wrong. And who are we protecting?

Summation:

Falling home prices due to too much inventory and non-qualified borrowers = foreclosures & short sales = more falling home prices & less motivated home owners = more foreclosures & short sales = more falling prices & less ability to stay in home .... I think you get the idea.

Appraisers used to be held to a level of accountability by the banks that would utilize "approved appraiser lists". If an appraiser was caught in fraudulent activity or other indiscretions, they lost their ability to do work for that lender and perhaps even their licensing. We keep over-correcting the problems while creating greater problems. This HVCC won't work long term and again puts too much control in the hands of the BIG BANKS who created the problems we are currently experiencing.

Equity – Our Motivation to Repay a Mortgage

Equity in a piece of property provides motivation for a borrower to keep paying the mortgage loan. Our current lending crisis resulted from the many100% financed properties. Subprime lending, neg am loans, and interest-only loans have all taken the fall for the primary reason behind this crisis. We let too many people purchase homes without any investment on their part. No vested equity at all.

Builders helped to fuel this "lack of motivation" by contributing money to self serving non-profit organizations that provided down-payment funding to many of their first time homebuyers. This is a slimy little fact that few knew about. It looked on paper like a person was bringing money into the transaction in buying a new home when in reality these funds were coming from outside sources. How easy it was for the builders to inflate the price of homes, provide the down-payment funds (via the non-profit organization that they helped to establish) and put the banks on the hook for fully mortgaged properties. Congress has since abolished this practice (a little late – the damage is already done). Also, maybe a little hypocritical since it was our legislators who were the ones pressuring Fannie and Freddie into providing high risk loans to no-down payment borrowers in the interest of making all Americans homeowners.

A person's *equity* in the property being mortgaged should be evaluated as follows:

1. How much cash are they putting down on the property (if a purchase) or how much did they put down originally?

2. How much has the person invested into the property in the way of improvements (either in cash or in sweat equity)?

3. How many years have they lived in this property (emotional investment)?

4. Have they taken out massive cash in the past few years and if so was this cash reinvested into the property or into other things?

In other words, what is their stake in the home? We need to be able to evaluate a person's motivation to repay a loan by a better measuring system than just currently deflated appraised values. Will Juan walk away from his $250,000 investment? Will Lucy give up on the home she has continually improved with the sweat equity of her labor? Will someone who has lived in a home for years just walk away because the economy is rough?

Are we punishing the 94% of homeowners who are paying their mortgages faithfully because of the 6% who are not?

12

<u>Overdrawn at the House of ATM</u>

<u>Solutions for the Defaulted Home Loans</u>

Our banking system is crumbling and laying in ruin. Wall Street has effectively collapsed, having been poisoned by their own "toxic" mortgages. Our equity has eroded and there is no more "House of ATM". Our entire economy lays at the brink of a potential "depression" if answers are not rapid in coming. The Feds have thrown billions of dollars into the economy, only to see it magically vanish. The legislators are passing bill after bill with no recovery in sight. There is no quick and easy solution.

The underlying problem is the defaulting mortgage loans, as we see this house of cards tumble. The first section of this book identified how we got into this mess in the first place. In the previous few chapters, I have offered tangible solutions to the various aspects of this lending crisis. However, we must deal swiftly with the homeowners who are in default before we can truly heal our wounds.

<u>What is the cost of Foreclosure to the Banks and the Market?</u>

The process of taking a mortgage holder into foreclosure is very costly to the lender and ultimately, to our economy. There are many months where no payments are being made on the defaulted loans and no earnings are being generated to the bank. The legal process of executing a foreclosure and subsequent sale of the property is obscenely expensive. In order for the lender to resell the property they must absorb the costs of realtor fees, escrow fees, title charges and all associated selling costs that diminish what they will actually get for their debt. Neighborhoods suffer from yet another foreclosure, weakening property values further. The cost of leaving a property vacant and vulnerable to vandals is certainly not an option. With homes selling for a fraction of their previous worth, it is a guarantee that the bank will only see a meager amount from this action, given the magnitude of foreclosures that are facing our country. A bank will lose potentially tens of thousands of dollars for any execution of a foreclosure in this current market. So let's get creative! We must look for alternatives to "buy" the recovery for our future. I feel confident, given enough time, and I am sure we are speaking years and not months, that home prices will eventually stabilize and then start increasing from these false lows. We just need time!

Stop Modifying Loans into 30 Year Fixed-Rate Mortgages:

The Federal Government has been "encouraging" lenders to provide loan modifications to the many homeowners of America who are struggling to keep up with their payments. In fact, the government is paying lenders to provide this service. According to the media, it is not working. They are reporting that newly modified loans are in default from payment number one. Why is this? If you take a loan that is in default because a borrower cannot afford the monthly payment and then raise their monthly payment, isn't it obvious that no solution was achieved? But that is what is being done. Lenders are taking the deficiency balance of what has gone in arrears and tacked it onto the current principal balance and then put the defaulted borrower into a stable 30 year fully-amortized loan. Doesn't work! Fully amortized loans are not necessarily the answer to our current affordability problems. In chapter 15, I introduce a mortgage loan that has all of the safeguards of a 30 year fixed-rate loan with initial lower monthly payments. Take a look. It will work.

Evaluate Defaulted Borrowers on a Case-by-Case Basis before offering a loan modification – Not every defaulted Homeowner should get modified:

Many defaulted homeowners are enjoying a free ride at taxpayer expense. Some of them have gone over a year without making any house payment at all. Many homeowners who went into default found that the lender was not quick to execute the foreclosure papers, and then a moratorium went into effect to temporarily stop these foreclosures from being finalized. Free housing - not a bad deal. Many of these individuals are the people who could not afford to buy the home initially and are now capitalizing on the crisis to "get theirs". Some of these free riders are the same ones who are going back into default immediately after a modification is granted. "Let's see how long we can ride this gravy train" is obviously their motivation. Maybe this is their way to get their share of the *bail-out* money. In any case, they do not ever intend to pay on the mortgage.

It is important for a lender to evaluate the motivation and agenda of any mortgagor who is seeking assistance to renegotiate their mortgage loan. Did the borrower recently purchase the home and not have the ability to pay on the mortgage in the first place? Is this a primary residence or a property purchased as an investment? How long has the individual owned the house and how much cold hard cash did they invest, if any? What is their emotional investment in this home? Are they suffering from a momentary loss of income or loss of job due to the current housing crisis and can they recoup given time to do so? Is the potential default due to a mortgage reset and if payments were affordable could they handle them? Is this person seeking to profit at the expense of the devalued market when they really are in a position to pay their contracted debt? All of these questions and more need to be addressed in order to see whether a modification agreement is necessary and/or even possible. Ultimately, a person's motivation for keeping the home will determine if they are "worth this risk". For example, an investor is going to be less motivated than an owner-occupant homeowner would be. Maybe we could take the tax dollars that we are paying the "Hope Now" crowd and employ case workers to investigate individual situations to determine the best use of our resources.

Stop requiring mortgagors to go delinquent before reviewing their loan needs and offering assistance.

Companies have sprung up overnight, many of the employees being the former subprime gangs who caused this mess to begin with, who are now actually helping people go into default and offering to assist them in getting the lenders to modify their loans – for a fee. Hundreds of thousands of dollars are being spent by desperate homeowners who wish to capitalize on this opportunity to get their loans modified. What a racket! Is anyone policing this? These people are selling homeowners on the idea of defaulting on their loans. Shouldn't this be illegal? It is certainly not helping the situation any.

Borrowers who need help and some who don't are going into default in record numbers. I am told that mortgage lenders can offer no assistance unless the borrowers are two months in arrears on their payments. This is forcing some people to voluntarily go into default in order to get mortgage relief. Not all of the people going into default are necessarily in need and we may find that the numbers are not as dire as originally thought. Some people are listening to the media who report that loans are being rewritten and some of the principal may be waived if they make this call. Who doesn't want their mortgage balance reduced? However, we are creating a precedent that is skewing the true picture of how many foreclosures we will actually see. Default does not necessarily mean foreclosure if the person applying for help is just "using the system". We must stop this practice immediately. The massive volume of default notices are causing more fear and panic and may not be a true reflection of how many bad mortgage loans are still out there.

Give a several month waiver on house payments for unemployed or underemployed borrowers and add the payments to the end of the loan, lengthening the term of the loan by the months waived.

Many people are suffering from lack of employment (or lack of income) that is directly attributable to this housing crisis. As soon as we get sanity restored to the lending markets then some of these people will be able to get back to work. This is a momentary setback, providing we fix the underlying problem. If a person is out of work, it is reasonable to assume that they cannot afford any size mortgage payment unless there are other working family members. If someone can show that they have a vested interest in staying in their home, for example, a large down payment, years in the property, etc. then consider giving them a six to twelve month respite with no housing payments and add the balance to the end of the mortgage note, extending the term of the loan.

Do not set a precedent of lowering mortgage balances; instead, find a way to lower monthly payments if necessary.

As suggested in the previous chapter, we need to find a way, outside of market valuation, to determine a property's true worth. An appraisal based on the cost approach of the home could assist a lender in determining how out of balance a mortgage loan really is. At this juncture, so many homes seem to be upside down in value as *false* lows, established by hardship sales, have skewed the true equity picture. If a value can be established showing a homeowner the true potential of their home's value, they may be more motivated to hold on and not feel so helpless. Under no circumstances should lenders start negotiating on the balance of the mortgage note, unless perhaps in cases of negatively amortizing loans where balances are so out of proportion to the actual value of the properties. This imbalance however, should be on replacement cost and not on market value. Lowering of mortgage balances will set a precedent that will open the gates for all homeowners who will bang down lender doors in droves wanting the same privilege. It is downright discriminatory and rewards the person who is defaulting while punishing the homeowner who is struggling to maintain their high balance loans. It will only exacerbate the problem and lengthen our recovery time. All negotiations should be to the payments and future modification of the note until recovery is possible. We are a payment-driven society and with a lower interest rate, or a longer loan term, homeowners will be able to stay in their homes. The ability to gain on the equity is a cost they will bear in the future, but we will not have to absorb it today.

We need sweeping regulatory reform to allow banks the necessary tools to effectively negotiate better terms for the mortgagors in need. Whether lowering interest rates to near zero for a time, or lengthening the term of the loan to 50 years, let's keep things moving. Adding defaulted payments to the end of the mortgage note or giving an unspecified time period with a payment forgiveness factor, are all practical solutions that should be considered. We need to avoid more potential foreclosures whenever possible. Let's issue some "get out of jail free" cards but no "free rides". These modifications will save potentially hundreds of thousands of dollars per loan and multiple billions to the economy. We need time to recuperate from this housing crisis.

Make homeowners, in high foreclosure areas, leasers to the bank for a specified time period.

As a **last** resort to avoiding another foreclosure consider making the homeowner – the renter. This action, although not conventional, will avoid increasing the over-supply of homes for sale, vacancies, and vandalism issues. If it is obvious that the homeowner cannot afford this home under any other circumstances, then perhaps, allowing them to stay in the home by leasing the property for a specified time period can relieve the immediacy of executing a foreclosure. This would be more applicable in areas where there are already too many properties in foreclosure and that are resulting in vacant homes not being sold. Perhaps counties could waive property tax payments for a time by taking a note against the future sale of the home.

If we can avoid foreclosures, then the banks will retain the underlying value of the property as collateral and thus shore up their balance sheets. What good is it to sell off an asset for a few pennies on the dollar? Use the pennies to grow the dollars. The homeowners will adapt to modifications to their housing payments, giving them the time to get back on their feet. The housing market will stabilize from the free fall it is in. Jobs in the housing and lending industry will return and help to grow the economy once again. The world markets will have more confidence, knowing that the good ol' US of A. is not a faltering giant about to fall on them.

We must rebuild confidence where fear now resides.

13

<u>Understanding Interest Rates</u>

<u>*Warning- this Chapter will raise Blood Pressure*</u>

$$\$200,000 \text{ X } 7.0\% = \$1,330$$

$$\$225,000 \text{ X } 6.0\% = \$1,348$$

$$\$250,000 \text{ X } 5.0\% = \$1,342$$

The above examples show the dramatic effect that interest rates can have on a typical mortgage lending scenario. The monthly payments shown are based on a standard 30 year fixed-rate mortgage loan. As this illustration shows, the lower the rate, the higher the amount of mortgage that you can afford. The difference of 2% in interest rate at the loan amount of $200,000 can buy you $50,000 more in loan amount for a mere $12.00 more per month. So what can $12 actually buy? How about that extra bedroom and bath? Will it buy a home in a better location? Want to take a dip in your new swimming pool? If the interest rate is low, you can buy so much more for your money. Likewise:

$$\$250,000 \text{ X } 5.0\% = \$1,342$$

$$\$250,000 \text{ X } 6.0\% = \$1,498$$

$$\$250,000 \text{ X } 7.0\% = \$1,663$$

The effects of lowering interest rates can give you many of the things that you desire but the raising of interest rates can take it all away just as fast. How can 2% affect you? Let's assume that during the falling rates of 2003 you were able to increase your borrowing power and obtained a mortgage loan of $250,000. Suppose your loan was on an adjustable rate mortgage and the rates continued to climb. You could easily find yourself paying $321 more per month for that same mortgage loan. If you are on a tight budget, that increase in payment could mean disaster.

The role of interest rates on mortgage lending is critical to affordability.

Pick up a newspaper on any given day and interest rates on mortgage loans are posted by various lenders. What do these rates actually mean? Can you assume that if you walk into the lobby of a mortgage lender's office that you can get the rate that you saw in that morning's newspaper? Probably not! The rates as shown are history by the time they reach the newsstands. Most lenders quote rates that are based on a 15 day delivery. That means your loan would have to close within a 15 day time period in order to get that rate. The reality is most loans from start to finish will take approximately 30 to 60 days to finalize. So how do we get these wonderful rates? Is time the only factor in loan pricing? How much will that wonderful rate cost? What is the APR? When one lender quotes significantly lower rates than the other lenders, are we dealing with a "bait and switch" scenario?

The general public has no idea how complicated today's pricing of mortgage loans actually is. Each morning, lenders publish rate sheets and send them to their wholesale brokers or inside loan officers. Rates change every day and in a volatile market, they can change multiple times in a single day. Lenders do not want the public to see these rate sheets and it is therefore the job of the loan officer to advise you as to what pricing is available for what product. This chapter will attempt to make you, the consumer, much wiser on the subject of interest rates. It may also serve to raise your blood pressure and anxiety level so have your Prozac handy, just in case.

In order to understand loan pricing, I have attached a mock rate sheet that could be from any lender. This particular rate sheet is based on actual pricing from one lender's rate sheet as of 3/20/2009 to illustrate how the pricing of loans is done. Most lenders are priced similarly but depending on the loan product, there can be variations. This is wholesale pricing which is given to mortgage brokers and is not the same as retail pricing, which you would get if you went directly to the lender. Wholesale pricing is designed to be at least one percentage point less (in cost) than retail so the broker can add his/her fee to this pricing and still be consistent with the rate you would receive if you were not using a broker. That is, *if* the broker is charging you fairly for the loan you are seeking. Using a broker can allow you to avail yourself of all lenders and a reputable broker knows the best days to lock in your interest rate. They are ultimately aware of which lender has the best pricing for what loan product. A reputable and experienced broker can be very valuable to you and a great source of advice when needed.

The example shown is an actual rate sheet on a standard 30 year fixed-rate loan. The interest rates are shown down the left hand column of the grid and most lenders post rates in eighths of a percent (.125). The time period across the top of the sheet refers to the "lock-in" period of the loan request. For example, if you are purchasing a home that is scheduled to close in the next 30 days, then the broker/loan officer would probably lock your loan under the 30 day pricing. If your loan transaction is scheduled to close within the next 45 days, then the pricing under that category would apply. As you can see - the shorter the lock term - the better the price. Loans can be locked, securing a particular interest rate, for even longer time periods, but the further out you go in time, the higher the interest rate. Many brokers elect for their clients to "float" and not lock in a rate until they can get into the 15 day period to maximize the best rate for their clients. This is very feasible when rates are stable.

Lender Rate Sheet
30 year fixed-rate loans
Pricing Sheet as of 3/20/09

Rate	15 day	30 day	45 day
4.250	1.755	1.837	1.987
4.375	1.066	1.136	1.286
4.50	0.637	0.740	0.890
4.625	0.450	0.570	0.720
4.75	0.000	0.100	0.250
4.875	(0.525)	(0.479)	(0.329)
5.00	(0.850)	(0.719)	(0.569)
5.125	(0.905)	(0.786)	(0.636)
5.250	(1.10)	(0.906)	(0.756)
5.375	(1.450)	(1.32)	(1.175)
5.50	(1.530)	(1.40)	(1.250)
5.625	(1.575)	(1.450)	(1.300)
5.750	(1.620)	(1.500)	(1.350)
5.875	(1.73)	(1.626)	(1.475)
6.00	(1.85)	(1.700)	(1.550)
6.125	(1.875)	(1.775)	(1.625)

Amount shown inside of parenthesis is called a rebate. It is a credit from the lender.   Amount outside of parenthesis is a charge.

If you review the attached rate sheet you may be surprised to understand that **ALL** of these rates are available to you as a borrower. The lower in rate that you go, the higher the cost of obtaining that rate. Conversely, the higher the interest rate, the lower the cost.

EXAMPLE:

Lending Scenario:

Sales Price of New Home:	$300,000
Down Payment of 20%	$ 60,000
Loan Amount of 80%:	$240,000

You are purchasing a home that is going to close within the next 30 days and you are borrowing $240,000 which represents an 80% loan to the purchase price of $300,000 (called LTV or loan amount to value of home). You decide that you want an interest rate of 4.875%. Going to the column for 30 day pricing you see that the lender is giving a rebate of .479% on this day. Rebates are monies paid to the broker/loan officer. Since this is wholesale pricing and your broker needs at least 1% as his fee, then he will typically charge you the difference (1.0 less .479 = .521)

4.875% Rate =	0.479 Rebate from lender to Broker ($1,149.60)
Broker Fee =	0.521 Charge to you to get that rate ($1,250.40)

$240,000 loan amount x (.479 plus .521) = $2,400 total or 1% of loan amount

You receive an interest rate of 4.875% for a 30 year fixed-rate loan at a cost of .521% (good deal)

The broker makes an industry standard fee of 1% through a combination of rebate from the lender and a cost to you. Often it is easier to round these numbers and the broker may offer you this rate for .50% or what is known as ½ of a point. One point equals 1% of a loan amount.

Now let's assume that you don't want to pay any points (which is also known as buying down the rate), in which case you would be looking at a rate of 5.25% to 5.375% depending on the broker that you are working with (or sometimes on how difficult you are as a client). This rate would allow the lender to pay the broker either .906% or 1.32% respectively. This is called par pricing and allows the broker/loan officer to get his entire fee from the lender. Remember, this is wholesale pricing and if the broker is only getting approximately 1% commission you are not paying any more than if you went to the lender directly, but you have the added benefit of using a broker who can shop all the lenders on your behalf.

5.25% Rate =   (.906%) Rebate to the Broker

5.375% Rate=   (1.32%) Rebate to the Broker

Loan amount of $240,000 x .906% = $2,174.40 Lender pays broker – no cost to you.

Loan amount of $240,000 x 1.32% = $3,168.00 Lender pays broker – no cost to you.

Again, all of the rates shown on that pricing chart are an option to you as a borrower, depending on how much or how little you want to spend for a rate. In the recent past, if you had elected to have a "no cost" loan, where all of the fees on the loan were paid by the lender/broker, then you would go to the place on the rate sheet where there is sufficient rebate to cover closing costs plus pay the broker at least a 1% fee. This option is clearly not available on this day and hasn't been for a while without increasing the rate significantly. In the olden "golden" days of not many years ago, a .25% increase in rate would get you a no-cost loan if your loan amount was high enough.

For example:

6.125% Rate =   (1.775%) Rebate from Lender or $4,260 Gross

Less Broker Fee =   1.0 or $2,400

Overage to pay closing costs   .775% or $1,860

$4,260 - $2,400 = $1,860 : Credit towards your closing costs

As you can see, you pay the cost, either in cash or in rate. Never be fooled by those loan advertisements again telling you that there is no cost on the loan. Every loan costs money as there are so many participants in a lending transaction. Closing costs are the amounts charged by the various providers of services. On every loan, there are many people and companies who work on your behalf in making a loan happen. Just to list a few: credit reporting agency, appraisal firm, title company, escrow company or attorney, notary, lender/broker staff of processor, underwriter, document drawer, funder, etc. It is surprising how many people it takes to complete a loan transaction. If the loan is for a purchase, there are also realtors, transaction coordinators, inspectors, surveyors, and the list can go on even more, depending on the particulars of a transaction.

<u>Now, that was the past and here comes the present with the new Fannie - Freddie additions to the pricing:</u>

Fannie Mae Additions To Pricing

Loan-to-Value Percentages

FICO Score Addition:

	<60%	60-70%	70-75%	75-80%	80-85%	85-90%	90-95%	>95%
>740	-0.25%	0	0	0	0	0	0	0
720-739	-0.25%	0	0	0.25%	0	0	0	0
700-719	-0.25%	0.50%	0.50%	0.75%	0.50%	0.50%	0.50%	0.50%
680-699	0	0.50%	1.00%	1.50%	1.00%	0.75%	0.75%	0.50%
660-679	0	1.00%	2.00%	2.50%	2.25%	1.75%	1.75%	1.25%
640-659	0.50%	1.25%	2.50%	3.00%	2.75%	2.25%	2.25%	1.75%
620-639	0.50%	1.50%	3.00%	3.00%	3.00%	2.75%	2.75%	2.50%
<620	0.50%	1.50%	3.00%	3.00%	3.00%	3.00%	3.00%	3.00%

Cash Out Adds:

	<60%	60-70%	70-75%	75-80%	80-85%	85-90%	90-95%	>95%
>740	0	0.25%	0.25%	0.50%	0.63%	0.63%	-	-
720-739	0	0.63%	0.63%	0.75%	1.50%	1.00%	-	-
700-719	0	0.63%	0.63%	0.75%	1.50%	1.00%	-	-
680-699	0	0.75%	0.75%	1.38%	2.50%	2.00%	-	-
660-679	0.25%	0.75%	0.75%	1.50%	2.50%	2.00%	-	-
640-659	0.25%	1.25%	1.25%	2.25%	3.00%	2.50%	-	-
620-639	0.25%	1.25%	1.25%	2.75%	3.00%	2.50%	-	-
<620	1.25%	2.25%	2.25%	2.75%	3.00%	3.00%	-	-

Interest Only Adds:

	<60%	60-70%	70-75%	75-80%	80-85%	85-90%	90-95%	>95%
	0	0	0	0.75%	0.75%	0.75%	0.75%	0.75%

Condo Adds:

	<60%	60-70%	70-75%	75-80%	80-85%	85-90%	90-95%	>95%
	0%	0%	0%	0.75%	0.75%	0.75%	0.75%	0.75%

Example, continued:

Now, assuming the same scenario as above, you are purchasing a home with 20% down and a loan amount of $240,000.

Your fico score is 679.

The pricing adjustment for an 80% loan with a FICO score of 679 is an additional fee of 2.5% of the loan amount. That is an **additional** pricing (add on) to whatever the rate sheet shows. On a loan amount of $240,000 x 2.5% =$6,000.00.

If this property happens to be a condominium add an additional .75% or $1800.00 to that also.

ARE YOU *%&*#(&*%^&* KIDDING ME?

Here is where the Prozac comes in..........

These pricing additions are not the result of some lunatic lender gone nuts.....this is the pricing of Fannie Mae and Freddie Mac under the current direction of our US Government, or you and I the taxpayers. More Prozac?

And you thought the five o'clock news was reporting the wonderful low interest rates! These are the most expensive interest rates that we have ever seen.

Most rate sheets state: "This information is strictly confidential and not to be disclosed to the general public". Why is this pricing of loans such a carefully guarded secret? Maybe they don't want gun-toting citizens coming in and shooting up the place out of sheer madness.

The honest and reputable brokers want you to know this information, as recent legislation has mandated that their income be fully disclosed on the closing statement. You know exactly what a broker is making on a transaction but who is reporting what the lender or the agencies (Fannie and Freddie) are making? This is outrageous fee income. Are the CEOs of these companies setting us up for their next round of bonuses? Is this the money they need to fill the politician's pockets so they keep voting in their favor? More Prozac anyone?

Example, continued:

Going back to the original lender rate sheet you will see that there is not an interest rate high enough to absorb this additional fee. You could take a rate of 6.125% and this would be the scenario:

Rate 6.125%	-1.775	(rebate or no cost to you)
Broker Fee: Less +1.00 charge=	-.775	(still no cost to you)
Pricing Adjustment for 80% loan with FICO score of 679 +	2.50	(charge)
= Net Cost to You of:	+1.725%	(this is the final cost to you)

$240,000 x 1.725% = $4,140

The best you can do on this pricing day is to take a rate of 6.125% for a cost of: $4,140.00 (not very cheap – is it?)

There is no way for you to avoid paying an origination fee under the current additions to pricing with this very conservative example. To avoid paying too much initially, you must now accept a significantly higher interest rate.

Now, the possibility of getting a "no-cost" loan is long gone.

The origination fee does not include the additional loan charges that will probably exceed $3,000, which are the fees charged by all of the providers of services as I indicated previously. Let us not forget about the prepaid items: interest charged per day, property insurance for the first year and property taxes that may be due. Let us use a conservative amount of $2,000 for all of these items (and that is very conservative).

Funds Needed to Close the Transaction:

Down Payment:	$60,000
Closing Costs:	$ 3,000
Prepaid Items:	$ 2,000
Total Costs before interest rate charge:	$65,000

@4.875% rate cost of .50 (broker fee) plus 2.5 (FICO add) = 3.00 or $7,200.

     Payment at 4.875% $1,270

@6.125% rate cost of 1.725 or $4,140.

     Payment at 6.125% $1,458

All of this is based on the very conservative loan amount of $240,000. Multiply that several times over for higher lending scenarios.

Note the following:

If your credit score was one point higher, you would pay $2400 (1%) less for this very same loan – this is a massive penalty since you already have a decent credit score. Could this be discrimination?

The highest additions to pricing occur at the 75-80% loan-to-value column. This is pure insanity. It is true that loans over 80% have mortgage insurance to negate the risk liability; however, would you assume that someone who is putting down a full 20-25% of the value of the property is a high risk? The pricing adjustments do, and are exorbitant in this category. We are being told that 75 -80% loans have been identified as the highest delinquency loans. Is this because the loans at 80% had a 20% 2nd Trust Deed behind them, making them 100% financing? No wonder we can't get out of this mess and no one can afford a loan these days. If someone is plunking down $60,000 to buy a piece of property, do you think there is a risk of default? Come on, someone's getting rich here and it ain't us!

Agency Jumbo Loans

All of the above pricing was for loan amounts under $417,000. If your loan amount exceeds that, but is in the "agency jumbo" category, then keep adding up the pricing additions even more. Remember, the agency jumbo loans are those loans in high cost areas where the loan amounts can be factored up according to the median home prices and up to a set ceiling amount. Also, keep in mind, these high cost areas are experiencing the highest foreclosure rates and need the help the most. These pricing adjustments vary so much from lender to lender that I did not include a chart on them. Some lenders start with higher base pricing and others just add to the conforming pricing. Suffice to assume that they will pay a minimum of .25% higher in rate than their conforming counterparts.

I gave a detailed example in chapter 6 to illustrate how difficult it is for current homeowners to access this jumbo agency financing program while trying to refinance their homes. Very few can even avail themselves of this financing since the values of their homes have dropped so much in price. Our legislators can vote in every imaginable solution in the world, but if it doesn't work, what good is it?

Real Jumbo Loans:

The real jumbo loans, those outside of the GSE limits, are priced so high that they are truly unaffordable. Most lenders are only offering this financing if you are willing and able to pay high 8's and 9's for this privilege. I am not talking here about wealthy individuals who can afford to pay the higher payments; I am talking about middle class Americans who can't. For example, in Riverside County, a county where the foreclosure rates are amongst the highest in the nation, and where the agency jumbo only goes up to a maximum loan amount of $500,000, there are many homeowners who owe much more than that. They need to get out from under highly adjustable loans but cannot do so. Their only current solution is to default and either walk away or have the lender reduce their loan balance. Is this really the solution we want? Many of these people want to retain their homes and to better their financing. How can they do this honorably with our current lending rules, lack of financial products, and interest rate pricing that penalizes them for the greed of our government (Fannie and Freddie)?

Summation:

The interest rate information that I have provided here is not being reported on the 5 o'clock news, but low rates are. The only individuals that are qualifying for these very low rates are those whose equity is strong, credit scores are high and income is documentable. In other words, the people who have not been seriously affected by the horrors of the past couple of years can now enjoy the benefits of very low interest rates. Who is helping the rest of us? Is it any wonder that those of us who make our living in the mortgage industry are either gone, sedating ourselves into numbness or living in a constant state of "pissed off" as we try and explain this insanity to our clients?

Washington – Is this taxation without representation? Do we need another tea party?

14

__Understanding Mortgage Loans__

Mortgages 101

The loan drought of 2008 caused by Wall Street pulling out of the lending market and the GSE's over-tightening of the credit criteria have left us desolate and withering away while our homes are carted off to the auction block. We must find a way to open up the lending floodgates and let it gush out to the potential buyers of these homes that are just sitting there on the market. Many of these unsold homes are lying vacant and being vandalized, reminding us of the misery that we all face if this crisis is not soon solved. We need loans, credible responsible loans!

- ✓ **Higher loan-to-value loans**
- ✓ **Jumbo loans**
- ✓ **Higher conforming loan amounts that are not restricted by the false lows of the foreclosure market**
- ✓ **Affordable loans without all the unnecessary add-ons to pricing**
- ✓ **Lower initial payment loans**
- ✓ **Stated income loans**
- ✓ **Investor loans**

We need loans for purchasing distressed properties on the market. We need loans to refinance existing properties into more affordable payments and more stable products. We need loans to meet a vast array of situations.

Washington, we need loans.

Now, you might be thinking that this is contradictory to what I have said in the previous chapters. However, when fire fighters go to a raging, out of control fire, they often set controlled fires around the perimeter to stop its further spread. They fight fire with fire. We need to fight the lending crisis that resulted from the issuance of bad loans with a blitz of good loans. Now I am not talking about the irresponsible lending practices of the past several years, but a return to responsible lending with common sense underwriting guidelines.

The over-tightening of the credit markets and lack of loans and types of loans during this past two years has created an inferno that is totally out of control. Realtors tell us that homes have sold only to go back on the market because there was no financing available. Most potential home buyers do not have sufficient cash to pay for properties, even if they are bargain priced. We need financing. There are too many buyers on the sidelines waiting for the lending streams to open up. As soon as we get the surplus of properties sold, the supply/demand balance will come back in line and home prices will stabilize. It is just that simple.

Financing is also needed for existing homeowners. Sadly many homeowners no longer *qualify* for their *existing* mortgage loans, based on all of the unreasonable underwriting criteria that I have outlined in previous chapters. Many of these homeowners may become part of the foreclosure statistics if they cannot refinance their current unstable mortgage loans into more affordable ones.

Understanding Mortgage Loan Products:

It is estimated that there were over 200 different loan products offered in the past few years to meet the varying needs of the borrowing public. Many of these loans were good solid products, while others were destined to fail because of design flaws. Despite the many variations, all of these loans fit into a few basic categories. It is impossible to discuss all the variations between these loans, but a simple outline of loan product types is offered here to assist you in understanding the fundamental differences between these loans.

Fixed Rate Loans:

Loans that have the same interest rate for the life of the loan, the same monthly payment, and fully amortize (pay off) over the loan term are called fixed-rate loans. These loans can have different amortization periods but fully pay off during the lifetime of the loan. They come in 10, 15, 20, 25, 30 and 40 year terms. The monthly payments on these loans remain the same every month for the entire duration of the loan. Generally, the shorter the amortization term, the lower the interest rate charged. The most common term for this type of loan is the standard 30 year fixed-rate mortgage.

Adjustable Rate Loans:

Loans that have interest rates tied to an index that is not fixed are called adjustable rate loans. These loans may fluctuate in interest rate and/or payment from month to month or may have a fixed portion of the loan prior to the interest rate becoming variable. There are several different indices that interest rates can be tied to such as: Prime, Libor, 11th District Cost of Funds (COFI) and Monthly Treasury Average (MTA). These indexes move monthly with the markets. In the resource section of this book you can see the historical averages of these various indexes. The actual interest rates on the mortgage notes are based on the index plus a predetermined margin (profit factor) at the time the loan is originated. When the loan becomes variable (adjusts) the interest rate is then calculated by adding the margin to the index.

Index + Margin = Interest Rate

The terms of the note determine how often the interest rate fluctuates. In some cases it is monthly, others are set annually. Generally, the initial interest rate on these loans is priced around a quarter to a full percentage point less in rate than standard fixed-rate loans being offered at that time, making them a more affordable and attractive alternative. The well-designed "adjustable rate loans" have "caps" that limit the amount of the initial payment increase or decrease when an adjustment is first made. Yes, I said decrease. Contrary to most people's understanding, these loans can actually decrease in rate from their original term and many of the loans turning variable now are doing just that. The current indexes on these loans are at an all time low. The "caps" on these loans also limit the future interest rates from ever exceeding a set predetermined rate. For example, most of the adjustable rate loans have a lifetime cap of 5%, meaning that under even the worst of circumstances, the rate would never go 5% over what it started at and yes, never go lower than 5% of where the initial rate began. As an example, if you took an adjustable loan with an initial rate of 6.25% then your loan could never go higher in rate than 11.25% (that would be scary) or ever go lower than 1.25% (that would be payday). Over the past several years there have been many different types of adjustable loans, making up the over 200 variations of loans available, but the most commonly used adjustable rate loans are outlined here.

Fixed-Term Adjustable Rate Loans:

The most widely used adjustable rate mortgage loans have a fixed interest rate period of anywhere from two years up to ten years in term. As a rule, the shorter the term of the fixed period, the lower the interest rate. Most of the prime loans (as opposed to sub-prime) have fixed periods of 3, 5, 7, or even 10 years of fixed interest rate payments, followed by the remaining term of the loan becoming fully adjustable. The monthly payment on the initial fixed period is a payment that is based on a 30 year amortization. Most of these loans are 30 years in duration, but only the initial period of the loan has a fixed interest rate. Most people who utilize this type of loan are looking for a lower interest rate for the short-term with the intent of either selling the home or refinancing when the mortgage rate becomes adjustable.

Interest-Only Payment Adjustable Loans:

A very popular loan of the past several years was the "interest only" loan. These loans are the very same as the last category, with the exception that the monthly minimum payment is based only on the interest that is due. You can pay more if you choose. If you only pay the interest on the loan due, then at the end of the term you will still owe the full amount of the original loan.

Subprime Adjustable Loans:

Subprime lending fell under the adjustable loan category and may be responsible for all of the bad press that adjustable rate loans are getting. This grouping of loans was designed to assist people who couldn't qualify for a prime (A paper) loan; however, many prime borrowers got sucked into these loans unknowingly (or uncaringly). This class of loans was designed with an inherent flaw from their very conception. All of them were written as two or three year initial fixed-rate loans. No problem there. The initial fixed-rate period on these loans was often very attractive and could lure in unsuspecting borrowers into believing that they could afford these loans. The theory was that you could "fix" whatever problem you had (that caused you to not fit into the prime lending category) prior to having to refinance into the next loan.

1. If you had horrible credit, then given two or three years you could change a lifetime of sloppy payment history into an *on-time* payer so that you could refinance into a prime loan before the loan became adjustable.
2. Assuming that equity prices would continue to rise, you could sell for a profit if you could not afford the loan once it became adjustable.
3. Maybe you could *start* earning the income that you *stated* you made in order to qualify for this loan.

All these loans carried very stiff prepayment penalties during the fixed portion of the loan. Since the interest rate on this portion of the loan was so low, the prepayment penalty was a guarantee of a premium, should the loan try to pay off too soon. The margins on these loans were very high and allowed the rates, once adjustable, to soar way beyond the initial payment of the previous fixed period. The margins on these loans were determined by the following:

✓ The higher the loan to value of the property, the higher the margins, thus the 100% financed loans had very high margins

✓ The lower the credit score, the higher the margin

✓ The more compensation paid to the agent, the higher the margin

The companies that specialized in this type of lending were making a financial killing at the borrower's expense. Borrowers typically were unaware of just how high their adjusted payment would go after the fixed portion of the loan ended, and didn't necessarily care because they assumed they could always refinance into another subprime loan when this one expired, if needed. Looking back, this short- sightedness on behalf of the lenders who allowed the compensation of these loans to be tied to the margins are to blame for the KABOOM factor.

Negatively Amortizing Loans:

Another financing vehicle that was horribly abused during the recent past was the negatively amortizing loans. These loans, also called cash-flow arms or pay-option arms, have been around for almost thirty years. They have been used successfully by self-employed individuals to manage monthly cash flows and seasonal income variations. This loan was designed to offer four monthly payment options as follows:

Payment Option 1: a teaser payment that was set at the time of loan origination. This low monthly payment would increase incrementally on an annual basis for the next five years. If you elected to make this teaser-payment option, then generally (but not always), it was not sufficient to pay even the interest. Any unpaid interest was then added to the principal balance of the loan.

Payment Option 2: was the amount of money required to pay the full interest payment on the loan.

Payment Option 3: was the amount of interest and principal to fully pay off the loan on a 30-year amortization schedule.

Payment Option 4: was the amount of interest and principal to fully pay off the loan on a 15-year amortization schedule.

Each month a borrower would have the option of making any one of the above referenced payments as long as they paid at least option number one. The potentially negative amortizing loan was a sophisticated loan that had been highly successful for many years and especially utilized by savvy borrowers who wanted to control their cash flows throughout the year. In all of my years in this industry, I have never seen a client "max out" this loan during the low payment phase where there is the potential for negative amortization (first 5 years of the loan), that is UNTIL the past couple of years. This loan was designed to cap any potential negative amortization to a maximum of 115% of the original loan amount. In other words, if you borrowed $200,000, the maximum that the loan could grow to would be $230,000, or 115% of the original amount. Once the loan hits that maximum amount, it then becomes a fully amortizing loan, subject to the remaining terms of the loan and the current interest rates.

This was not a loan for the masses. It was a highly specialized loan product that required a high level of expertise as to how to best benefit from it. People that had variations in their cash flow, like accountants, who made the majority of their income during one portion of the year, could pay minimum payments throughout some of the year and then "catch up" when the big paychecks arrived. It was never intended that the loan go negative consistently. It was intended to manage cash flows.

In the past, this loan had built-in safeguards that protected a homeowner from abusing this product. For example, there were limits to the loan amounts compared to the values of the property (LTV). Historically these loans could not be written for over 80% of the current value of the property at the time that the loan was originated. Thus, if you were purchasing a property and wanting to use this financing vehicle, you would be required to have at least a 20% down payment. It was certainly not a financing vehicle for low down payment loans or 100% financing. The initial start or teaser rate was not that much lower than the current interest rates being offered on the market (maybe one to two percentage points). The size of the margins and lifetime caps were limited. These loans were traditionally tied to the "monthly treasury average" MTA or the "cost of funds index" COFI, both very stable indexes – not the Libor, which is more volatile. They were considered portfolio loans to the very few lenders that offered them.

All of a sudden, the neg-am loans became the poster child for affordability and were advertised on every medium. Many lenders wanted to profit from this once-specialized loan product and disregarded the safeguards that had been their benchmark. They began *"pushing"* these *"affordable"* loans to the masses, leading many borrowers to believe that the interest rates on these loans were a mere 1%. Many banks were even offering added incentives to the brokers and loan officers who would bring them this product (same thing applied to HELOCs). Why sell a buyer on a 30 year fixed-rate loan if you could make double the money by selling this specialized loan. Buyer beware!!! It is my understanding that the lender was somehow able to "put on their books" earnings that were not yet even realized due to the negative amortization.

As a side note: You in Congress may want to check this out as I suspect the same thing is happening with "Reverse Mortgages" that are now being advertised on every channel. The only reason for lenders to *push* a product is that they are making a *killing* on it. Despite the advertising claims that "It is time that our homes paid us back", the oldsters should know that nothing is for free.

I guess the high profit potential of these specialized loans must have skewed their better judgment. The lenders did not limit what an agent could make on this loan product and the higher the margin – the higher the paycheck, which is **a definite recipe for disaster**. To my knowledge, it was Countrywide that first dropped the start rate on this loan to an unbelievable 1% rate. Interest rates had remained very low in the Greenspan era and as they started inching up, so too did the actual rates on these neg-am loans. The minimum teaser rate soon became so significantly below the actual interest rate on the loan that I had one person contact me within 18 months of taking out his neg-am loan and it had actually gone to its full maximum of 115% of the starting balance. Maxed out in 18 months? By making the lowest payment (that the lender had arranged) it had eaten up the equity in his home and he now owed more on the loan than the property was worth, in only 18 months time. The new amortized payment on this loan was higher than he could afford and he could not refinance without equity. The agent who had arranged this loan had saddled him with a very high margin on a highly volatile LIBOR index during a time of ascending interest rates and also a prepayment penalty to boot (these prepays also added to the compensation of the agent). Last I heard he was still struggling to stay on the property that he had owned for over two decades.

The teaser rates (those below the interest due on the loan) were highly advertised and sold to the public as a panacea. People falsely assumed this very low payment was the only payment needed on these loans, and buyers rushed in to acquire homes via these very volatile loans, without any knowledge of their true risk potential. This loan has now been vilified by the media and has been abandoned by virtually all lenders. I doubt we will ever see this loan product offered again, but the industry has lost one of the best financing vehicles for the self-employed clientele.

HELOC – Home Equity Lines of Credit:

During the years of explosive growth in equity, lenders began *pushing* equity lines of credit to every customer. These wonderful credit cards, attached to your home, allowed you to instantly satisfy any spending whim that could arise. The initial idea of an equity line of credit was to have a source of ready cash for emergencies that might occur. You could write a check tied to your home's equity to allow you to make that unexpected repair or carry you through an income interruption of short duration. It was insurance against calamity.

These lines of credit had interest rates that were tied to the prime rate and at one point the rates on these equity lines were so low that they were cheaper than most primary trust deeds. I know of many individuals who paid off stable financing with these very volatile lines of credit. Who knew rates could go higher?

The use of these credit lines allowed consumers to purchase homes with little or no money down without paying the exorbitant cost of mortgage insurance. Loans were written as 80/20's (80% first trust deed loan and 20% equity line of credit) or 75/25's and with no equity to guarantee the repayment of loan debts, the lenders also did not have the safeguard of an insurer to back them up. I'm not sure how the mortgage insurance companies survived this era, but I can tell you they are back with a vengeance right now, calling all the shots. As I mentioned in the last chapter, Fannie Mae has identified the 75-

80% loans as having the highest default ratios. Did they not know that there was 20 -25% second trust deeds behind them? Hmmm.

Many of these equity lines were written up to the maximum value of the property and therefore left no margin of error should a housing price correction happen. Guess what???? These once liquid forms of salvation are now being *frozen* by the very lenders that once pushed them on us. Even when there is sufficient equity to support the line of credit, and homeowners have faithfully made their payments, the lenders are closing them. It seems the banks now prefer the unsecured lines of credit that are held in plastic cards and have "the sky's the limit" interest rate potentials.

Current Problem: *The loans now available are "one size fits all".*

Ever since August of 2007, when all of the investor-originated loans vanished, we have had virtually one lending option, and that is the GSE's (Government Sponsored Enterprise) of Fannie Mae, Freddie Mac and FHA conforming loans. For the most part, these are all 30 year, fixed-rate, fully amortizable loans. These GSE agencies do offer some adjustable short-term, fixed-rate loans, but sadly, on most days, these loans are priced as high, or even higher, than the 30 year fixed-rate loans. What good is that? There is no advantage in taking a shorter-term, fixed-rate loan unless it is priced lower than its 30 year fixed alternative, or if it has less stringent underwriting guidelines. Recently, they have started offering interest-only loans again; however, there is such a huge pricing hit, often as high as 1.75% that it makes the interest rates on these loans very unattractive and defeats the purpose that they were designed for. Why bother???? This is a "one shoe fits all" mentality that isn't working.

Fixed-rate, fully amortizable loans have always been considered the most stable, safe loans on the market. You never have to worry about interest rate fluctuations, there is no guessing as to what your monthly payment will be during the coming years, and you know that if you keep making those monthly set payments, your home will be paid off at the end of the term. These loans have and do serve their purpose. Presumably, when you purchase your home with a fixed-rate mortgage it is assumed that you will stay in that mortgage until it is fully paid off. However, historically, even before the insanity of the past decade, statistics show that the average homeowner either sells their home or refinances their mortgage within the first five to seven years of the loan. We are one of the very few countries that even offer a 30 year fixed-rate term mortgage. In Canada, for example, the longest term that you can secure on a fixed rate is five years then the mortgage must be renewed.

Common Sense Reasoning:

During an era when home prices have escalated so much faster than the average person's income, we have become accustomed to and **need** loans with initial lower monthly payments. Does it make any sense that we should pay on month "1" of any loan, the same payment that we will pay on month "360"? Can we safely assume that during the next 30 years of our lives, given inflation and other economic considerations, we should be in a position to pay a higher amount in the future? **It is important to note** that the vast majority of people commonly purchase their first home when their financial needs are the greatest. Generally speaking, we want to settle down in our own home when the children start appearing. The time period of our lives when we are raising our children is certainly the most expensive years. It is also during this time period where our needs for larger homes and the location of homes in relationship to both school districts and employment centers are significant factors. With this being considered, affordability may be more important at this phase of life than being debt-free is. It was in response to this need for lower monthly payments that we originally got the adjustable rate mortgage loans.

Adjustable interest rate loans are not the villains they are being portrayed in the media. If they are responsibly designed and offer lesser monthly payments, then they serve their purpose. Different people have differing needs and so the many varieties of loans were designed. For example, the interest-only loans of the past several years have offered many homebuyers the opportunity to pay less monthly for more home initially. The only problem with these loans is that you never gain on the unpaid principal balance if you only make the minimum payment. As seen in our current economic crisis, our home prices do not always appreciate either. If you continually pay the interest-only payments on a loan over its lifetime, then you are just a RENTER, without the benefit of a landlord. You will never be a home OWNER. I am always amazed when a client comes back after four or five years in an interest-only loan to discover that they have made zero pay-down on the original principal balance. This seems to be true even when the client is in a financial position to pay higher monthly amounts. Additional principal payments were/are allowed on these loans, but only the interest portion has to be paid monthly. It would seem that if the minimum payment says you pay $$$, then that is what you pay. There is no real incentive to pay more than the minimum due each month.

Although monthly payments on adjustable loans can be stabilized for a fixed period of time, there is always going to be a day of reckoning when the payment will have to adjust to allow the loan to fully amortize over the remaining term. These loans are subject to the fluctuations of the market, both high and low. A simple 5/25 variable loan would have a fixed interest rate for a period of 5 years and then would become fully adjustable for the remaining 25 years of the loan. The payment can go up or down depending on the interest rate, but must amortize fully over the remaining life of the loan. In recent years, with the very low interest rates, many of these adjustable loans have seen current monthly payments drop even lower than the previous fixed rate. Again, well designed loans need not be scary if you know what lending vehicle you are using and why.

With the disappearance of so many financing vehicles, we are left with very few options and very little hope of solving our current lending crisis. We need a loan product that will satisfy the industry needs while making it affordable for people to purchase new homes and refinance existing loans.

The answer is here in the "L.A.M.P." loan.

15

<u>Say YES to the LAMP Loan</u>

<u>"Your Easy Solution" - "Loan with Affordable Monthly Payments".</u>

Out of the darkness comes a ray of light in the LAMP loan.   It is a loan product that provides a common sense solution to our current lending dilemma. The idea came to me quite by surprise, but not without a lot of earnest soul searching for a mortgage product that would creatively solve the needs of the lending industry and that of the borrower. People have become so accustomed to interest-only and negatively amortizing loans that the payment shock of a fully amortized loan is quite out of reach for many. The longer-term amortization loans have been available, for example, the 40 year loans, but they are priced so much higher in rate that it often negates the purpose of taking more time to pay them off. It seems like only the banker benefits in this case.

The enclosed loan program that I have designed balances the need of the borrower with the need of the financier in the following ways.

✓ The interest rate is fixed for the duration of the loan.

✓ The loan is fully amortizable over the 30 year period.

✓ The initial payment on the loan is slightly above the interest-only payment but does allow for principal reduction, even if ever so slightly.

✓ The increase in monthly payment on the 61st month (5th year) is minimal and affordable. The maximum increased payment is known at the time that the mortgage is originated. Additional principal reductions during the first five years of the loan will lower this new payment amount.

✓ The final increase in monthly payment happens ten full years after the mortgage is originated. Again, the maximum payment at this adjustment is known at the time of loan origination and not subject to market conditions in the future. The monthly final payment can be lowered by principal reductions of the balance. The 20 year amortized payment should be very affordable to a family who has ten years to prepare for it.

If bankers encourage additional principal pay-downs of as little as $25.00 per month they will significantly impact the final 20 year payment.

This loan would carry the security of a 30 year fixed-rate mortgage with the initial payment option of little more than an interest-only loan. There is no worry of market fluctuations, of principal balances increasing, and there should be no pre-payment penalties.

I have included examples of various loan amounts to show how the payments adjust and a comparison to other loan products.

"LAMP" Loan

Loan with Affordable Monthly Payments

$200,000 @ 6%

30-year fixed rate mortgage loan with graduated payments

Payment Years 1-5 $1052.81
60 monthly payments calculated on a 50-year Amortization Schedule
Loan balance at the end of 60 months (5 years) payments: $196,315.47

Payment Years 6-10 $1080.15
60 monthly payments calculated on a 40-year Amortization Schedule
Loan balance at the end of 120 months (10 years) payments: $189,437.74

Payment Years 11-30 * $1357.19
240 monthly payments calculated on a 20-year Amortization Rate
Loan balance at the end of 360 months (30 years) payments: **PAID IN FULL**

*Monthly payment less if additional principal reduction made during first ten years of loan

Compare to:

Traditional 30-year fixed rate loan fully
amortized payment=   **$1199.10**

30-year Interest Only (IO) payment=   **$1000.00**
Fixed rate for an initial term of 5-10 years ONLY. Balance
amortized over the remaining life of the loan, fully adjustable at
market rate. No principal reduction during first IO term of the loan.

"LAMP" Loan

Loan with Affordable Monthly Payments

$300,000 @ 6%

30-year fixed rate mortgage loan with graduated payments

Payment Years 1-5 $1579.21
60 monthly payments calculated on a 50-year Amortization Schedule
Loan balance at the end of 60 months (5 years) payments: $294,473.21

Payment Years 6-10 $1620.23
60 monthly payments calculated on a 40-year Amortization Schedule
Loan balance at the end of 120 months (10 years) payments: $284,156.61

Payment Years 11-30 * $2035.79
240 monthly payments calculated on a 20-year Amortization Rate
Loan balance at the end of 360 months (30 years) payments: **PAID IN FULL**

*Monthly payment less if additional principal reduction made during first ten years of loan

Compare to:

Traditional 30-year fixed rate loan fully
amortized payment=   **$1798.65**

30-year Interest Only (IO) payment=   **$1250.00**
Fixed rate for an initial term of 5-10 years ONLY. Balance
amortized over the remaining life of the loan, fully adjustable at
market rate. No principal reduction during first IO term of the loan.

"LAMP" Loan

Loan with Affordable Monthly Payments

$400,000 @ 6%

30-year fixed rate mortgage loan with graduated payments

Payment Years 1-5 $2105.62

60 monthly payments calculated on a 50-year Amortization Schedule
Loan balance at the end of 60 months (5 years) payments: $392,630.95

Payment Years 6-10 $2160.31

60 monthly payments calculated on a 40-year Amortization Schedule
Loan balance at the end of 120 months (10 years) payments: $378,875.49

Payment Years 11-30 * $2714.38

240 monthly payments calculated on a 20-year Amortization Rate
Loan balance at the end of 360 months (30 years) payments: **PAID IN FULL**

*Monthly payment less if additional principal reduction made during first ten years of loan

Compare to:

Traditional 30-year fixed rate loan fully
amortized payment=   **$2398.20**

30-year Interest Only (IO) payment=   **$2000.00**
Fixed rate for an initial term of 5-10 years ONLY. Balance
amortized over the remaining life of the loan, fully adjustable at
market rate. No principal reduction during first IO term of the loan.

"LAMP" Loan

Loan with Affordable Monthly Payments

$500,000 @ 6%

30-year fixed rate mortgage loan with graduated payments

Payment Years 1-5 — $2632.02
60 monthly payments calculated on a 50-year Amortization Schedule
Loan balance at the end of 60 months (5 years) payments: $490,788.68

Payment Years 6-10 — $2700.39
60 monthly payments calculated on a 40-year Amortization Schedule
Loan balance at the end of 120 months (10 years) payments: $473,597.35

Payment Years 11-30 * — $3392.98
240 monthly payments calculated on a 20-year Amortization Rate
Loan balance at the end of 360 months (30 years) payments: **PAID IN FULL**

**Monthly payment less if additional principal reduction made during first ten years of loan*

Compare to:

Traditional 30-year fixed rate loan fully
amortized payment=   **$2997.75**

30-year Interest Only (IO) payment=   **$2500.00**
Fixed rate for an initial term of 5-10 years ONLY. Balance
amortized over the remaining life of the loan, fully adjustable at
market rate. No principal reduction during first IO term of the loan.

16

Where Fear Now Resides

The Summary

The sudden reversal of fortune has caused demoralizing fear and we truly are *Stunned in America* by the events of the past two years. We fear losing our homes. We fear losing our jobs. We fear the loss of assets in our investment and retirement accounts by the collapse of Wall Street. We fear losing the standard of living that we have become accustomed to. We fear not being able to send our kids to college. We fear not being able to retire. We are living in a state of constant fear.

Fear causes panic. Panic causes us to react. The recent run on banks was caused by panic. Many people have stopped making purchases, even when they can afford to do so, as they fear the future. This sudden embargo on buying "stuff" is self-propagating. No purchases, no manufacturing. No manufacturing, no stuff to sell. No sales, no profits. No profits, then employee layoffs and no jobs. No jobs and no income result in no purchasing power. No purchases, no profits, more layoffs. We are watching the daily collapse of industries as they suffer from the effects of this recent turn of events. We no longer know if the auto manufacturers will be there to warrant our new vehicles, so we stop buying them. The banks have frozen or closed our credit lines and our credit cards, limiting our purchasing power even further. The massive layoffs in various industries cause us fear as we wonder when we will be the next casualty of this crisis, if we aren't already. We are reacting to fear. We have lost faith in our banking system, Wall Street, our American corporations, and now the U.S. Government. To restore faith and banish fear, our leaders must take deliberate and responsible actions to re-establish our faith. Faith is the opposite of fear.

None of the new rules of mortgage lending make any *common sense,* but then again, how would private jet travelling legislators understand common sense solutions? Are they too far removed, too rich, too self-serving, to see the needs of the common man? Are there pockets so full of lobbyist dollars that they clang as they walk and vote their pockets over principles? We the American people want to be your *"special interest"*! While billions flow to the guilty, the innocent are left to pay the bill. We need a hand up and not a hand out. I have shown the recklessness of our recent legislative decisions and what the results of those decisions have been. Government is not the answer; it is a part of the problem. While each party points their fingers at the other it should be mentioned, that our banking system fell apart during the watch of the Republican Party and President George W. Bush. It should also be noted that deregulation of the banking system occurred under the administration of the Democratic Party and President William Jefferson Clinton. The only constant here is the many oldsters who occupy the seats of congress. Anyone for mandatory retirement age and term limits? Do others need to keep ole Duke Cunningham company in his jail cell?

We need responsible decision makers who know the mortgage business and understand the problems that we are facing. As the old saying goes, understanding is half of the battle. We need leaders who can put the interest of our citizens above that of their own paychecks. Asking the Angelo Mozilo's of this world how to fix this lending crisis is like asking the wolf to guard the hen house. We need solutions that are workable in the streets and not just on paper. The current solutions proposed by Washington will not work and will not fix the lending problems. Time is running out. We need simple common sense to prevail.

My interest in writing this book was not just to expose the indiscretions of our industry and leaders, but to offer concrete viable solutions that will get us back on track. I am not concerned with CEO bonus packages, shareholder stock prices, or whether or not my party will be in office after the next election. I am only concerned with improving our currently ineffective lending industry and our inability by reason of the new rules to help homeowners who deserve better. I'm also concerned with my own financial future, my home's value, and my family's ability to survive this crisis.

Federal Reserve Statistics:

If you go online to www.federalreserve.gov you will find all of the statistical information that you would ever want to know. One of the areas outlined on this website is the past and present residential mortgage information.

As of the end of the 4th Quarter of 2008, there was over 14 trillion dollars in total debt throughout all of the various channels that hold mortgage loans in the United States.

At this same website, you can find the Charge-Off and Delinquency Rates of all Residential and Commercial Real Estate Loans (as well as other types of loans) at the following link:

www.federalreserve.gov/Releases/ChargeOff/delallnsa.htm

Looking at the information given from third quarter of 1999 through the second quarter of 2003 (16 months) you will see that the average delinquency rate on residential mortgage loans was 2.12%. The average from third quarter of 2003 through second quarter of 2007 (16 months) was 1.69%. This lower delinquency rate was due to the free-flowing money that was being loaned to anyone, creditworthy or not, who applied for financing. In the third quarter of 2007 the plug was pulled from the lending streams and delinquency rates started increasing with each subsequent quarter. Overnight, somebody yelled "the party is over, everybody out of the pool!"

It is interesting to note that the delinquency rate during the third quarter of 2007 (and this includes all borrowers who have missed even one month payment) was only 2.35%. Not exactly earth shattering! This was the quarter that ushered in the freeze on financing. HUH!! Therefore 97.65% of all mortgage holders were still paying their loans on time. What was the event that caused such a dramatic standstill on financing? I doubt we will never know the true answer to this question but I have my suspicions. Did the banks of America in conjunction with Wall Street investment firms pull off the biggest Ponzi scheme in the world? What aren't we being told?

Despite how we got here we need solutions to get us back on track. Throughout this book I have offered multiple ways to "fix" the lending dilemma and get money back into the mortgage market. Here is a review of the solutions that I recommend.

Summary of Common Sense Solutions to Fix the Mortgage Lending Industry:

1. We need loan programs with initial low monthly payments to help homeowners afford the mortgages that they are already burdened with.

2. We need a variety of loan products to offer multiple lending options.

3. We need the L.A.M.P. loan.

4. Restore underwriting into the hands of qualified and trained human underwriters. Give them the ability to weigh the pros and cons of a loan applicant and make an informed decision as to a person's creditworthiness. Human underwriters need to be given authority to make decisions based on credible underwriting standards as opposed to the current computer software models that cannot use reasoning skills.

5. Restore common sense to the underwriting function without fear of regulator wrath.

6. Get rid of hard and fast rules of lending, in favor of responsible guidelines that don't exclude credit-worthy individuals from the mortgage market.

7. Get rid of credit scoring entirely, as it is not a reliable reflection of credit-worthiness. Absolutely, stop pricing to a faulty scoring system.

    a. Credit scoring discriminates against the individuals, especially the elderly who don't use credit anymore or those who deal on a cash only basis.

    b. Credit scoring unfairly punishes an individual who is shopping for good credit terms. Multiple credit inquiries do not mean multiple loans.

    c. Faulty credit information should not be allowed to rule over your ability to obtain financing or cost you thousands of dollars in penalty charges.

    d. Credit scoring unfairly punishes the creditworthy for items on their credit report that they have no knowledge of, that they do not owe, and that are not even their responsibility.

    e. Credit scoring does not allow for a "one-time" occurrence where someone could not make payments on time due to an extraordinary circumstance. Credit scoring is inhumane.

    f. Credit scoring rewards a person for having a lot of open credit, and punishes someone who has too little, especially if they know the formula.

g. Credit scores do not recognize errors in reporting.

h. Collection agencies can ruin your good credit history without notifying you in advance that they are reporting you.

i. How reliable are credit scores when you can pay others to "fix" them?

8. Get rid of the current Fannie/Freddie pricing additions that only serve to provide fee income. Establish only true "risk-based" pricing additions. A person who is bringing in a 20% down payment should not pay higher pricing than someone who is not.

9. Restore stated income loans using the safeguards of equity, reserves and credit history. Reverse the law that insists that income must be verified in order to obtain a mortgage loan.

10. Grant more flexibility in the underwriting of income to allow self-employed individuals the same opportunity as salary workers. Just because a salary worker can't write off some of their expenses on their tax returns does not mean that they do not have them. Don't punish the self-employed for enjoying the tax benefits granted by the legislators.

11. Bring income verification into the 21st Century.

12. Consider cash in the bank as an offset to high ratios when a person has the ability to pay off debts through resources already at their disposal.

13. Value the liquidity of a borrower who can demonstrate the discipline of not spending everything they have.

14. Use the cost approach to value real estate under the current economic downturn so to not discriminate against homeowners who overpaid for their homes.

15. Allow homeowners an opportunity to refinance their current loans based on previous loan–to-value ratios and not on the artificial low prices of the foreclosure markets. People need to be able to get out from under bad loans before they become default candidates. They should not be penalized by higher pricing or mortgage insurance when all they are doing is seeking better terms.

16. Get rid of the HVCC (Home Value Code of Conduct). It is creating more problems in the market place and penalizing innocent homeowners in both needless fees and useless values. Give us back our trusted appraisers.

17. Never allow people to purchase property without any investment on their part. Abolish 100% financing.

18. Evaluate a borrower's motivation to repay a loan by the true equity that they have

in a property, not just the paper value of an appraisal.

19. Stop modifying defaulted mortgages into higher monthly payment 30 year fixed-rate loans.

20. Only modify current mortgage loans upon a thorough review of each applicant to determine that they are truthfully in need of a loan modification. Too many homeowners are being "sold" a bill of goods by loan modification companies who are profiting at homeowner expense. Too many may be using this crisis for self benefit at all of our expense.

21. Get rid of loan modification companies who are hurting our current mortgage markets for the sake of fast cash.

22. Don't require homeowners to be in default before reviewing their need for a loan modification.

23. Make all modification of loans to the monthly payment and not to the principal balance of the loan to avoid setting a precedence that will further exacerbate our crisis.

24. Give payment waivers (without destroying someone's credit history) to any individual who finds themselves unemployed or under employed due to this current economic crisis.

25. Consider making defaulted homeowners, renters in their own property saving one more vacancy and foreclosure sale until the market stabilizes.

26. Roll back underwriting standards to the pre-2000 era when mortgage lending was still credible and worked.

Conclusion:

Stunned is a good description of the state of our current psyche. Wasn't it just yesterday that we all had houses worth more than what we paid for them, free flowing cash, bulging retirement accounts, job opportunities where we could afford to be picky? Wealth for almost everyone!!!! What happened? It is like we woke up to find a bomb exploded on our financial lives. And we are stunned! Our house of ATM has become a House of Horror and everywhere we look we see a distorted view of where we are compared to where we were. And we are stunned!

We must be *Stunned in America* because we are not doing anything to change the cycle of events that have cascaded into a repression of our individual rights and freedom of democracy. The last generation to openly protest was the baby boomers who went to the streets with picket signs in open rebellion against an unjust war. Ironic isn't it, since it is the boomers who have orchestrated much our current economic chaos? Are we so stunned by the events of the last two years that we sit complacently by, watching more "tax & spend" policies that will only create greater financial hardships for our children to carry? We have the power to change this crisis and stop it from taking us into another "great depression". Should we start by sending a collective message to Washington that we are "mad as hell and not going to take it anymore"? Maybe we need to vote out all of the politicians who no longer represent "we the people" in favor of those who do. If politicians won't vote in term limits, we the voters need to enforce it by voting out all elected officials who have served more than two terms in office. America is still a democracy. Let's keep it that way.

All of us need to contact our elected officials and make our voices heard. You can find the contact information for them at: www.usa.gov/contact/elected.shtml. If you don't know who your representative is then try the following resource: www.house.gov/zip/zip2rep.html.

I asked the question in Chapter 1 – "did this greed originate with us or did it trickle down"? We have just seen greed in operation on a scale large enough to destroy the American way of life. Maybe the time has come for us to reevaluate our priorities and realign ourselves with what is really important. They say "the man who dies with the most toys wins" – I say – he's still dead. This financial crisis has stopped most of us "dead" in our tracks; maybe good can come out of it. Doing the right thing is better than having all things. It takes adversity to show us what we are made of. This country was founded by brave men and women who no longer wished to live under the tyranny of bad government. They wanted a country that provided freedom. We will only be free when we stop being slaves. Greed makes us a slave to a way of life that will never bring happiness or freedom. For the sake of all of our little Z's, let's start doing the right thing ourselves and demand honor from our leadership.

Section III:

The Start

Workbook

17

How Much Mortgage Can I Afford?

You Be the Judge

Purchasing a home is possibly the most important *financial* decision that you will ever make. You are about to commit a sizeable percentage of your income to a very long-term debt. Therefore, don't trust others to tell you what you can afford. You need to be the judge.

The decision to go from being a renter to being a homeowner is an extremely big jump. A renter knows exactly how much money is dedicated to their housing expense each and every month and there are seldom any surprises. A homeowner however, may not anticipate all of the expenses that they will incur and preparedness is essential. When you are a renter you have a landlord to call whenever something isn't working correctly. A homeowner must bear the responsibility for all ongoing maintenance and repairs. They must also meet the rising costs of insurance, tax assessments and many other unexpected financial outlays. Even if you have previously been a homeowner and are ready to make an upward move, you need to prepare for just how much additional expense you can afford.

Our personal value system, within the confines of our income limitations, should dictate what we are willing and able to commit to any expenditure. For some people, having their children in private school is an expense they are willing to justify when public school is available for free. Other people judge success by the clothes they wear while they live in a very modest home. Some like to drive the latest vehicles while others are content with models that are many years out of date. There are people who want to travel and their freedom is most meaningful to them. I know of individuals who hate to cook and eating out is a necessary staple in their budget. One thing is for certain we can't afford everything and therefore must determine our priorities when it comes to our spending.

Our lending professionals should be able to tell us, looking only at basic dollars and cents, if we can afford the loan that we are applying for. Obviously our lending system has failed us in this regard over the past several years. No system however, can establish our values and tell us what priority to place on what expenditure. For this reason WE personally need to be the judge of our income resources and how we are going to spend this money based on what expenditures that WE deem necessary.

Many people are in serious financial trouble because they thought they could afford it all. Some don't even know what they can afford because they don't know how, or don't take the time to evaluate their income and expenses. Have you ever gone shopping for a car and been talked into payments that were almost double what you expected them to be before you started looking. After the newness of that "must have" vehicle wears off you may live to regret the seven additional years of payments, especially after the vehicle gets its first major scratch. We get into trouble when we go shopping without a plan and without a budget. Shopping for a home **cannot** be an impulse purchase.

For most of us our largest monthly outlay is our housing expense and therefore we need to take the necessary time *before* we start shopping to know what we are willing and able to spend. During the mid 2000's when home prices were rising so quickly, many people rushed to purchase before they understood the consequences of their financial obligation. For too many people now, their homes are their prison as they lost their freedom the minute they committed to purchase the home that they couldn't really afford. Why then do we let others tell us how much we should be spending for a house? When you inform the real estate agent that you are looking for a home in the $$$ category, don't even look at the homes that are beyond your reach. Stretching may be good for muscles but if your budget is stretched every month, soreness, if not injury, is sure to follow. Also, the same thing applies when speaking with a mortgage loan professional. They may be able to arrange financing for loans, but just because they can arrange it, doesn't mean you can afford it. This workbook is designed to enable YOU to decide how much house you *want* to afford with your own personal value system. So let's get started.

Evaluate Your Priorities:

Think long term. It is always exciting to get something new that is, until the newness wears off. The new home (new to you) may not be so exciting if you have to work two jobs just to keep up with the payments. Life if more than just a house and you need to be aware of the *other things* equally important to you. Using the list provided put a number from one and upwards beside each item in order of the priority that you place on these things for you and your family. Let number one be the highest priority on your value system. Your priorities differ according to the stage of life that you are in. While your children are still young, paying for their education may be more important to you than saving for your retirement. As you get older, retirement may become number one. This is something that you should do on an annual basis to determine if you are putting your money where your values are. Sometimes just looking at things in writing helps you to establish spending priorities.

Do this exercise together with a spouse or partner so you can balance each other. A husband may put a higher worth on golfing while the wife can't live without salon services. Determine together if you are currently spending your hard earned dollars in conjunction with your personal values. Many people spend until there is nothing left and therefore never accomplish what they really dream about. Others are so bound by debt for impulsive purchases they are no longer enjoying, but still paying for, that they can't afford to save towards what is really important to them.

Do this exercise with some real "soul searching" and discussion. There is no right or wrong answers as this is YOUR list. Place your numbers as you **want** your priorities to become, even if they are not currently there. This is an exercise that may take days, if not weeks to ponder. Don't be in a hurry. Buying a home is a long-term commitment and you should give yourself sufficient prep time before deciding on how much house you can afford.

Worksheet #1

Evaluate your Spending Priorities

Housing /Rent or Own: _____

Retirement Savings: _____

Children's Education/Private School /College/Tutoring: _____

Investment/Savings: _____

Business Development (owning your own business): _____

Vehicle: _____

Insurance (life or health): _____

Travel: _____

Clothing/Accessories: _____

Entertainment/Recreation: _____

Disposable Cash (eating out, Starbucks, impulsive spending): _____

Support Services (housekeeper, babysitting, gardener, etc): _____

Health & Beauty (fitness clubs, salon services, massage, Chiropractor, plastic surgeon, supplements): _____

Athletics/Club Sports/Lessons/Social Clubs/Golfing/ Extra-curricular

activities for you or your children: _____

Debt Reduction: _____

Charity/Giving: _____

Other: _____

Other: _____

Where Does My Money Go?

Once you have completed exercise #1, then you are ready for the really big challenge. Where is your money currently going? The second exercise will take a significant amount of time if you do it correctly, but it is a very necessary step before you can determine how much home you can afford. Using the worksheet provided, record what you spend on a monthly basis in all of the categories listed. Don't guess – be as accurate as possible. Since not all expenses are paid on a monthly basis, finding all of them can be a challenge. The category of "other" is necessary as not all families have the same financial obligations. Some people are business owners and have significant expenses related to the production of income. Other families may care for an elderly parent. Also, many people have no idea what they actually spend for some items. The "latte factor" is a recent term that has been used to describe how much people *unconsciously* spend for the small items, like the daily coffee (and pastry) at the local coffee shop. A five dollar (with tip) purchase almost every day can add up to a significant amount on a monthly and annualized basis. The trivial expenditures could be costing you your dreams, a few dollars at a time. This is the moment to identify the "little foxes". Don't try and shortcut your way through this worksheet as it is imperative to know how much money you actually have left over at the end of a month or could have as discretionary income if a few changes were made. In this exercise don't record what you want it to be – record what it is. We will get to the "want to be" later. Again, this step may take a few hours or days to complete if you are serious about knowing where your money has been over the past twelve months. This is the first step to determine your budget and how much mortgage and home you can safely afford.

Worksheet #2

Current Monthly Expenditures

1. Payroll Taxes:
    a. Federal Tax Withholding: _____
    b. State Tax Withholding: _____
    c. FICA Withholding of SSI and Medicare: _____
    d. Union Dues: _____
2. Housing: Current Rent or Mortgage Payment: _____
3. House Insurance: (if not included in above) _____
4. Property Taxes: (if not included in above) _____
5. Housing: (Homeowner dues, etc) _____
6. Utilities:
    a. Gas _____
    b. Electric _____
    c. Water _____
    d. Sewer _____
    e. Garbage _____
7. Communications
    a. Cable: _____
    b. Internet: _____
    c. Phone: _____
    d. Cell Phone: _____
8. Retirement Savings
(may be taken out directly from paycheck): _____
9. Education/Private School /College/Tutoring: _____
10. Vehicle Payments: _____
11. Transportation Costs: (insurance, gas, parking, tolls) _____
12. Insurance: Health _____
13. Insurance: Life _____

14. Travel: _____

15. Clothing/Accessories: _____

16. Entertainment/Recreation: _____

17. Support Services:

    a. Housekeeper: _____

    b. Childcare: _____

    c. Gardener: _____

18. Health & Beauty:

    a. Fitness clubs: _____

    b. Salon services: _____

    c. Massage, chiropractor, plastic surgeon: _____

19. Athletics/Club Sports/Lessons/Social Clubs/Golfing/ Extra-curricular activities for you or your children: _____

20. Charity: _____

21. Food, Cleaning products, Weekly necessities: _____

22. Investment/Savings: _____

23. Medical/Dental/Vision – not covered by insurance: _____

24. Home Repair/Maintenance: _____

25. Disposable Cash (dining out, coffee, impulsive spending _____

26. Debt Reduction: (installment loans such as education loans) _____

27. Debt Reduction: (credit card payments) _____

28. Debt Reduction: _____

29. Debt Reduction: _____

30. Business Expenses: _____

31. Other: _____

32. Other: _____

33. Other: _____

34. Other: _____

35. Other: _____

36. Other: _____

Monthly Total Expenditures: (A) _____

The completion of worksheet #2 may have served as a rude awakening. Did you notice that this list is much longer than the list of our priorities? There are things that we must pay for that is not a priority to us, but a necessity none the less. How do you rank Uncle Sam's chunk that is taken automatically out of your paycheck? A big zero would be my guess. Payroll taxes: including social security, state and federal, are as inevitable as death and are listed as the number one expense. Utility costs are a needed evil of life unless you don't mind living in the dark and cold. Food, essential to staying alive, may not be a fun expense but must be in your budget also. Do you eat to live or live to eat?

If you took this exercise seriously and really wrote down all of your expenses, including those that are paid less frequently than monthly, then you, like many others, may have one big surprise awaiting you. Did your monthly expenditures exceed your income? For many Americans this is a reality. Why is this? They don't live on a budget. That means they don't have a plan.

How Much Do I Make?

Before we can start formulating "The Plan" we must first take inventory of what we actually earn. Thankfully, for most people, this will be an easy exercise. However, just like in Worksheet #2, accuracy is important. You may need to gather last year's tax return to complete this assignment unless all of your earnings are from wages. Also assemble your W-2's and paystubs to record your earnings exactly. We are looking for gross earnings here and not just what you get paid after deductions.

Also, you need to consider all <u>documentable</u> sources of "cash flow" that come into your home on a consistent and ongoing basis. Since the purpose of this exercise is to determine how much mortgage you will qualify for, we will only be using income that the lenders will allow.

Worksheet #3

Monthly Income and Cash Flows

Salary/Wages: (refer to Note 1) _____

Overtime: (refer to Note 2) _____

Commission: (refer to Note 3) _____

Bonus: (refer to Note 4) _____

Stock Options: (refer to Note 5) _____

Self Employment Income: (refer to Note 6) _____

Interest: (refer to Note 7) _____

Dividends: (refer to Note 7) _____

Net Rental Income: (refer to Note 8) _____

Social Security: (refer to Note 9) _____

Alimony/Child Support: (refer to Note 10) _____

Pension/Retirement Income: (refer to Note 11) _____

Investment: (refer to Note 12) _____

Other: _____

Other: _____

Other: _____

Other: _____

Total Monthly Income: (B) _____

Helping You Compute Your Earnings:

Note 1: Salary/Wages:

It is important to know whether you are paid on a monthly, bi-weekly, or bi-monthly basis. Use your paystubs to assist in getting this number correct. If you are paid monthly, that is the amount of the gross earnings (before any deductions) that you put on this line. If you are paid bi-weekly (every two weeks), then multiply the gross earnings by 26 and then divide by 12 to get your monthly income. If you are paid twice a month, (typically on the 15th and 30th), then multiply your gross earnings by two to get your monthly earnings. We are only using base pay in this line. If your pay is from hourly wages then you will have to use an average of what your earnings have been for the last 12 months. This is especially difficult since you may have experienced an increase in hourly rate during that time. Divide your total earnings by the months that are represented.

Note 2: Overtime Earnings:

In some occupations, overtime earnings are consistent and a regular source of ongoing income. In order to use these earnings for mortgage loan qualification purposes it must be proved that this is a regular part of your income. The best way to calculate what a lender will allow you to use is to take your most recent full year's income and be able to show what percentage of that income was from overtime as opposed to other types of income. Be prepared to have your last paystub of the previous year as typically overtime earnings are not broken down on a W-2 form. Your employer can often assist you with getting these numbers. Overtime earnings will generally be averaged using the most current tax year plus the months into the current year when you are applying for the loan. Divide only overtime earnings over the appropriate number of months to show an average of your earnings from this source.

Note 3: Commission Earnings:

Many sales people derive a significant portion of their earnings from commission. The minute an underwriter sees commission earnings, they will require you to provide your tax returns. They are looking for expenses associated with sales earnings. It is very common for sales individuals to "write-off" expenses on their tax returns associated with travel, entertainment, supplies or other associated costs not reimbursed by the employer. If your earnings are reported on a W-2 tax form, then you would be able to write-off any sales expenses on the schedule 'A' form of your tax returns. If you are paid on a 1099 basis, as a non-employee, then you typically would file your income on a schedule 'C' as a self-employed individual. Look at the schedule 'A' of your most current tax year to see if you deducted any employee non-reimbursed expenses. You will need to calculate the *percentage* that you took as expenses as that will be used against current commission earnings. For example, if your total expenses as shown on schedule 'A' equals 10% of your total gross earnings, then you will need to deduct the same percentage on your current year to date earnings. Assuming this is May and your most current earnings are through April, then you will need to deduct 10% from January through April earnings to allow for the cost of producing that income. Since income from commission earnings will need to be averaged, and if your current year earnings are through April, the lender will *probably* use the most recent 16 months of earnings (last year plus 4 months into this year), less expenses, to calculate what you make. Be aware of this for the coming tax year if you are planning on purchasing a home. You may not want to be as liberal in deducting expenses as they will be reducing your qualifying income by these expenses.

Note 4: Bonus Income:

Bonus income can be tricky because it is often paid at the end of a quarter or the end of a year. Most employers will not guarantee that bonuses will be awarded on a forward basis. In order to use this as income in your qualification of a home loan it must be proven that you have a history of earning a bonus, must be deemed as ongoing, and must be averaged.

Note 5: Stock Options:

Unfortunately, if stock options are a part of your regular and ongoing income, you probably won't be able to use them in order to qualify for your mortgage loan. Stock option income is only income when the options are exercised (sold). It is especially difficult right now that the stock market is so depressed and many people want to wait until the market is right in order to exercise their options. Due to the nature of stock options and the pricing of the same, it is very difficult to use this as income, but the sale of stock can be used for a down payment resource if you choose to sell them. If you do have a consistent history of selling your options then you may be able to use an averaged amount in the calculation, provided you can prove that you receive these options regularly and do exercise them.

Note 6: Self-Employment Income:

This area is especially difficult for the average individual to extrapolate income as there are so many variables. Being self-employed can be as simple as filing income on a schedule 'C' of your personal tax returns, to being an owner in a corporation. If you own greater than 25% of any business then you are considered to be self-employed.

Schedule 'C' filers: If you file your income on a schedule 'C' form of your tax returns, then typically you will only get to use the income that you pay tax on. This is your "net" income after expenses. You do not get to use your gross income in this case. Two items that can be added back into your net income are any deduction that you take for an "in-home" office and any depreciation of items. Generally if you are self-employed, you will be required to furnish the most current two years of tax returns in order to determine an average of your income. Unfortunately, most self-employed individuals have more spendable income than they can use for qualification purposes.

S-Corp: The same rules apply for people that utilize an S-Corp for filing of taxes that apply to the schedule 'C' filers, but you will need to provide both years S-Corp returns in addition to personal returns.

Corporation: Owners of a corporation are typically paid on a W-2 basis, but if you own more than 25% of the corporation, then full corporate tax returns as well as personal tax returns will be required. Your personal income will be increased or decreased by the profit or loss that you report, according to your percentage of ownership.

Partnership: Again, the full partnership tax returns will be required if you own more than 25% of the partnership. Your income is reported on a K-1 statement and this is the earnings that will be used for your qualification. Many people have minority interests in partnerships and can use that income for their qualification if it is deemed ongoing. Some people have losses from partnerships that do not require any ongoing financial contribution, but provide a tax savings. These losses will need to be shown as tax losses only.

Note 7: Interest and Dividend Earnings:

Income from interest and dividends can be used if it is a consistent and on-going source of income. However, you must still have the assets that support this income. If you are planning on using your savings for a down payment then you will lose a portion, or all, of the source of the asset for this income. Income from this source must also be averaged over a 24-month period.

Note 8: Rental Income:

There are a couple of ways that we have of utilizing rental income. First, if a person owns one or more rental properties, they can provide the lender with the most current lease agreement on the property(s) to show current rents. If this source of verification is used then the lender will take only 75% of the gross rental income and then deduct the full mortgage payment, taxes and insurance from the rents. The amount remaining, if positive, is added to income. If the amount is negative, then it is calculated as a debt. The reason that the lender only uses 75% of gross rents is to allow for any vacancy factors and maintenance on the property. Currently, lenders are requiring a copy of the most current tax returns if a person owns even one rental property. Income as shown on a schedule 'E' of the tax return can also be used in qualification, before the deduction for depreciation on the property.

Note 9: Social Security Income:

Each year you receive an award letter that states the income for the following year. Use the gross amount of the monthly award.

Note 10: Alimony/Child Support:

Although many people are entitled to alimony and child support earnings, it can only be used if you can prove that you receive it on a regular basis. If the ex is a "dead-beat" then you can only use what you have actually received from them.

Note 11: Pension /Retirement:

Use the gross amount of monthly income before any deductions.

Note 12: Investment/ Other Income:

There are so many possibilities of other income such as: gas and oil leases, trust funds, renting out a room, note income and a whole host of other ways in which people get money. Keep in mind that any money that you receive must be verified and considered as ongoing for at least five years. Also be aware that if you don't pay tax on it, chances are, it can't be used as income.

Earnings Summary:

Total up all of the income on this report and you will have your gross monthly household qualifying income for mortgage loan purposes. This is also important information for you to have before you can establish a legitimate budget. The more time you invest in calculating your own earnings will assist you in providing the appropriate documentation that a lender will need in order to qualify you for a mortgage loan. Never assume that a lender understands your earnings better than you do. You are the authority on how much money that you actually earn. You just have to be able to prove it. If you are a self-employed person and can only use net earnings for income qualification, be aware that any expenses you listed on Worksheet #2 that are paid or expensed out of your business earnings can be taken out of your personal expense worksheet. Providing that you can prove that these are business expenses, the lender will not use them in your personal qualifications. Again the optimum word here is "prove".

What Assets Do You Have?

The next step in planning for a potential home purchase, is being aware of how much money you have available for a down payment on a home. In addition to the down payment, you also need funds for closing costs and a sufficient amount remaining for reserves. Reserves are the funds you have left after the down payment and closing costs have been paid. This is your emergency money and is a necessity of being a homeowner. Complete the enclosed sheet to determine how many assets that you can turn into cash.

Worksheet #4

Assets

Cash on hand: _____

Checking Accounts: _____

Savings Accounts: _____

Stocks (cash value): _____

Bonds (cash value): _____

Mutual Funds: _____

Retirement Accounts (cash available) _____

Life Insurance (cash value): _____

Gift Funds from family: _____

Saleable Assets: _____

Collectibles: _____

Other: _____

Other: _____

Total Assets Available: (C) _____

Asset Summary

Knowing what cash you have available for a purchase is crucial. The more money you have for a down payment the cheaper the cost of the financing. It is also important that you have money left after the purchase of a home for all of the unexpected "life events" that may happen.

Don't overlook any assets you have that may be turned into cash. Every family is different. Your age and life circumstances may help you to decide which assets are better liquidated and invested in a home as opposed to just taking up space. For example, the coin collection that you may have been saving may better be used as a cash down payment. Life insurance policies often have cash value that doesn't affect your insurance in the event that it was needed. Some retirement accounts will allow you to draw out proceeds, without penalty, if you are using it for a home purchase. Many families have relatives that offer to help with a down payment. This exercise can help you think in terms of what you really have at your disposal if you choose to use it in this manner. Don't overlook anything. It could be time to clean out the garage and do an EBay posting.

Are You Ready for Home Ownership?

You are on a fact finding mission to help you better understand your OWN financial circumstances. Now that you have assembled all of your financial data, it is time to start analyzing. Ask yourself the following questions:

1. Based on worksheet #2 (expenses), how much of your monthly income from worksheet #3 (income) is already committed?

2. Are you happy with where your money is currently allocated and what changes could you make immediately?

3. Is your current spending in conjunction with "Your Value System" from Worksheet #1?

4. What adjustments to your spending do you need to make before you can become a homeowner or move up in house expense?

5. If you have discretionary income (money left over after payment of all expenses), how much can you apply towards an additional housing expense?

6. If you paid down some or all of your debt, how much more could you afford towards a higher housing payment?

7. If you are not already a homeowner, are you aware that the money you pay in interest on a mortgage payment (and most of the payment is interest) and all of your property tax payments are deductable from your taxable income. With the potential decrease in tax liability, how much will this increase your monthly available income?

8. If you are looking towards a larger home purchase, don't forget to calculate higher utility costs.

9. Are your cash assets sufficient to provide a down payment, closing costs and still have money left over for an emergency fund?

Calculating Your Potential Housing Payment:

The following two examples show a variety of housing payments that a person/family would potentially qualify for based on two different earning scenarios. Use the total of earnings from Worksheet #3 (income) item (B) to calculate *your* payment potentials. I have used a range from 33%, being very conservative, to a high of 50% (ouch) of your gross income as a possible future housing payment. Fannie Mae will often allow you to commit more than 50% of your gross income to your PITI payment. Unless you are a very large wage earner, this is a recipe for a potential disaster. Don't forget, this is gross earnings prior to taxes and all other monthly expenses that you have identified in Worksheet #2.

Based on the examples provided, if you made a gross income of $5,000 per month, then your potential housing payment could be anywhere from $1,650 up to $2,500 per month. If your household income was $10,000 per month then you could possibly afford a housing payment range from $3,300 and up to $5,000. By using the various percentages, we can determine the **maximum** mortgage loan that *you* should be considering.

Example #1:

Using the Gross Monthly Income Totals from Worksheet #3, complete the following:

Housing-to-Income Ratios:

(B) _____ $5,000 _____ X 33% = $1,650 _____ (D1) PITI

(B) _____ $5,000 _____ X 35% = $1,750 _____ (D2) PITI

(B) _____ $5,000 _____ X 38% = $1,900 _____ (D3) PITI

(B) _____ $5,000 _____ X 40% = $2,000 _____ (D4) PITI

(B) _____ $5,000 _____ X 44% = $2,200 _____ (D5) PITI

(B) _____ $5,000 _____ X 48% = $2,400 _____ (D6) PITI

(B) _____ $5,000 _____ X 50% = $2,500 _____ (D7) PITI

(B) equals the total gross income from worksheet #3

(D) equals the total amount of a mortgage loan payment (PITI) at the specified percentage. PITI is the amount of monthly payment including: principal and interest on the mortgage loan, the monthly property taxes and the monthly insurance. Item (D) is the amount of PITI that you should be able to qualify for based on the gross percentages listed.

Example #2:

Using the Gross Monthly Income Totals from Worksheet #3, complete the following:

Housing-to-Income Ratios:

(B) _____$10,000_____ X 33% = _$3,300_____(D1) PITI

(B) _____$10,000_____ X 35% = _$3,500_____(D2) PITI

(B) _____$10,000_____ X 38% = _$3,800_____(D3) PITI

(B) _____$10,000_____ X 40% = _$4,000_____(D4) PITI

(B) _____$10,000_____ X 44% = _$4,400_____(D5) PITI

(B) _____$10,000_____ X 48% = _$4,800_____(D6) PITI

(B) _____$10,000_____ X 50% = _$5,000_____(D7) PITI

(B) equals the total gross income from worksheet #3

(D) equals the total amount of a mortgage loan payment (PITI) at the specified percentage. PITI is the amount of monthly payment including: principal and interest on the mortgage loan, the monthly property taxes and the monthly insurance. Item (D) is the amount of PITI that you should be able to qualify for based on the gross percentages listed.

Worksheet #5

How Much Mortgage Expense Can I Afford?

Using the Gross Monthly Income Totals from Worksheet #3, complete the following:

Housing-to-Income Ratios:

(B) _____ X 33% = _____ (D1) PITI

(B) _____ X 35% = _____ (D2) PITI

(B) _____ X 38% = _____ (D3) PITI

(B) _____ X 40% = _____ (D4) PITI

(B) _____ X 44% = _____ (D5) PITI

(B) _____ X 48% = _____ (D6) PITI

(B) _____ X 50% = _____ (D7) PITI

(B) equals the total gross income from worksheet #3

(D) equals the total amount of a mortgage loan payment (PITI) at the specified percentage. PITI is the amount of monthly payment including: principal and interest on the mortgage loan, the monthly property taxes and the monthly insurance. Item (D) is the amount of PITI that you should be able to qualify for based on the gross percentages listed.

Review Your Housing Payment Results to Discover Your Maximum Mortgage Loan Potential:

The enclosed chart titled "Housing Payment Table" will identify the monthly payment amounts of PITI that go with different loan amounts based on varying interest rates. Again, PITI is the total of: Principal, Interest, Taxes and Insurance payments. The amounts for taxes and insurance will vary from region to region, and state to state, but since we are using a *range* of monthly payments, then you will know the ballpark of what loan amount you should qualify for based on your household income level. Notice the difference in monthly payments on varying loan amounts and how they fluctuate with the differing interest rates. The lower the interest rate - the more loan amount that you can afford. Since there are so many variables to consider when purchasing a home, we are simply trying to identify the **maximum** amount of mortgage loan that you should be considering. It is critically important to see how the potential monthly payment fits into your current expenses as identified in Worksheet #2. Also, is this increase or decrease in housing payment consistent with your priority values as identified in Worksheet #1? Playing with the numbers on paper isvery time consuming initially, but save you untold suffering in the end.

Example #1

At 33% of income, this family would be able to afford a monthly payment of approximately $1,650. Using the Housing Payment Table, the following would be the *closest* monthly payments at the various rates:

@4.5%   PITI of $1,598 would equal a loan amount of $240,000

@5.0%   PITI of $1,670 would equal a loan amount of $240,000

@5.5%   PITI of $1,453 would equal a loan amount of $200,000

@6.0%   PITI of $1,520 would equal a loan amount of $200,000

@6.5%   PITI of $1,583 would equal a loan amount of $200,000

Therefore, if this family was comfortable in this price range then they should be looking to borrow no more than $240,000 if rates are low, but less if they are higher.

At 40% of income the monthly payment of $2,000 applies and the following would be the closest payments at the various rates:

@4.5%   PITI of $1,864 would equal a loan amount of $280,000

@5.0%   PITI of $1,948 would equal a loan amount of $280,000

@5.5%   PITI of $2,035 would equal a loan amount of $280,000

@6.0%   PITI of $1,824 would equal a loan amount of $240,000

@6.5%   PITI of $1,902 would equal a loan amount of $240,000

If you look at these numbers you will see that the interest rate can make a big difference. For example, at 4.5% the payment at$280,000 is almost the same as the 6.0% payment at $240,000. That is a significant difference in borrowing power just based on rate alone.

Housing Payment Table-PITI

Loan Amount	4.5%	5%	5.5%	6%	6.5%
80,000	532	556	581	607	633
100,000	665	696	727	760	793
120,000	799	835	872	912	951
140,000	931	974	1017	1064	1106
160,000	1065	1113	1162	1216	1268
200,000	1331	1392	1453	1520	1583
240,000	1598	1670	1745	1824	1902
280,000	1864	1948	2035	2128	2219
320,000	2130	2227	2326	2431	2535
360,000	2397	2506	2617	2735	2852
400,000	2663	2783	2853	3038	3168
440,000	2930	3063	3199	3342	3485
480,000	3197	3342	3490	3646	3802
520,000	3463	3619	3780	3949	4118
560,000	3729	3898	4072	4253	4435
600,000	3996	4177	4363	4556	4751
640,000	4262	4455	4653	4860	5068
680,000	4528	4733	4944	5163	5385
720,000	4795	5012	5235	5467	5701
760,000	5061	5290	5525	5770	6018
800,000	5327	5569	5816	6042	6334

*PITI based on 20% down-no MI

"Housing Payment Table"

<u>Are We Done Yet?</u>

NO! You have just made a very important discovery through all of these worksheets. You now know the *maximum amount* of a mortgage loan that you can qualify for based only on your household income level. However, this is not the only criteria that you have to consider. If you have debt, then your housing payment is going to be limited by the amount of the payments on that debt.

Another Worksheet???? You bet!

Worksheet #6

Your Monthly Debt Payments

Using this worksheet, add up all of the monthly payments that you have on any debt that you carry. This is not monthly expenses, but debt payments only.

Credit Card (minimum monthly payment) _____

Credit Card _____

Credit Card _____

Credit Card _____

Vehicle Loan _____

Vehicle Loan _____

Installment Loan _____

School/Education Loan _____

Alimony _____

Child Support _____

Co-signed Debt _____

Negative Rental Property Expense

(if you own other property) _____

Other _____

Other _____

Total Monthly DEBT: (E) _____

Debt Summary:

The debts that you have listed in Worksheet #6 should be the debts that will be reflected on your credit report. Any money that you have *borrowed* and needs to be repaid is to be included in this list of expenses. Do not include the loan that you owe to Aunt Bertha or any other personal loans that will not show on your credit report. However, in your personal list of expenditures, I certainly hope that this is a debt that you intend to take care of. If you have co-signed for someone else and this debt is on your credit report, you will also have to include it as if it were you making the payments. Any loan that will be paid off in less than 10 months can be excluded from this list. Credit card payments are never excluded, even if you pay off your cards monthly. The lender will use a monthly payment of at least 5% of the unpaid balance in their calculation of your debt-ratio. If you are obligated for alimony or child support payments, then these amounts are also treated as debts and will reduce your borrowing power.

Once you have added up all of your monthly debt payments then we can see the net amount that you can use towards your housing payment.

From Worksheet #5 take the PITI payments (D1) through (D7) and subtract (E) as follows:

Example #1

Final Monthly Housing Payment

Using this worksheet, deduct your total monthly debt payments (E) on Worksheet #6, from your previously allowable housing payments (D) on Worksheet #5:

33% (D1) PITI $1,650 -   Debt Pmts (E) of $450 = (F1) $1,200

35% (D2) PITI $1,750 -   Debt Pmts (E) of $450 = (F2) $1,300

38% (D3) PITI $1,900 -   Debt Pmts (E) of $450 = (F3) $1,450

40% (D4) PITI $2,000 -   Debt Pmts (E) of $450 = (F4) $1,550

44% (D5) PITI $2,200 -   Debt Pmts (E) of $450 = (F5) $1,750

48% (D6) PITI $2,400 -   Debt Pmts (E) of $450 = (F6) $1,950

50% (D7) PITI $2,500 -   Debt Pmts (E) of $450 = (F7) $2,050

The amounts listed in (F1) through (F7) are now the new potential housing payment limitations based on your income level at the proposed percentage of income PITI payments.

Worksheet #7

Final Monthly Housing Payment

Using this worksheet, deduct your total monthly debt payments (E) on Worksheet #6, from your previously allowable housing payments (D) on Worksheet #5:

33% (D1) PITI _____ - Debt Pmts (E) of _____ = (F1) _____

35% (D2) PITI _____ - Debt Pmts (E) of _____ = (F2) _____

38% (D3) PITI _____ - Debt Pmts (E) of _____ = (F3) _____

40% (D4) PITI _____ - Debt Pmts (E) of _____ = (F4) _____

44% (D5) PITI _____ - Debt Pmts (E) of _____ = (F5) _____

48% (D6) PITI _____ - Debt Pmts (E) of _____ = (F6) _____

50% (D7) PITI _____ - Debt Pmts (E) of _____ = (F7) _____

The amounts listed in (F1) through (F7) are now the new potential housing payment limitations based on your income level at the proposed percentage of income PITI payments.

Final Monthly Housing Payment Range:

The amounts represented by (F1) through (F7) are the potential housing payments that you should be able to afford (theoretically) based on your household income and current debt levels. Using this range of payments, refer back to the chart called: <u>Housing Payment Table</u> and once again look at the corresponding loan amounts. Recall that the interest rate plays a significant role in how much of a mortgage that you can handle. It is easy to look up the current 30 year fixed-rate mortgage loan rates in the newspapers. The rates shown in the newspapers or on the internet are usually lower than the average person can obtain so always add .5%-1% higher in your personal calculations. Remember you are just starting your quest. Be conservative.

Example #1

Assuming this family has $450 in monthly debt repayments, let us see how that will affect their borrowing power for a mortgage loan.

At 33% of household income, the new mortgage payment would be lowered from $1,650 to $1200 per month and the closest loan amount scenario would be as follows:

@4.5%   PITI of $1,065 would equal a loan amount of $160,000

@5.5%   PITI of $1,162 would equal a loan amount of $160,000

@6.5%   PITI of $1,268 would equal a loan amount of $160,000

At 40% of household income, the new mortgage payment would be lowered from $2,000 to $1,550 per month and the closest loan amount scenario would be as follows:

@4.5%   PITI of $1,598 would equal a loan amount of $240,000

@5.5%   PITI of $1,392 would equal a loan amount of $200,000

@6.5%   PITI of $1,583 would equal a loan amount of $200,000

Whereas in the first set of examples, the family could easily afford the $240,000 loan amount range, now they would be pushing it at the $200,000 amount. The amount of monthly debt ($450) has significantly affected their potential borrowing power for a home loan.

Review YOUR Monthly Payments with YOUR Current Monthly Expenses:

Reviewing the revised potential monthly payments of (F1) through (F7), go back to Worksheet #2 and see how these numbers fit into your current household expenses. There are three items listed in Worksheet #2 (#2, 3 and 4) that reflect your current payments for your housing. Are the new numbers higher or lower than you are currently paying? Can you afford this new payment?

You will want to play with these numbers to get a feel for what you can handle on an ongoing basis. Keep in mind your values and what you want to prioritize for your future.

Deciding on a monthly payment and the corresponding loan amount is the first step in deciding how much of a home that you can truthfully afford. There is however, still one more major item to be considered.

Available Cash for Down Payment Can Limit Your Home Purchase:

While your income will determine how much mortgage you can afford, your cash will determine how much home you can buy. You have now successfully decided on the amount of mortgage that you feel comfortable in carrying, but how much you have to put down on a house will determine the price range of home that you should be shopping for.

Only one more worksheet -

Example #1

Price of Home Based on Down Payment

Step #1   Use Worksheet #7 (monthly housing payment) to identify the mortgage amount that most conservatively is represented by the payment that you can afford.

Loan Amount of: $240,000

Step #2   From Worksheet #4 (assets) how much cash can you reasonably use as a down payment.

Down Payment Amount: $16,000

Step #3   Add the down payment amount to the loan amount that you can safely handle to arrive at the home price that you can afford.

Approximate Price of Home: $256,000

Step #4   Take the amount of the down payment and divide by the price of the home to get the percentage of down payment being used.

Down Payment: $16,000 divided by: Price of Home: $256,000

Equals: 6.3 % Percent of Down Payment to Home Price

Example#2

Price of Home Based on Down Payment

Step #1   Use Worksheet #7 (monthly housing payment) to identify the mortgage amount that most conservatively is represented by the payment that you can afford.

Loan Amount of: $240,000

Step #2   From Worksheet #4 (assets) how much cash can you reasonably use as a down payment.

Down Payment Amount: $200,000

Step #3   Add the down payment amount to the loan amount that you can safely handle to arrive at the home price that you can afford.

Approximate Price of Home: $440,000

Step #4   Take the amount of the down payment and divide by the price of the home to get the percentage of down payment being used.

Down Payment: $200,000 divided by: Price of Home: $440,000

Equals: 45%   Percent of Down Payment to Home Price

Worksheet #8

Price of Home Based on Down Payment

Step #1   Use Worksheet #7 (monthly housing payment) to identify the mortgage amount that most conservatively is represented by the payment that you can afford.

Loan Amount of: _____

Step #2   From Worksheet #4(assets) how much cash can you reasonably use as a down payment.

Down Payment Amount: _____

Step #3   Add the down payment amount to the loan amount that you can safely handle to arrive at the home price that you can afford.

Approximate Price of Home: _____

Step #4   Take the amount of the down payment and divide by the price of the home to get the percentage of down payment being used.

Down Payment: _____ divided by: Price of Home: _____

Equals: _____ Percent of Down Payment to Home Price

Down Payment Percentage:

The more down-payment you have, the better the terms of the financing. If you do not have at least a 20% down payment, then you will also be paying for mortgage insurance on a monthly basis to protect the lender in the event that you default on your loan. The minimum that you can put down on a home is 3%, although this keeps changing in our current lending environment. The minimal down is also subject to very strict limitations and loan amounts. The more that you put down, the less you will have to pay in mortgage insurance costs and interest rate. In addition to your down payment you will also have to pay closing costs, prepaid items and have an amount left over for cash reserves.

Qualification Charts

Following this section are individual qualification charts at various interest rates and various loan amounts. These charts break down the actual monthly amounts for principal and interest, property taxes, and property insurance. We have used 1.25% of the sales price as a factor for property taxes. This amount may be higher or lower than your local area. Check in advance as to the property tax rates so you can hone in more accurately on what your actual monthly payment would be. There are some areas that pay additional property taxes such as a community tax for the support of schools, roads, services, etc. In California many areas have a tax known as Mello-Roos which is a tax that builders would normally pay in the development of an area in order to reimburse the community for the additional support services needed by their homeowners. Builders have found a way to pass this tax on to the homeowner in the form of a 30 year bond payment. Check all of these hidden taxes before you decide on the area that you want to start looking in. For property insurance we have used a factor of .35% of the loan amount. Again this may be high or low depending on the area that you live in.

If you do not have a down payment of at least 20% then you will be paying mortgage insurance. This is a very difficult payment to anticipate as it has many variables. Allow additional for this monthly expense.

If you are purchasing in a planned unit development (PUD) such as a condominium then you will also have to allocate monthly funds for a homeowner association fee. All of these added expenses will further limit what you can afford in the way of a maximum mortgage payment and ultimately a home purchase price.

How Much Are Closing Costs:

Closing costs can vary depending on the area that you live and the type of services that are needed. There are financing costs for obtaining a mortgage loan and also potential costs not paid by the seller that you will have to absorb. Always estimate high so you will be prepared. A local realtor should be able to assist you with estimating these charges. In addition, some of the costs may be negotiable with the seller.

Financing charges will include: appraisal, credit report, escrow or attorney fee, title charges, notary, recording fees, lender charges, etc. Also, if you plan to pay points in order to get a lower interest rate, this will add to these fees.

Other fees that you may expect to pay are: inspection fees, termite services or other costs relating to the purchase of a piece of property.

What Are Prepaid Items?

There are at least three items that will be prepaid at the time of a home purchase. The interest on the new loan will be charged from the day of funding until the end of the month. For example, if you close your loan on the 15th day of any month, then you will have approximately 15 days of interest that you will prepay on the loan. The first of the next month you will not have a housing payment due. You will be expected to purchase an insurance policy that will cover you for the first year of home-ownership. After the first year then you can set it up monthly or quarterly if you wish. Also, depending on the time of year that you purchase a home, you may be expected to pay a portion of the property tax bill. Other potential prepaid items could be a proration for association fees if they are relative to your purchase.

How Much in Reserves Should I Have?

The minimum amount of cash reserves after accounting for the down payment, closing costs and prepaid items is at least three months worth of PITI. If you have done all of the worksheets you will know the approximate amount of monthly payment for principal, interest, taxes, insurance and if there is any mortgage insurance that you will be obligating yourself for. Plan to have at least three months worth of this amount of money left over after everything else has been paid. Over estimating is always better than finding yourself short on funds.

What Role Do Credit Scores Play?

You have assessed your income, your debt and your cash available, but the final part of the financing equation is becoming aware of what your credit scores are. Having your credit report checked at this juncture is wise so you will have time to <u>fix</u> any little problem that may be on your report. You may also be able to pay down or pay off some of the debt being reported that can hinder you from fully qualifying for the amount of mortgage that you will need for the purchase. Avoid over using credit cards at this stage, especially if you pay them off every month as any unpaid balance that shows on your credit will require a monthly payment in the ratio calculation.

Formulating the Plan

Congratulations, you made it this far. Now you should know where you are in the preparation stage for purchasing a home.

If your results are positive and you are ready to take the plunge now…..then please consider the following:

1. Decide *before* you start shopping what your **maximum** purchase price should be, based on the maximum loan amount that you will qualify for, and how much money you have available for the down-payment and closing costs. Avoid the temptation to just "look at" the home that is over your budget. If you fall in love with a house that you really can't afford, you may have difficulty exercising your better judgment.

2. Don't forget to keep a sizeable amount of cash for reserves after the purchase of your home.

    a. If buying a new home then you will need money for landscaping, painting, decorating, window coverings and many items that you may not anticipate.

    b. If your purchase is an older home then you may need money for renovation, upkeep and certainly the unexpected.

    c. Emergency funds are essential as <u>things</u> happen.

3. Seek the assistance of a professional for both a mortgage lender and a realtor. This is not the time to "let your fingers do the walking" through the yellow pages. Ask around to see if any of your family, friends or co-workers knows somebody they trust to handle their real estate affairs. Any person can show you a house, but an experienced and trustworthy realtor is going to negotiate on your behalf. Their

experience can save you not only dollars but also grief if you end up buying a home with undisclosed maintenance issues, etc. Most important is to find an experienced and honorable mortgage professional. I recommend an independent broker who can advise you as to the loan programs that you will qualify for and is approved with many lenders so they can shop your loan for the best in terms. Even before you find that perfect home, find the agent who can work with you in advance so you can plan together.

If the results of these worksheets indicate that you are not yet ready for home ownership then start your future plan NOW. Decide what needs to be done to make it happen. There are typically only three major obstacles to your owning a home:

1. Not enough cash

2. Not enough income

3. Too much debt

You be the JUDGE!!!!

20% Down-Qualification Chart@4.5%

Sales Price	Down Payment @ 20%	Loan Amount	Principal Interest @4.5%	Property Taxes Estimate	Hazard Insurance Estimate	Total Payment PITI
100,000	20,000	80,000	405	104	23	532
125,000	25,000	100,000	506	130	29	665
150,000	30,000	120,000	608	156	35	799
175,000	35,000	140,000	709	182	40	931
200,000	40,000	160,000	811	208	46	1,065
250,000	50,000	200,000	1,013	260	58	1,331
300,000	60,000	240,000	1,216	312	70	1,598
350,000	70,000	280,000	1,419	364	81	1,864
400,000	80,000	320,000	1,621	416	93	2,130
450,000	90,000	360,000	1,824	468	105	2,397
500,000	100,000	400,000	2,027	520	116	2,663
550,000	110,000	440,000	2,229	573	128	2,930
600,000	120,000	480,000	2,432	625	140	3,197
650,000	130,000	520,000	2,635	677	151	3,463
700,000	140,000	560,000	2,837	729	163	3,729
750,000	150,000	600,000	3,040	781	175	3,996
800,000	160,000	640,000	3,243	833	186	4,262
850,000	170,000	680,000	3,445	885	198	4,528
900,000	180,000	720,000	3,648	937	210	4,795
950,000	190,000	760,000	3,851	989	221	5,061
1 Million	200,000	800,000	4,053	1,041	233	5,327

*property tax estimate figured at 1.25% of the purchase price
*hazard insurance figured at .35% of the loan amount
*total PITI=Total Principal, Interest, Taxes and Insurance

20% Down-Qualification Chart@4.75%

Sales Price	Down Payment @ 20%	Loan Amount	Principal Interest @4.75%	Property Taxes Estimate	Hazard Insurance Estimate	Total Payment PITI
100,000	20,000	80,000	417	104	23	544
125,000	25,000	100,000	522	130	29	681
150,000	30,000	120,000	626	156	35	817
175,000	35,000	140,000	730	182	40	952
200,000	40,000	160,000	835	208	46	1,089
250,000	50,000	200,000	1,043	260	58	1,361
300,000	60,000	240,000	1,252	312	70	1,634
350,000	70,000	280,000	1,461	364	81	1,906
400,000	80,000	320,000	1,669	416	93	2,178
450,000	90,000	360,000	1,878	468	105	2,451
500,000	100,000	400,000	2,087	520	116	2,723
550,000	110,000	440,000	2,295	573	128	2,996
600,000	120,000	480,000	2,504	625	140	3,269
650,000	130,000	520,000	2,713	677	151	3,541
700,000	140,000	560,000	2,921	729	163	3,813
750,000	150,000	600,000	3,130	781	175	4,086
800,000	160,000	640,000	3,339	833	186	4,358
850,000	170,000	680,000	3,547	885	198	4,630
900,000	180,000	720,000	3,756	937	210	4,903
950,000	190,000	760,000	3,964	989	221	5,174
1 Million	200,000	800,000	4,173	1,041	233	5,447

*property tax estimate figured at 1.25% of the purchase price
*hazard insurance figured at .35% of the loan amount
*total PITI=Total Principal, Interest, Taxes and Insurance

20% Down-Qualification Chart@5%

Sales Price	Down Payment @ 20%	Loan Amount	Principal Interest @5%	Property Taxes Estimate	Hazard Insurance Estimate	Total Payment PITI
100,000	20,000	80,000	429	104	23	556
125,000	25,000	100,000	537	130	29	696
150,000	30,000	120,000	644	156	35	835
175,000	35,000	140,000	752	182	40	974
200,000	40,000	160,000	859	208	46	1,113
250,000	50,000	200,000	1,074	260	58	1,392
300,000	60,000	240,000	1,288	312	70	1,670
350,000	70,000	280,000	1,503	364	81	1,948
400,000	80,000	320,000	1,718	416	93	2,227
450,000	90,000	360,000	1,933	468	105	2,506
500,000	100,000	400,000	2,147	520	116	2,783
550,000	110,000	440,000	2,362	573	128	3,063
600,000	120,000	480,000	2,577	625	140	3,342
650,000	130,000	520,000	2,791	677	151	3,619
700,000	140,000	560,000	3,006	729	163	3,898
750,000	150,000	600,000	3,221	781	175	4,177
800,000	160,000	640,000	3,436	833	186	4,455
850,000	170,000	680,000	3,650	885	198	4,733
900,000	180,000	720,000	3,865	937	210	5,012
950,000	190,000	760,000	4,080	989	221	5,290
1 Million	200,000	800,000	4,295	1,041	233	5,569

*property tax estimate figured at 1.25% of the purchase price
*hazard insurance figured at .35% of the loan amount
*total PITI=Total Principal, Interest, Taxes and Insurance

20% Down-Qualification Chart@5.25%

Sales Price	Down Payment @ 20%	Loan Amount	Principal Interest @5.25%	Property Taxes Estimate	Hazard Insurance Estimate	Total Payment PITI
100,000	20,000	80,000	442	104	23	569
125,000	25,000	100,000	552	130	29	711
150,000	30,000	120,000	663	156	35	854
175,000	35,000	140,000	773	182	40	995
200,000	40,000	160,000	884	208	46	1,138
250,000	50,000	200,000	1,104	260	58	1,422
300,000	60,000	240,000	1,325	312	70	1,707
350,000	70,000	280,000	1,546	364	81	1,991
400,000	80,000	320,000	1,767	416	93	2,276
450,000	90,000	360,000	1,988	468	105	2,561
500,000	100,000	400,000	2,209	520	116	2,845
550,000	110,000	440,000	2,430	573	128	3,131
600,000	120,000	480,000	2,651	625	140	3,416
650,000	130,000	520,000	2,871	677	151	3,699
700,000	140,000	560,000	3,092	729	163	3,984
750,000	150,000	600,000	3,313	781	175	4,269
800,000	160,000	640,000	3,534	833	186	4,553
850,000	170,000	680,000	3,755	885	198	4,838
900,000	180,000	720,000	3,976	937	210	5,123
950,000	190,000	760,000	4,197	989	221	5,407
1 Million	200,000	800,000	4,418	1,041	233	5,692

*property tax estimate figured at 1.25% of the purchase price
*hazard insurance figured at .35% of the loan amount
*total PITI=Total Principal, Interest, Taxes and Insurance

20% Down-Qualification Chart@5.5%

Sales Price	Down Payment @ 20%	Loan Amount	Principal Interest @5.5%	Property Taxes Estimate	Hazard Insurance Estimate	Total Payment PITI
100,000	20,000	80,000	454	104	23	581
125,000	25,000	100,000	568	130	29	727
150,000	30,000	120,000	681	156	35	872
175,000	35,000	140,000	795	182	40	1,017
200,000	40,000	160,000	908	208	46	1,162
250,000	50,000	200,000	1,135	260	58	1,453
300,000	60,000	240,000	1,363	312	70	1,745
350,000	70,000	280,000	1,590	364	81	2,035
400,000	80,000	320,000	1,817	416	93	2,326
450,000	90,000	360,000	2,044	468	105	2,617
500,000	100,000	400,000	2,271	520	116	2,853
550,000	110,000	440,000	2,498	573	128	3,199
600,000	120,000	480,000	2,725	625	140	3,490
650,000	130,000	520,000	2,952	677	151	3,780
700,000	140,000	560,000	3,180	729	163	4,072
750,000	150,000	600,000	3,407	781	175	4,363
800,000	160,000	640,000	3,634	833	186	4,653
850,000	170,000	680,000	3,861	885	198	4,944
900,000	180,000	720,000	4,088	937	210	5,235
950,000	190,000	760,000	4,315	989	221	5,525
1 Million	200,000	800,000	4,542	1,041	233	5,816

*property tax estimate figured at 1.25% of the purchase price
*hazard insurance figured at .35% of the loan amount
*total PITI=Total Principal, Interest, Taxes and Insurance

20% Down-Qualification Chart@5.75%

Sales Price	Down Payment @ 20%	Loan Amount	Principal Interest @5.75%	Property Taxes Estimate	Hazard Insurance Estimate	Total Payment PITI
100,000	20,000	80,000	454	104	23	581
125,000	25,000	100,000	568	130	29	727
150,000	30,000	120,000	681	156	35	872
175,000	35,000	140,000	795	182	40	1,017
200,000	40,000	160,000	908	208	46	1,162
250,000	50,000	200,000	1,136	260	58	1,454
300,000	60,000	240,000	1,363	312	70	1,745
350,000	70,000	280,000	1,590	364	81	2,035
400,000	80,000	320,000	1,817	416	93	2,326
450,000	90,000	360,000	2,044	468	105	2,617
500,000	100,000	400,000	2,271	520	116	2,853
550,000	110,000	440,000	2,498	573	128	3,199
600,000	120,000	480,000	2,725	625	140	3,490
650,000	130,000	520,000	2,953	677	151	3,781
700,000	140,000	560,000	3,180	729	163	4,072
750,000	150,000	600,000	3,407	781	175	4,363
800,000	160,000	640,000	3,634	833	186	4,653
850,000	170,000	680,000	3,861	885	198	4,944
900,000	180,000	720,000	4,088	937	210	5,235
950,000	190,000	760,000	4,315	989	221	5,525
1 Million	200,000	800,000	4,542	1,041	233	5,816

*property tax estimate figured at 1.25% of the purchase price
*hazard insurance figured at .35% of the loan amount
*total PITI=Total Principal, Interest, Taxes and Insurance

20% Down-Qualification Chart@6%

Sales Price	Down Payment @ 20%	Loan Amount	Principal Interest @6%	Property Taxes Estimate	Hazard Insurance Estimate	Total Payment PITI
100,000	20,000	80,000	480	104	23	607
125,000	25,000	100,000	599	130	29	760
150,000	30,000	120,000	719	156	35	912
175,000	35,000	140,000	839	182	40	1,064
200,000	40,000	160,000	959	208	46	1,216
250,000	50,000	200,000	1,199	260	58	1,520
300,000	60,000	240,000	1,439	312	70	1,824
350,000	70,000	280,000	1,679	364	81	2,128
400,000	80,000	320,000	1,918	416	93	2,431
450,000	90,000	360,000	2,158	468	105	2,735
500,000	100,000	400,000	2,398	520	116	3,038
550,000	110,000	440,000	2,638	573	128	3,342
600,000	120,000	480,000	2,878	625	140	3,646
650,000	130,000	520,000	3,117	677	151	3,949
700,000	140,000	560,000	3,357	729	163	4,253
750,000	150,000	600,000	3,597	781	175	4,556
800,000	160,000	640,000	3,837	833	186	4,860
850,000	170,000	680,000	4,077	885	198	5,163
900,000	180,000	720,000	4,316	937	210	5,467
950,000	190,000	760,000	4,556	989	221	5,770
1 Million	200,000	800,000	4,796	1,041	233	6,042

*property tax estimate figured at 1.25% of the purchase price
*hazard insurance figured at .35% of the loan amount
*total PITI=Total Principal, Interest, Taxes and Insurance

20% Down-Qualification Chart@6.25%

Sales Price	Down Payment @ 20%	Loan Amount	Principal Interest @6.25%	Property Taxes Estimate	Hazard Insurance Estimate	Total Payment PITI
100,000	20,000	80,000	492	104	23	620
125,000	25,000	100,000	616	130	29	776
150,000	30,000	120,000	739	156	35	931
175,000	35,000	140,000	862	182	40	1,086
200,000	40,000	160,000	985	208	46	1,241
250,000	50,000	200,000	1,231	260	58	1,553
300,000	60,000	240,000	1,478	312	70	1,863
350,000	70,000	280,000	1,724	364	81	2,173
400,000	80,000	320,000	1,970	416	93	2,483
450,000	90,000	360,000	2,216	468	105	2,793
500,000	100,000	400,000	2,463	520	116	3,103
550,000	110,000	440,000	2,709	573	128	3,413
600,000	120,000	480,000	2,955	625	140	3,723
650,000	130,000	520,000	3,202	677	151	4,033
700,000	140,000	560,000	3,448	729	163	4,343
750,000	150,000	600,000	3,694	781	175	4,653
800,000	160,000	640,000	3,940	833	186	4,963
850,000	170,000	680,000	4,187	885	198	5,273
900,000	180,000	720,000	4,433	937	210	5,583
950,000	190,000	760,000	4,679	989	221	5,893
1 Million	200,000	800,000	4,926	1,041	233	6,203

*property tax estimate figured at 1.25% of the purchase price
*hazard insurance figured at .35% of the loan amount
*total PITI=Total Principal, Interest, Taxes and Insurance

20% Down-Qualification Chart@6.5%

Sales Price	Down Payment @ 20%	Loan Amount	Principal Interest @6.5%	Property Taxes Estimate	Hazard Insurance Estimate	Total Payment PITI
100,000	20,000	80,000	505	104	23	633
125,000	25,000	100,000	632	130	29	793
150,000	30,000	120,000	758	156	35	951
175,000	35,000	140,000	885	182	40	1,106
200,000	40,000	160,000	1,011	208	46	1,268
250,000	50,000	200,000	1,264	260	58	1,583
300,000	60,000	240,000	1,517	312	70	1,902
350,000	70,000	280,000	1,770	364	81	2,219
400,000	80,000	320,000	2,022	416	93	2,535
450,000	90,000	360,000	2,275	468	105	2,852
500,000	100,000	400,000	2,528	520	116	3,168
550,000	110,000	440,000	2,781	573	128	3,485
600,000	120,000	480,000	3,034	625	140	3,802
650,000	130,000	520,000	3,287	677	151	4,118
700,000	140,000	560,000	3,539	729	163	4,435
750,000	150,000	600,000	3,792	781	175	4,751
800,000	160,000	640,000	4,045	833	186	5,068
850,000	170,000	680,000	4,298	885	198	5,385
900,000	180,000	720,000	4,551	937	210	5,701
950,000	190,000	760,000	4,804	989	221	6,018
1 Million	200,000	800,000	5,056	1,041	233	6,334

*property tax estimate figured at 1.25% of the purchase price
*hazard insurance figured at .35% of the loan amount
*total PITI=Total Principal, Interest, Taxes and Insurance

20% Down-Qualification Chart@6.75%

Sales Price	Down Payment @ 20%	Loan Amount	Principal Interest @6.75%	Property Taxes Estimate	Hazard Insurance Estimate	Total Payment PITI
100,000	20,000	80,000	519	104	23	646
125,000	25,000	100,000	648	130	29	804
150,000	30,000	120,000	778	156	35	971
175,000	35,000	140,000	908	182	40	1,132
200,000	40,000	160,000	1,038	208	46	1,294
250,000	50,000	200,000	1,297	260	58	1,619
300,000	60,000	240,000	1,556	312	70	1,942
350,000	70,000	280,000	1,816	364	81	2,265
400,000	80,000	320,000	2,075	416	93	2,588
450,000	90,000	360,000	2,335	468	105	2,914
500,000	100,000	400,000	2,594	520	116	3,235
550,000	110,000	440,000	2,854	573	128	3,558
600,000	120,000	480,000	3,113	625	140	3,881
650,000	130,000	520,000	3,372	677	151	4,204
700,000	140,000	560,000	3,632	729	163	4,527
750,000	150,000	600,000	3,891	781	175	4,851
800,000	160,000	640,000	4,151	833	186	5,174
850,000	170,000	680,000	4,410	885	198	5,497
900,000	180,000	720,000	4,670	937	210	5,820
950,000	190,000	760,000	4,929	989	221	6,143
1 Million	200,000	800,000	5,189	1,041	233	6,466

*property tax estimate figured at 1.25% of the purchase price
*hazard insurance figured at .35% of the loan amount
*total PITI=Total Principlal, Interest, Taxes and Insurance

10% Down-Qualification Chart@4.5%

Sales Price	Down Payment @ 10%	Loan Amount	Principal Interest @4.5%	Property Taxes Estimate	Hazard Ins. Est.	Mort. Ins. Est.	Total Pmt. PITI-MI
100,000	10,000	90,000	456	104	26	50	636
125,000	12,500	112,500	570	130	33	63	796
150,000	15,000	135,000	684	156	39	75	954
175,000	17,500	157,500	798	182	46	88	1,114
200,000	20,000	180,000	912	208	52	100	1,272
250,000	25,000	225,000	1,140	260	66	125	1,591
300,000	30,000	270,000	1,368	312	79	150	1,909
350,000	35,000	315,000	1,596	364	92	176	2,228
400,000	40,000	360,000	1,824	416	105	201	2,546
450,000	45,000	405,000	2,052	468	118	226	2,864
500,000	50,000	450,000	2,280	520	131	251	3,182
550,000	55,000	495,000	2,508	573	144	276	3,501
600,000	60,000	540,000	2,736	625	157	301	3,819
650,000	65,000	585,000	2,964	677	171	326	4,138
700,000	70,000	630,000	3,192	729	184	352	4,457
750,000	75,000	675,000	3,420	781	197	377	4,775
800,000	80,000	720,000	3,648	833	210	402	5,093
850,000	85,000	765,000	3,876	885	223	427	5,411
900,000	90,000	810,000	4,104	937	236	452	5,729
950,000	95,000	855,000	4,332	989	249	477	6,047
1 Million	100,000	900,000	4,560	1,041	262	502	6,365

Property tax estimate based on 1.25% of purchase price

Hazard insurance based on .35% of loan amount

Mortgage insurance payments are estimates based on factor of .67%. Actual payment may vary based on loan type and fico scores

Total payment is total of principal, interest,taxes, insurance & mortgage insurance

10% Down-Qualification Chart@4.75%

Sales Price	Down Payment @ 10%	Loan Amount	Principal Interest @4.75%	Property Taxes Estimate	Hazard Ins. Est.	Mort. Ins. Est.	Total Pmt. PITI-MI
100,000	10,000	90,000	469	104	26	50	649
125,000	12,500	112,500	587	130	33	63	813
150,000	15,000	135,000	704	156	39	75	974
175,000	17,500	157,500	822	182	46	88	1,138
200,000	20,000	180,000	939	208	52	100	1,299
250,000	25,000	225,000	1,174	260	66	125	1,625
300,000	30,000	270,000	1,408	312	79	150	1,949
350,000	35,000	315,000	1,643	364	92	176	2,275
400,000	40,000	360,000	1,878	416	105	201	2,600
450,000	45,000	405,000	2,113	468	118	226	2,925
500,000	50,000	450,000	2,347	520	131	251	3,249
550,000	55,000	495,000	2,582	573	144	276	3,575
600,000	60,000	540,000	2,817	625	157	301	3,900
650,000	65,000	585,000	3,052	677	171	326	4,226
700,000	70,000	630,000	3,286	729	184	352	4,551
750,000	75,000	675,000	3,521	781	197	377	4,876
800,000	80,000	720,000	3,756	833	210	402	5,201
850,000	85,000	765,000	3,990	885	223	427	5,525
900,000	90,000	810,000	4,225	937	236	452	5,850
950,000	95,000	855,000	4,460	989	249	477	6,175
1 Million	100,000	900,000	4,695	1,041	262	502	6,500

Property tax estimate based on 1.25% of purchase price

Hazard insurance based on .35% of loan amount

Mortgage insurance payments are estimates based on factor of .67%. Actual payment may vary based on loan type and fico scores

Total payment is total of principal, interest,taxes, insurance & mortgage insurance

10% Down-Qualification Chart@5%

Sales Price	Down Payment @ 10%	Loan Amount	Principal Interest @5%	Property Taxes Estimate	Hazard Ins. Est.	Mort. Ins. Est.	Total Pmt. PITI-MI
100,000	10,000	90,000	483	104	26	50	663
125,000	12,500	112,500	604	130	33	63	830
150,000	15,000	135,000	725	156	39	75	995
175,000	17,500	157,500	845	182	46	88	1,161
200,000	20,000	180,000	966	208	52	100	1,326
250,000	25,000	225,000	1,208	260	66	125	1,659
300,000	30,000	270,000	1,449	312	79	150	1,990
350,000	35,000	315,000	1,691	364	92	176	2,323
400,000	40,000	360,000	1,933	416	105	201	2,655
450,000	45,000	405,000	2,174	468	118	226	2,986
500,000	50,000	450,000	2,416	520	131	251	3,318
550,000	55,000	495,000	2,657	573	144	276	3,650
600,000	60,000	540,000	2,899	625	157	301	3,982
650,000	65,000	585,000	3,140	677	171	326	4,314
700,000	70,000	630,000	3,382	729	184	352	4,647
750,000	75,000	675,000	3,624	781	197	377	4,979
800,000	80,000	720,000	3,865	833	210	402	5,310
850,000	85,000	765,000	4,107	885	223	427	5,642
900,000	90,000	810,000	4,348	937	236	452	5,973
950,000	95,000	855,000	4,590	989	249	477	6,305
1 Million	100,000	900,000	4,831	1,041	262	502	6,636

Property tax estimate based on 1.25% of purchase price

Hazard insurance based on .35% of loan amount

Mortgage insurance payments are estimates based on factor of .67%. Actual payment may vary based on loan type and fico scores

Total payment is total of principal, interest,taxes, insurance & mortgage insurance

10% Down-Qualification Chart@5.25%

Sales Price	Down Payment @ 10%	Loan Amount	Principal Interest @5.25%	Property Taxes Estimate	Hazard Ins. Est.	Mort. Ins. Est.	Total Pmt. PITI-MI
100,000	10,000	90,000	497	104	26	50	677
125,000	12,500	112,500	621	130	33	63	847
150,000	15,000	135,000	745	156	39	75	1,015
175,000	17,500	157,500	870	182	46	88	1,186
200,000	20,000	180,000	994	208	52	100	1,354
250,000	25,000	225,000	1,242	260	66	125	1,693
300,000	30,000	270,000	1,491	312	79	150	2,032
350,000	35,000	315,000	1,739	364	92	176	2,371
400,000	40,000	360,000	1,988	416	105	201	2,710
450,000	45,000	405,000	2,236	468	118	226	3,048
500,000	50,000	450,000	2,485	520	131	251	3,387
550,000	55,000	495,000	2,733	573	144	276	3,726
600,000	60,000	540,000	2,982	625	157	301	4,065
650,000	65,000	585,000	3,230	677	171	326	4,404
700,000	70,000	630,000	3,479	729	184	352	4,744
750,000	75,000	675,000	3,727	781	197	377	5,082
800,000	80,000	720,000	3,976	833	210	402	5,421
850,000	85,000	765,000	4,224	885	223	427	5,759
900,000	90,000	810,000	4,473	937	236	452	6,098
950,000	95,000	855,000	4,721	989	249	477	6,436
1 Million	100,000	900,000	4,970	1,041	262	502	6,775

Property tax estimate based on 1.25% of purchase price
Hazard insurance based on .35% of loan amount
Mortgage insurance payments are estimates based on factor of .67%. Actual payment may vary based on loan type and fico scores
Total payment is total of principal, interest,taxes, insurance & mortgage insurance

10% Down-Qualification Chart@5.5%

Sales Price	Down Payment @ 10%	Loan Amount	Principal Interest @5.5%	Property Taxes Estimate	Hazard Ins. Est.	Mort. Ins. Est.	Total Pmt. PITI-MI
100,000	10,000	90,000	511	104	26	50	691
125,000	12,500	112,500	639	130	33	63	865
150,000	15,000	135,000	767	156	39	75	1,037
175,000	17,500	157,500	894	182	46	88	1,210
200,000	20,000	180,000	1,022	208	52	100	1,382
250,000	25,000	225,000	1,278	260	66	125	1,729
300,000	30,000	270,000	1,533	312	79	150	2,074
350,000	35,000	315,000	1,789	364	92	176	2,421
400,000	40,000	360,000	2,044	416	105	201	2,766
450,000	45,000	405,000	2,300	468	118	226	3,112
500,000	50,000	450,000	2,555	520	131	251	3,457
550,000	55,000	495,000	2,811	573	144	276	3,804
600,000	60,000	540,000	3,066	625	157	301	4,149
650,000	65,000	585,000	3,322	677	171	326	4,496
700,000	70,000	630,000	3,577	729	184	352	4,842
750,000	75,000	675,000	3,833	781	197	377	5,188
800,000	80,000	720,000	4,088	833	210	402	5,533
850,000	85,000	765,000	4,344	885	223	427	5,879
900,000	90,000	810,000	4,599	937	236	452	6,224
950,000	95,000	855,000	4,855	989	249	477	6,570
1 Million	100,000	900,000	5,110	1,041	262	502	6,915

Property tax estimate based on 1.25% of purchase price

Hazard insurance based on .35% of loan amount

Mortgage insurance payments are estimates based on factor of .67%. Actual payment may vary based on loan type and fico scores

Total payment is total of principal, interest,taxes, insurance & mortgage insurance

10% Down-Qualification Chart@5.75%

Sales Price	Down Payment @ 10%	Loan Amount	Principal Interest @5.75%	Property Taxes Estimate	Hazard Ins. Est.	Mort. Ins. Est.	Total Pmt. PITI-MI
100,000	10,000	90,000	525	104	26	50	705
125,000	12,500	112,500	657	130	33	63	883
150,000	15,000	135,000	788	156	39	75	1,058
175,000	17,500	157,500	919	182	46	88	1,235
200,000	20,000	180,000	1,053	208	52	100	1,413
250,000	25,000	225,000	1,313	260	66	125	1,764
300,000	30,000	270,000	1,576	312	79	150	2,117
350,000	35,000	315,000	1,838	364	92	176	2,470
400,000	40,000	360,000	2,101	416	105	201	2,823
450,000	45,000	405,000	2,363	468	118	226	3,175
500,000	50,000	450,000	2,626	520	131	251	3,528
550,000	55,000	495,000	2,889	573	144	276	3,882
600,000	60,000	540,000	3,151	625	157	301	4,234
650,000	65,000	585,000	3,414	677	171	326	4,588
700,000	70,000	630,000	3,677	729	184	352	4,942
750,000	75,000	675,000	3,939	781	197	377	5,294
800,000	80,000	720,000	4,202	833	210	402	5,647
850,000	85,000	765,000	4,464	885	223	427	5,999
900,000	90,000	810,000	4,727	937	236	452	6,352
950,000	95,000	855,000	4,990	989	249	477	6,705
1 Million	100,000	900,000	5,252	1,041	262	502	7,057

Property tax estimate based on 1.25% of purchase price

Hazard insurance based on .35% of loan amount

Mortgage insurance payments are estimates based on factor of .67%. Actual payment may vary based on loan type and fico scores

Total payment is total of principal, interest,taxes, insurance & mortgage insurance

10% Down-Qualification Chart@6%

Sales Price	Down Payment @ 10%	Loan Amount	Principal Interest @6%	Property Taxes Estimate	Hazard Ins. Est.	Mort. Ins. Est.	Total Pmt. PITI-MI
100,000	10,000	90,000	540	104	26	50	720
125,000	12,500	112,500	674	130	33	63	900
150,000	15,000	135,000	809	156	39	75	1,079
175,000	17,500	157,500	944	182	46	88	1,260
200,000	20,000	180,000	1,079	208	52	100	1,439
250,000	25,000	225,000	1,349	260	66	125	1,800
300,000	30,000	270,000	1,619	312	79	150	2,160
350,000	35,000	315,000	1,889	364	92	176	2,521
400,000	40,000	360,000	2,158	416	105	201	2,880
450,000	45,000	405,000	2,428	468	118	226	3,240
500,000	50,000	450,000	2,698	520	131	251	3,600
550,000	55,000	495,000	2,968	573	144	276	3,961
600,000	60,000	540,000	3,238	625	157	301	4,321
650,000	65,000	585,000	3,507	677	171	326	4,681
700,000	70,000	630,000	3,777	729	184	352	5,042
750,000	75,000	675,000	4,047	781	197	377	5,402
800,000	80,000	720,000	4,317	833	210	402	5,762
850,000	85,000	765,000	4,587	885	223	427	6,122
900,000	90,000	810,000	4,856	937	236	452	6,481
950,000	95,000	855,000	5,126	989	249	477	6,841
1 Million	100,000	900,000	5,396	1,041	262	502	7,201

Property tax estimate based on 1.25% of purchase price

Hazard insurance based on .35% of loan amount

Mortgage insurance payments are estimates based on factor of .67%. Actual payment may vary based on loan type and fico scores

Total payment is total of principal, interest,taxes, insurance & mortgage insurance

10% Down-Qualification Chart@6.25%

Sales Price	Down Payment @ 10%	Loan Amount	Principal Interest @6.25%	Property Taxes Estimate	Hazard Ins. Est.	Mort. Ins. Est.	Total Pmt. PITI-MI
100,000	10,000	90,000	554	104	26	50	734
125,000	12,500	112,500	693	130	33	63	919
150,000	15,000	135,000	831	156	39	75	1,101
175,000	17,500	157,500	970	182	46	88	1,286
200,000	20,000	180,000	1,108	208	52	100	1,468
250,000	25,000	225,000	1,385	260	66	125	1,836
300,000	30,000	270,000	1,662	312	79	150	2,203
350,000	35,000	315,000	1,940	364	92	176	2,572
400,000	40,000	360,000	2,217	416	105	201	2,939
450,000	45,000	405,000	2,494	468	118	226	3,306
500,000	50,000	450,000	2,771	520	131	251	3,673
550,000	55,000	495,000	3,048	573	144	276	4,041
600,000	60,000	540,000	3,325	625	157	301	4,408
650,000	65,000	585,000	3,602	677	171	326	4,776
700,000	70,000	630,000	3,879	729	184	352	5,144
750,000	75,000	675,000	4,156	781	197	377	5,511
800,000	80,000	720,000	4,433	833	210	402	5,878
850,000	85,000	765,000	4,710	885	223	427	6,245
900,000	90,000	810,000	4,987	937	236	452	6,612
950,000	95,000	855,000	5,264	989	249	477	6,979
1 Million	100,000	900,000	5,541	1,041	262	502	7,346

Property tax estimate based on 1.25% of purchase price

Hazard insurance based on .35% of loan amount

Mortgage insurance payments are estimates based on factor of .67%. Actual payment may vary based on loan type and fico scores

Total payment is total of principal, interest,taxes, insurance & mortgage insurance

10% Down-Qualification Chart@6.5%

Sales Price	Down Payment @ 10%	Loan Amount	Principal Interest @6.5%	Property Taxes Estimate	Hazard Ins. Est.	Mort. Ins. Est.	Total Pmt. PITI-MI
100,000	10,000	90,000	569	104	26	50	749
125,000	12,500	112,500	711	130	33	63	937
150,000	15,000	135,000	853	156	39	75	1,123
175,000	17,500	157,500	996	182	46	88	1,312
200,000	20,000	180,000	1,138	208	52	100	1,498
250,000	25,000	225,000	1,422	260	66	125	1,873
300,000	30,000	270,000	1,707	312	79	150	2,248
350,000	35,000	315,000	1,991	364	92	176	2,623
400,000	40,000	360,000	2,275	416	105	201	2,997
450,000	45,000	405,000	2,560	468	118	226	3,372
500,000	50,000	450,000	2,844	520	131	251	3,746
550,000	55,000	495,000	3,129	573	144	276	4,122
600,000	60,000	540,000	3,413	625	157	301	4,496
650,000	65,000	585,000	3,698	677	171	326	4,872
700,000	70,000	630,000	3,982	729	184	352	5,247
750,000	75,000	675,000	4,266	781	197	377	5,621
800,000	80,000	720,000	4,551	833	210	402	5,996
850,000	85,000	765,000	4,835	885	223	427	6,370
900,000	90,000	810,000	5,120	937	236	452	6,745
950,000	95,000	855,000	5,404	989	249	477	7,119
1 Million	100,000	900,000	5,689	1,041	262	502	7,494

Property tax estimate based on 1.25% of purchase price

Hazard insurance based on .35% of loan amount

Mortgage insurance payments are estimates based on factor of .67%. Actual payment may vary based on loan type and fico scores

Total payment is total of principal, interest,taxes, insurance & mortgage insurance

10% Down-Qualification Chart@6.75%

Sales Price	Down Payment @ 10%	Loan Amount	Principal Interest @6.75%	Property Taxes Estimate	Hazard Ins. Est.	Mort. Ins. Est.	Total Pmt. PITI-MI
100,000	10,000	90,000	584	104	26	50	764
125,000	12,500	112,500	730	130	33	63	956
150,000	15,000	135,000	876	156	39	75	1,146
175,000	17,500	157,500	1,022	182	46	88	1,338
200,000	20,000	180,000	1,167	208	52	100	1,527
250,000	25,000	225,000	1,459	260	66	125	1,910
300,000	30,000	270,000	1,751	312	79	150	2,292
350,000	35,000	315,000	2,043	364	92	176	2,675
400,000	40,000	360,000	2,335	416	105	201	3,057
450,000	45,000	405,000	2,627	468	118	226	3,439
500,000	50,000	450,000	2,919	520	131	251	3,821
550,000	55,000	495,000	3,211	573	144	276	4,204
600,000	60,000	540,000	3,502	625	157	301	4,585
650,000	65,000	585,000	3,794	677	171	326	4,968
700,000	70,000	630,000	4,086	729	184	352	5,351
750,000	75,000	675,000	4,378	781	197	377	5,733
800,000	80,000	720,000	4,670	833	210	402	6,115
850,000	85,000	765,000	4,962	885	223	427	6,497
900,000	90,000	810,000	5,254	937	236	452	6,879
950,000	95,000	855,000	5,546	989	249	477	7,261
1 Million	100,000	900,000	5,837	1,041	262	502	7,642

Property tax estimate based on 1.25% of purchase price

Hazard insurance based on .35% of loan amount

Mortgage insurance payments are estimates based on factor of .67%. Actual payment may vary based on loan type and fico scores

Total payment is total of principal, interest,taxes, insurance & mortgage insurance

Section IV

Supplemental

HVCC

Home
Valuation
Code
Of
Conduct

Home Valuation
Code of Conduct

I. No employee, director, officer, or agent of the lender, or any other third party acting as joint venture partner, independent contractor, appraisal management company, or partner on behalf of the lender, shall influence or attempt to influence the development, reporting, result, or review of an appraisal through coercion, extortion, collusion, compensation, instruction, inducement, intimidation, bribery, or in any other manner including but not limited to:

    1)   withholding or threatening to withhold timely payment for an appraisal report;

    2)   withholding or threatening to withhold future business for an appraiser, or demoting or terminating or threatening to demote or terminate an appraiser[1];

    3)   expressly or impliedly promising future business, promotions, or increased compensation for an appraiser;

    4)   conditioning the ordering of an appraisal report or the payment of an appraisal fee or salary or bonus on the opinion, conclusion, or valuation to be reached, or on a preliminary estimate requested from an appraiser;

    5)   requesting that an appraiser provide an estimated, predetermined, or desired valuation in an appraisal report, or provide estimated values or comparable sales at any time prior to the appraiser's completion of an appraisal report;

    6)   providing to an appraiser an anticipated, estimated, encouraged, or desired value for a subject property or a proposed or target amount to be loaned to the borrower, except that a copy of the sales contract for purchase transactions may be provided;

    7)   providing to an appraiser, appraisal management company, or any entity or person related to the appraiser or appraisal management company, stock or other financial or non-financial benefits;

    8)   allowing the removal of an appraiser from a list of qualified appraisers used by any entity, without prior written notice to such appraiser, which notice shall include written evidence of the appraiser's illegal conduct, a violation of the Uniform Standards of Professional Appraisal Practice

---

[1]   An "Appraiser" must be licensed or certified by the state in which the property to be appraised is located.

(USPAP) or state licensing standards, substandard performance, or otherwise improper or unprofessional behavior;

9)   ordering, obtaining, using, or paying for a second or subsequent appraisal or automated valuation model in connection with a mortgage financing transaction unless there is a reasonable basis to believe that the initial appraisal was flawed or tainted and such basis is clearly and appropriately noted in the loan file, or unless such appraisal or automated valuation model is done pursuant to a bona fide pre- or post-funding appraisal review or quality control process; or

10) any other act or practice that impairs or attempts to impair an appraiser's independence, objectivity, or impartiality.

Nothing in this section shall be construed as prohibiting the lender (or any third party acting on behalf of the lender) from requesting that an appraiser (i) provide additional information or explanation about the basis for a valuation, or (ii) correct objective factual errors in an appraisal report.

II.   The lender shall ensure that the borrower is provided, free of charge, a copy of any appraisal report concerning the borrower's subject property immediately upon completion, and in any event no less than three days prior to the closing of the loan. The borrower may waive this three-day requirement. The lender may require the borrower to reimburse the lender for the cost of the appraisal.

III. The lender or any third-party specifically authorized by the lender (including, but not limited to, appraisal management companies and correspondent lenders) shall be responsible for selecting, retaining, and providing for payment of all compensation to the appraiser. The lender will not accept any appraisal report completed by an appraiser selected, retained, or compensated in any manner by any other third-party (including mortgage brokers and real estate agents).

IV.   All members of the lender's loan production staff, as well as any person (i) who is compensated on a commission basis upon the successful completion of a loan or (ii) who reports, ultimately, to any officer of the lender other than either the Chief Compliance Officer, General Counsel, or any officer who is not independent of the loan production staff and process, shall be forbidden from: (1) selecting, retaining, recommending, or influencing the selection of any appraiser for a particular appraisal assignment or for inclusion on a list or panel of appraisers approved to perform appraisals for the lender; (2) any communications with an appraiser, including ordering or managing an appraisal assignment; and (3) working together in the same organizational unit, or being directly supervised by the same manager, as any person who is involved in the selection, retention, recommendation of, or communication with any appraiser. If absolute lines of independence cannot be achieved as a result of the originator's small size and limited staff, the lender must be able to clearly demonstrate that it has prudent safeguards to isolate its collateral evaluation process from influence or interference from its loan production process.

V.   Any employee of the lender (or if the lender retains an appraisal management company, any employee of that company) tasked with selecting appraisers for an approved panel or substantive appraisal review must be (1) appropriately trained and qualified in the area of real estate and appraisals, and (2) in the case of an employee of the lender, wholly independent of the loan production staff and process.

VI.   In underwriting a loan, the lender shall not utilize any appraisal report prepared by an appraiser employed by:

(1) the lender;

(2) an affiliate of the lender;

(3) an entity that is owned, in whole or in part, by the lender;

(4) an entity that owns, in whole or in part, the lender

(5) a real estate "settlement services" provider, as that term is defined in the Real Estate Settlement Procedures Act, 12 U.S.C.§ 2601 et seq.;

(6) an entity that is owned, in whole or in part, by a "settlement services" provider.

The lender also shall not use any appraisal report obtained by or through an appraisal management company that is owned by the lender or an affiliate of the lender, provided that the foregoing prohibitions do not apply where the lender has an ownership interest in the appraisal management company of 20% or less and where (i) the lender has no involvement in the day-to-day business operations of the appraisal management company, (ii) the appraisal management company is operated independently, and (iii) the lender plays no role in the selection of individual appraisers or any panel of approved appraisers used by the appraisal management company.

Notwithstanding these prohibitions, the lender may use in-house staff appraisers to (i) order appraisals, (ii) conduct appraisal reviews or other quality control, whether pre-funding or post-funding, (iii) develop, deploy, or use internal automated valuation models, or (iv) prepare appraisals in connection with transactions other than mortgage origination transactions (e.g. loan workouts).

VII.   The lender will establish a telephone hotline and an email address to receive any complaints from appraisers, individuals, or any other entities concerning the improper influencing or attempted improper influencing of appraisers or the appraisal process, which hotline and email address shall be attended only by a member of the office of the General Counsel, Chief Compliance Officer or other independent officer. In addition: (1) each appraiser now or hereafter on any list of approved appraisers, or, upon retention by the lender, will be notified, in a separate document, of the hotline and email address and their purpose; and (2) each borrower, as part of a cover letter accompanying the provided appraisal, will be notified of the hotline and email address and their purpose. Within 72 hours of receiving any complaint, the lender will begin a preliminary investigation of the complaint and upon completing the inquiry (or, after a period not to exceed 60 days, whichever shall come first) shall notify the Independent Valuation Protection Institute and any relevant regulatory bodies of any indication of improper conduct. The name and any identifying information of the person or entity that has filed such a complaint shall be kept in strictest confidence by the office of the General Counsel, Chief Compliance Officer or other independent officer, except as required by law. The lender shall not retaliate, in any manner or method, against the person or entity which makes such a complaint.

VIII. The lender agrees that it shall quality control test, by use of retroactive or additional appraisal reports or other appropriate method, of a randomly-selected 10 percent (or other bona fide statistically significant percentage) of the appraisals or valuations which are used by the lender, including the results of automated valuation models, broker's price opinions or "desktop" evaluations. The lender shall report the results of such quality control testing to the Independent Valuation Protection Institute and any relevant regulatory bodies.

IX. Any lender who has a reasonable basis to believe an appraiser is violating applicable laws, or is otherwise engaging in unethical conduct, shall promptly refer the matter to the Independent Valuation Protection Institute and to the applicable State appraiser certifying and licensing agency.

X. The lender shall certify, warrant and represent that the appraisal report was obtained in a manner consistent with this Code of Conduct.

XI. Nothing in this Code shall be construed to establish new requirements or obligations that (1) require a lender to obtain a property valuation, or to use any particular method for property valuation (such as an appraisal or automated valuation model) in connection with any mortgage loan or mortgage financing transaction, or (2) affect the acceptable scope of work for an appraiser in connection with a particular assignment.

Historical
Index
Charts

12 Month Treasury Average (12 MTA)										
Month	1999	2000	2001	2002	2003	2004	2005	2006	2007	2008	2009
Jan	4.991%	5.212%	5.999%	3.260%	1.935%	1.234%	2.022%	3.751%	4.983%	4.326%	1.633%
Feb	4.940%	5.338%	5.871%	3.056%	1.858%	1.229%	2.171%	3.888%	5.014%	4.076%	1.514%
Mar	4.889%	5.458%	5.711%	2.912%	1.747%	1.225%	2.347%	4.011%	5.027%	3.794%	1.439%
Apr	4.832%	5.580%	5.530%	2.787%	1.646%	1.238%	2.504%	4.143%	5.029%	3.528%	
May	4.783%	5.703%	5.318%	2.668%	1.548%	1.288%	2.633%	4.282%	5.022%	3.291%	
Jun	4.757%	5.793%	5.102%	2.553%	1.449%	1.381%	2.737%	4.432%	5.005%	3.079%	
Jul	4.729%	5.880%	4.897%	2.414%	1.379%	1.463%	2.865%	4.563%	4.983%	2.856%	
Aug	4.728%	5.962%	4.671%	2.272%	1.342%	1.522%	3.019%	4.664%	4.933%	2.665%	
Sep	4.773%	6.035%	4.395%	2.180%	1.302%	1.595%	3.163%	4.758%	4.863%	2.479%	
Oct	4.883%	6.083%	4.088%	2.123%	1.268%	1.677%	3.326%	4.827%	4.788%	2.256%	
Nov	4.968%	6.128%	3.763%	2.066%	1.256%	1.773%	3.478%	4.883%	4.662%	2.053%	
Dec	5.078%	6.108%	3.481%	2.002%	1.244%	1.887%	3.618%	4.933%	4.522%	1.823%	

11th District Cost of Funds Index

Month	1999	2000	2001	2002	2003	2004	2005	2006	2007	2008	2009
Jan	4.608%	4.901%	5.514%	2.823%	2.308%	1.811%	2.183%	3.347%	4.392%	3.970%	2.455%
Feb	4.562%	4.967%	5.426%	2.744%	2.257%	1.841%	2.317%	3.604%	4.376%	3.560%	2.003%
Mar	4.519%	5.002%	5.198%	2.653%	2.210%	1.815%	2.400%	3.624%	4.299%	3.280%	
Apr	4.490%	5.078%	4.946%	2.723%	2.208%	1.802%	2.515%	3.759%	4.224%	3.111%	
May	4.480%	5.196%	4.745%	2.772%	2.130%	1.708%	2.622%	3.884%	4.293%	2.918%	
Jun	4.504%	5.357%	4.498%	2.847%	2.113%	1.758%	2.676%	4.090%	4.283%	2.829%	
Jul	4.500%	5.456%	4.274%	2.821%	2.018%	1.816%	2.757%	4.177%	4.277%	2.698%	
Aug	4.562%	5.509%	4.106%	2.763%	1.946%	1.875%	2.870%	4.277%	4.359%	2.693%	
Sep	4.608%	5.548%	3.974%	2.759%	1.923%	1.931%	2.972%	4.382%	4.383%	2.769%	
Oct	4.666%	5.589%	3.628%	2.708%	1.909%	1.960%	3.074%	4.346%	4.233%	3.125%	
Nov	4.773%	5.607%	3.368%	2.537%	1.821%	2.025%	3.190%	4.358%	4.172%	3.155%	
Dec	4.852%	5.617%	3.074%	2.375%	1.902%	2.118%	3.296%	4.396%	4.072%	2.757%	

1 Year LIBOR

Month	1999	2000	2001	2002	2003	2004	2005	2006	2007	2008	2009
Jan	5.108%	6.659%	5.284%	2.420%	1.477%	1.461%	3.2710%	4.9412%	5.4414%	4.2238%	2.00375%
Feb	5.405%	6.760%	4.925%	2.496%	1.368%	1.365%	3.5114%	5.1526%	5.3328%	2.8494%	1.97500%
Mar	5.307%	6.970%	4.670%	3.006%	1.340%	1.340%	3.8420%	5.2476%	5.2009%	2.7088%	2.11938%
Apr	5.303%	6.964%	4.330%	2.613%	1.362%	1.808%	3.7101%	5.4217%	5.2967%	2.4863%	1.97188%
May	5.503%	7.453%	4.259%	2.634%	1.221%	2.0764%	3.7789%	5.4139%	5.3885%	3.0788%	
Jun	5.803%	7.214%	4.055%	2.251%	1.201%	2.4682%	3.8632%	5.7660%	5.4048%	3.1638%	
Jul	5.836%	7.047%	3.835%	2.070%	1.279%	2.4632%	4.1745%	5.5910%	5.4256%	3.31063%	
Aug	6.023%	6.978%	3.600%	1.943%	1.471%	2.3001%	4.3123%	5.4501%	5.2450%	3.25250%	
Sep	6.053%	6.811%	2.650%	1.813%	1.286%	2.4445%	4.4067%	5.2985%	5.2750%	3.20688%	
Oct	6.313%	6.725%	2.311%	1.664%	1.455%	2.5289%	4.6765%	5.3348%	4.9013%	3.96250%	
Nov	6.261%	6.618%	2.492%	1.705%	1.487%	2.9607%	4.7379%	5.2439%	4.6375%	3.17375%	
Dec	6.508%	5.997%	2.445%	1.447%	1.458%	3.1004%	4.8226%	5.3139%	4.4575%	2.76625%	

Fannie Mae
Historical Conventional Loan Limits
(Excludes Alaska, Hawaii, the Virgin Islands and Guam)

Year	1 Unit	2 Units	3 Units	4 Units	Seconds
1980	93,750	120,000	145,000	180,000	N/A*
1981	98,500	126,000	152,000	189,000	98,500*
1982	107,000	136,800	165,100	205,300	107,000*
1983	108,300	138,500	167,200	207,900	108,300*
1984	114,000	145,800	176,100	218,900	57,000
1985	115,300	147,500	178,200	221,500	57,650
1986	133,250	170,450	205,950	256,000	66,625
1987	153,100	195,850	236,650	294,150	76,550
1988	168,700	215,800	260,800	324,150	84,350
1989	187,600	239,950	290,000	360,450	93,800
1990	187,450	239,750	289,750	360,150	93,725
1991	191,250	244,650	295,650	367,500	95,625
1992	202,300	258,800	312,800	388,800	101,150
1993	203,150	259,850	314,100	390,400	101,575
1994	203,150	259,850	314,100	390,400	101,575
1995	203,150	259,850	314,100	390,400	101,575
1996	207,000	264,750	320,050	397,800	103,500
1997	214,600	274,550	331,850	412,450	107,300
1998	227,150	290,650	351,300	436,600	113,575
1999	240,000	307,100	371,200	461,350	120,000
2000	252,700	323,400	390,900	485,800	126,350
2001	275,000	351,950	425,400	528,700	137,500
2002	300,700	384,900	465,200	578,150	150,350
2003	322,700	413,100	499,300	620,500	161,350
2004	333,700	427,150	516,300	641,650	166,850
2005	359,650	460,400	556,500	691,600	179,825
2006	417,000	533,850	645,300	801,950	208,500
2007	417,000	533,850	645,300	801,950	208,500
2008**	417,000	533,850	645,300	801,950	208,500

Limits for Alaska, Guam, Hawaii, U.S. Virgin Islands are 50% higher.

*Prior to 1984, second mortgage limits were the same as first mortgage limits. Subsequent legislation reduced the limits to 50% of first mortgage limits. We had no second mortgage program before 1981.

**With passage of the economic stimulus package, Fannie Mae may temporarily purchase loans beyond the company's prevailing conventional loan limit in designated high-cost areas. The company may purchase loans with a maximum original principal obligation of up to 125 percent of the area median home price in high-cost areas, not to exceed $729,750 except in Alaska, Hawaii, Guam and the U.S. Virgin Islands where higher limits may apply.

Prepared by Executive Communications
Updated: March 6, 2008

"LAMP"
Loan
Examples

Lamp Loan @ 5.5%

Loan Amount	Years 1-5	Years 6-10	Years 11-30	Traditional 30 Year	Interest Only Payment
100,000	$489.85	$504.58	$646.33	$567.79	$458.33
150,000	$734.77	$756.86	$969.50	$851.68	$687.80
200,000	$979.69	$1,009.15	$1,292.66	$1,135.58	$916.66
250,000	$1,224.61	$1,261.44	$1,615.83	$1,419.47	$1,145.83
300,000	$1,469.54	$1,513.73	$1,939.00	$1,703.37	$1,375.00
350,000	$1,714.46	$1,766.01	$2,262.16	$1,987.26	$1,604.16
400,000	$1,959.38	$2,018.30	$2,585.33	$2,271.16	$1,833.33
450,000	$2,204.30	$2,270.59	$2,908.49	$2,555.05	$2,062.50
500,000	$2,449.23	$2,522.88	$3,231.66	$2,838.95	$2,291.66
550,000	$2,694.15	$2,775.16	$3,554.83	$3,122.84	$2,520.83
600,000	$2,939.07	$3,027.45	$3,877.99	$3,406.73	$2,750.00
625,000	$3,061.53	$3,153.59	$4,039.57	$3,548.68	$2,864.58

Lamp Loan @ 6%

Loan Amount	Years 1-5	Years 6-10	Years 11-30	Traditional 30 Year	Interest Only Payment
100,000	$526.40	$540.08	$678.60	$599.55	$500.00
150,000	$789.61	$810.12	$1,017.89	$899.33	$750.00
200,000	$1,052.81	$1,080.15	$1,357.19	$1,199.10	$1,000.00
250,000	$1,316.01	$1,350.19	$1,696.49	$1,498.88	$1,250.00
300,000	$1,579.21	$1,620.23	$2,035.79	$1,798.65	$1,250.00
350,000	$1,842.42	$1,890.27	$2,375.08	$2,098.43	$1,750.00
400,000	$2,105.62	$2,160.31	$2,714.38	$2,398.20	$2,000.00
450,000	$2,368.82	$2,430.35	$3,053.68	$2,697.98	$2,250.00
500,000	$2,632.02	$2,700.39	$3,392.98	$2,997.75	$2,500.00
550,000	$2,895.23	$2,970.42	$3,232.27	$3,297.53	$2,750.00
600,000	$3,158.43	$3,240.46	$4,071.57	$3,597.30	$3,000.00
625,000	$3,290.03	$3,375.48	$4,241.22	$3,747.19	$3,125.00

Lamp Loan @ 6.5%

Loan Amount	Years 1-5	Years 6-10	Years 11-30	Traditional 30 Year	Interest Only Payment
100,000	$563.72	$576.33	$711.24	$632.07	$541.66
150,000	$845.58	$864.50	$1,066.86	$948.10	$812.50
200,000	$1,127.43	$1,152.67	$1,422.48	$1,264.14	$1,083.33
250,000	$1,409.29	$1,440.83	$1,778.10	$1,580.17	$1,354.16
300,000	$1,691.15	$1,729.00	$2,133.72	$1,896.20	$1,625.00
350,000	$1,973.01	$2,017.17	$2,489.34	$2,212.24	$1,895.83
400,000	$2,254.87	$2,305.33	$2,844.96	$2,528.27	$2,166.66
450,000	$2,536.73	$2,593.50	$3,200.58	$2,844.31	$2,437.50
500,000	$2,818.58	$2,881.67	$3,556.20	$3,160.34	$2,708.33
550,000	$3,100.44	$3,169.83	$3,911.82	$3,476.37	$2,979.16
600,000	$3,382.30	$3,458.00	$4,267.44	$3,792.41	$3,250.00
625,000	$3,523.23	$3,602.08	$4,445.25	$3,950.43	$3,385.41

Know
Your
Mortgage
Terminology

Terminology

Adjustable Rate Mortgage-
> A loan in which the interest rate is adjusted periodically based on a preselected index. Indexes often used are: Prime, COFI, MTA, LIBOR.

Adverse Action-
> A formal denial of credit

Affidavit-
> A sworn written statement signed before a court officer, notary public, or other officer with authority to administer an oath.

American Land Title Association (ALTA)-Policy of Title Insurance
> An extended policy of title insurance, required by the lender. The coverage provides for physical aspects of the property that can be determined only by a property inspection. The buyer (owner) may also purchase this coverage.

Amortization-
> Equal principal reductions of a debt, by monthly payments in excess of the interest due.

Annual Percentage Rate-
> The cost of credit expressed as a yearly rate to the consumer. Calculated by including, among other things, (a) the yearly interest rate, (b) discount points charged to the purchaser and (c) certain costs related to closing such as mortgage insurance premiums.

Application-
> An oral or written request for an extension of credit, made in accordance with procedures established by a creditor for the type of credit requested.

Appraisal-
> A professional written evaluation of the value of real property by a licensed independent expert.

Appraisal Report-
> A written report by an appraiser containing an opinion as to the value of a property and the reasoning leading to this opinion. Comparables, appraisal formulas and the appraiser's qualifications are set forth.

Appraised Value-
> A professional appraiser's estimate of the value (worth) of property as of a specific date.

Assessed Value-
> The valuation placed upon real or personal property for purpose of taxation.

Asset-
> Items of value that can be used to pay debts. Entries on a balance sheet that express in terms of money the value of the intangible things or tangible rights which constitute the resources of a person or business as of a given date.

Assign-
> To transfer property, rights & interest.

Assumption of Mortgage-
> Contract by deed or other form through which a buyer undertakes the obligation of an existing mortgage. In some cases, the seller remains secondarily liable for the obligation unless released by the lender.

Attorney-in-Fact-
> A person who is given written authorization by another person to act as their agent and transact business out of court. Distinguished from attorney-at-law.

Balloon Mortgage Note-
> A mortgage note with an amortization schedule that does not extinguish the debt by the end of the mortgage term. A large (balloon) payment of the remaining principal balance must be paid at the end of the mortgage term.

Balloon Payment-
> The last payment on a loan which is substantially larger than the others.

Bankruptcy-
> The legal proceedings by which affairs of a bankrupt person, corporation or other legal entity are turned over to a trustee or receiver for administration in accordance with the bankruptcy act.

Basis Point-
> Often used to express interest rates, yields or margins. One basis point equals one-hundredth of one percent. For example, 300 basis points equal 3.00%. An index of 6.5% plus a margin of 300 basis points corresponds to a rate of 9.5%.

Beneficiary-

One for whose benefit a trust is created. In states where deeds of trust are commonly used instead of mortgages, the lender (mortgagee) is called the beneficiary.

Broker-

A real estate broker is a licensed agent engaged in negotiating the sale, purchase or lease of property for a fee or valuable consideration. A mortgage broker is a licensed agent who obtains financing on behalf of a borrower for a fee.

Bylaws-

Formal rules and regulations governing the operation and internal management of a corporate entity, as opposed to resolutions which are formal actions of the board of directors on particular matters. Also applicable to homeowner's associations.

California Land Title Association (CLTA)-Title Insurance Policy

The "standard" policy of title insurance of the California Land Title Association. It protects the insured against failure of title based on public records and off-record risks, such as forgery of deed and the lack of capacity of a party (a minor, for example) to execute a deed. The policy does not insure against the physical aspects of the property.

Capital Gains-

Profit from the sale of an asset that has been held for a certain period of time. Stocks, real property, etc.

Caps (Interest)-

A limit on the amount the interest rate on an adjustable rate mortgage can change per adjustment and/or over the life of the loan.

Closing-

The finalization of the loan transaction, where usually the deed of trust, promissory note and other loan documents are executed and delivered and funds are disbursed to the appropriate parties.

Closing costs-

Expenses incurred in connection with the sale of property and/or closing of a loan transaction. Generally includes things such as: an origination fee, discount points, sales commission, appraisal fee, credit report, cost of a termite report, recording fees, document preparation fee, processing, title insurance, mortgage insurance premiums, attorney or escrow fees, survey and prepaid items such as taxes and insurance escrow payments.

Closing Statement-
An accounting of funds received and disbursed at closing. Includes escrow deposits for taxes, hazard insurance and mortgage insurance for the escrow account. All FHA, VA and most conventional financing loans use a uniform closing or settlement statement commonly referred to as the Hud-1 settlement statement.

Collection-
The filing of an action against someone for non-payment of a debt. The procedure to bring a delinquent account current.

Commitment-
An agreement between a lender and a borrower specifying the terms and conditions of a loan.

Community Property-
Property acquired by a husband and/or wife during the marriage, which was not acquired as a gift or by inheritance.

Compensation-
Income or wages received for services rendered.

Compliance Inspection Report-
A report given to a lender by a designated compliance inspector that indicates whether or not construction or repairs satisfy conditions established by a prior inspection.

Condominium-
A structure of two or more units, the interior space of which is individually owned. The balance of the property (land and building) is owned in common by the owners of the individual units.

Conforming Loans-
Loans that meet salability requirements to Fannie Mae & Freddie Mac are called conforming loans. They have set maximum loan limits and set underwriting criteria.

Consolidation Loan-
An installment loan extended to enable a borrower to repay all smaller outstanding loans and have only one periodic payment rather than several smaller ones.

Contract-
> In real estate, a written agreement between two or more parties stating the contract or sales price and the terms or conditions of the sale.

Conventional Loan-
> Any mortgage loan that is not underwritten by a federal agency up to a certain pre-designated loan amount, generally sold to Fannie Mae & Freddie Mac.

Convey-
> To transfer title to real property from one person to another by an acceptable instrument.

Credit Bureau-
> A company that maintains creditor-reported information on personal and business financial obligations.

Credit Line-HELOC – Home Equity Line of Credit
> An agreement by a bank to have a specific amount of funds available when needed, based on the borrower's ability to repay.

Credit Report-
> A report to a lender on the credit history of a prospective borrower used to determine creditworthiness.

Creditworthiness-
> The ability and willingness to repay debts. Largely demonstrated by a credit history.

Debt-to-Income Ratio-
> The ratio, expressed as a percentage, which results when a borrower's monthly payment obligation on long-term debts is divided by his or her gross monthly income. See housing expenses to income ratio.

Deed of Trust-
> A security instrument which takes the place of a mortgage in many states. The legal title to real property is transferred to a third-party trustee to secure the repayment of the loan. When the debt is repaid, the trustee reconveys the title to the owner.

Default-
> With regard to a promissory note, the failure to make a payment either of principal or interest when due.

Deferred Interest-
>   Interest due on the loan which exceeds the amount of the regularly scheduled monthly payment. The difference is added to the loan balance and interest is charged on the entire amount.

Delinquency-
>   A loan payment that is overdue but within the grace period allowed before actual default is declared.

Demand Statement-
>   A letter from a lender showing the amount due in order to pay off a mortgage or trust deed.

Depreciation-
>   A loss of value in real property brought about by age, physical deterioration, functional or economic obsolescence.

Discount Points-
>   A fee (usually a percentage) charged by a lender to increase the lender's yield or effective interest rate.

Discount Rate-
>   The rate of interest charged by the federal reserve on loans to member banks. This influences rates that banks charge their customers.

Discretionary Income-
>   Income remaining after essential expenditures is made.

Documentary Transfer Tax-
>   A tax on recorded transfers of title to real property.

Down Payment-
>   The difference between the sales price of real estate and the loan amount.

Draft-
>   A signed, written order by which one party (the drawer) instructs another party (the drawee) to make a payment of a specified sum to a third party (the payee).

Due-on-Sale
>   A provision in a security instrument that allows the lender to call the mortgage due and payable in the event of sale or transfer of title by the borrower.

Duplex-
   A house divided into two living units.

Dwelling-
   A residential-type structure. Commonly implies one or more single-family housing units; can include a residential condominium unit.

Earnest Money-
   A cash deposit delivered with an offer to the seller or escrow officer by the purchaser of real estate as evidence of good faith.

Easement-
   The right of an individual, subdivision, utility or other to have access over a portion of a piece of real estate.

Economic Life-
   The "profitable" life of an improvement.

Eminent Domain-
   The governmental right to take private property for public use. The owner must be compensated justly.

Encroachment-
   A structure or construction on one property that intrudes illegally upon an adjoining property beyond proper or prescribed limits.

Encumbrance-
   Any claim, interest, or right in a piece of property, such as a lien, mortgage or easement.

Equal Credit Opportunity Act- ECOA
   A federal law requiring lenders and other creditors to make credit equally available without discrimination.

Equity-
   The interest or value an owner has in real estate less the amount of existing liens (indebtedness).

Escrow-
   An arrangement in which an impartial third party acts as custodian of documents and funds, holding or distributing them according to the instructions of the seller, buyer, borrower and lender.

Escrow Account-
    An account which holds that portion of a borrower's monthly payments which is set aside to pay for taxes, hazard insurance, and mortgage insurance as they come due. Also known as reserves or impounds.

Federal Deposit Insurance Corporation - FDIC
    A federal agency organized in 1933 to guarantee funds on deposit in member banks.
    The FDIC also makes loans or buys assets from member banks to help effect mergers or prevent bank failures.

Federal Home Loan Mortgage Corporation- FHLMC
    Known more commonly as Freddie Mac
    Created in 1970 as a private corporation to offer additional mortgage backed securities and to break the monopoly of Fannie Mae. As of September of 2008 this publically traded company is now under the conservatorship of the United States government.
    A government sponsored entity whose primary purpose is to establish a secondary market for conventional mortgage loans.

Federal Housing Administration- FHA
    A division of the department of Housing and Urban Development (HUD). It insures residential mortgage loans made by private lenders and sets standards for construction and underwriting. This government agency is the innovator of the long-term, amortized, minimum down payment home mortgage.

Federal National Mortgage Association-FNMA
    Known more commonly as Fannie Mae
    Fannie Mae was founded as a government agency in 1938 as part of Franklin Delano Roosevelt's New Deal to provide liquidity to the mortgage market.
    For the next 30 years, Fannie Mae held a virtual monopoly on the secondary mortgage market in the United States. In 1968, to remove the activity of Fannie Mae from the annual sheet of the federal budget, it was converted into a private corporation. As of September of 2008, it is back to being controlled by the United States government.
    Fannie Mae is a government sponsored enterprise (GSE) that is also a publically traded corporation that supplements private mortgage funds. It provides a secondary market for FHA, VA and conventional home mortgages.

Federal Reserve System-
    The central banking system that regulates the supply of money. It includes 12 regional "banker's banks", their branches, and all national and state banks that choose to be members.

Fee Simple-
>The largest interest or estate in real property a person may own. Sometimes known as fee simple absolute.

Fiduciary-
>One who holds a position of trust and confidence requiring scrupulous good faith and candor. One who acts in a financial role for the benefit of another.

Fiscal Year-
>An accounting year, which may be the calendar year or any other one year period.

Forbearance-
>To refrain from, cease and desist; the act of a creditor who refrains from enforcing a debt when it falls due.

Foreclosure-
>Enforcement of a lien by the sale of property given as security in an attempt to satisfy a debt.

Government National Mortgage Association - GNMA
>A federally owned corporation that invests in government mortgages. Administered by the U.S. Department of Housing and Urban Development (HUD), Ginnie Mae invests in relatively high risk mortgages.

GNMA Mortgaged Backed Securities-
>Securities guaranteed by GNMA and issued primarily by mortgage bankers. The holder of GNMA securities is protected by the "full faith and credit of the U.S. Government" because they are collateralized by FHA or VA mortgages.

Government Sponsored Enterprise GSE-
>Although Fannie Mae and Freddie Mac are shareholder held companies they are also considered government sponsored enterprises.

Grace Period-
>A formally specified extension of time beyond the due date for payment of insurance premiums, taxes or other obligations.

Grant Deed-
>A written instrument transferring title of real property. May also be used to add parties to an existing title.

Grantee (Buyer)-
>A person to whom property is transferred by deed or to whom property rights are granted by means of a trust instrument or some other document.

Grantor (Seller)-
>A person who transfers property by deed or who grants property rights by a trust instrument or some other document.

Gross Income-
>Total dollar amount of all income before deductions for taxes, etc.

Gross Rent Multiplier-
>A figure by which effective gross rental income is multiplied to obtain an amount that indicates the capital value of property.

Guaranteed Loan-
>A loan guaranteed by the veteran's administration that partially protects against the borrower's default.

Guarantor-
>The person or legal entity who offers a guaranty. Generally not required to hold title to the guaranteed property.

Guaranty-
>An agreement to answer for payment of another's debt in case of their default.

Hardscape-
>Permanent, outside home improvements including driveways, fences, retaining walls, patios, etc.

Hazard Insurance-
>Home insurance which protects the lender and borrower from specified hazards, such as fire, etc.

Home Improvement Loan- HELOC or Home Equity Line of Credit
>A loan for remodeling, repairs, renovations or improvements to residential property. Generally a junior lien behind a first trust deed.

Homeowner's Policy-
>An insurance policy for owner occupied primary residences that cover personal liability as well as home damages caused by fire, wind, hail or other disasters.

Homestead-
Laws in some states that protect a person's principal residence against judgments up to certain amounts.

Housing-to-Income Ratio-
The ratio, expressed as a percentage which results when a borrower's housing expenses are divided by his/her gross monthly income. See debt-to-income ratio.

Impound Account-
An account maintained by the lender to pay premiums for insurance and taxes on the property.

Income
Contractual-Income determined by contract before a service is rendered. Rent, wages and interest payments are contractual income.
Earned-Income received for work or services performed, as opposed to income from investments or rent.
Fixed-A steady level of income, such as that received from retirement payments or from a security that pays a constant amount at specific intervals.

Indemnify-
To agree to compensate or reimburse an individual or other legal entity in the event of a potential future loss.

Index-
An interest rate established and made publicly available by a source other than the lender used to determine future interest rates on an adjustable rate mortgage loan. Common indexes are COFI, LIBOR, MTA and Prime.

Installment Loan-
A note usually given in consumer and personal credit transactions. The principal is payable in specified installments, together with interest on the unpaid balance, until the note is paid in full.

Installment Payments-
Equal periodic payments.

Institutional Lender-
A federally regulated financial institution.

Insurance-
A contract whereby for a fee one party agrees to pay a sum to another party in the

event that the latter suffers a particular loss. The person or firm that undertakes the risk is the insurer. The party protected from loss is the insured party.

Insurance Binder-
A written evidence of temporary hazard or title coverage that only runs for a limited time and must be replaced by a permanent policy.

Insurance Company-
An institution whose primary business is insurance but which also may act as an important secondary mortgage holder by investing surplus funds in real estate and other loans.

Insured Closing Protection-
A document from a title company. It insures a lender against the failure of the title company's agent to perform duties according to the lender's instruction.

Insured Loan-
A loan insured by FHA or a private mortgage insurance company that partially protects the lender against the borrower's default.

Interest on the Unpaid Balance-
Interest charged at an agreed upon rate, calculated on the balance remaining on the obligation.

Interest Rate-
The percentage rate charge for the use of money, usually quoted as an annual rate.

Investor-
An individual or business entity that purchases securities with the intention to obtain income from the investment without losing the principal. Also applies to buyers of rental property.

Joint Tenancy-
The equal, undivided interest in property of two or more people in such a manner that upon death of one of the joint owners, the survivor(s) inherits the property. The term should be distinguished from tenancy in common.

Junior Mortgage-
A lien that is subordinate to the claims of the prior "senior" lien. A second mortgage is an example of a junior mortgage.

Jurat-
>A memorandum added to an affidavit stating when, before whom and, in some jurisdictions, where an oath was taken.

Leasehold-
>The estate or interest which a tenant has in real estate. Land held under lease.

Legal Description-
>A method accepted by real estate law for geographically identifying a parcel of land.

Legal Rate of Interest-
>A rate of interest established by law rather than by agreement (contract).

Lessee-
>A person who rents property from another; a tenant.

Level Payment Mortgage-
>A mortgage that provides for equal fixed payments to be paid periodically during a term of the loan. Part of the fixed payment is credited to interest, and the balance reduces the principal of the loan.

Liability-
>A debt, financial obligation or potential loss. In business, the claims of creditors and owners against the assets of a business.

Lien-
>A voluntary or involuntary encumbrance against property for money.

Liquidity-
>That condition of an individual or business, a high percentage of whose assets can be quickly converted into cash.

Loan Application-
>A form to record a potential borrower's formal request for a loan. It is designed to obtain all information required and allowed by law.

Loan Maturity-
>The date when a loan is due to be paid in full.

Loan-to-Value Ratio, LTV-
>The ratio, expressed as a percentage, between the loan amount and the property value.

Long Term Capital Gains-
Profits earned on assets held for more than the specified time.

Loss Payable Clause-
An endorsement to a property insurance policy specifying the lender as a payee in the event of property damage. Protects the lender's interest in the property in proportionate value to the loan outstanding.

Margin-
A specified number of percentage points the lender adds to the index rate to calculate the ARM interest rate at each adjustment.

Market Rates-
Rates of interest resulting from the demand for a supply of funds in the money market.

Market Value-
The price at which an asset may be sold in an open market.

Maturity-
The date that payment on a loan is due.

Mechanic's Lien-
A lien allowed by statute to contractors, laborers and suppliers to protect and secure the payment for labor performed or materials supplied.

Metes and Bounds-
A description of property that identifies boundaries through their terminal points and angles. Metes are the measurements and bounds are the boundaries of a tract of land.

Mineral Rights-
The right or title to all or to certain specified resources such as oil or gas coming from a tract of land with or without the right of surface entry.

Minimum Payment-
The smallest monthly payment a borrower can make and remain in compliance with the terms and conditions of a credit agreement.

Mortgage-

An instrument by which the borrower (mortgagor) gives the lender (mortgagee) a lien on property as security for the payment of an obligation. The borrower continues to use the property, and the lien is removed when the obligation is paid in full. If the subject matter of the lien is personal property other than securities (such as machinery tools, or other equipment) the mortgage is known as a chattel mortgage.

Mortgage Banking-

The origination, packaging and servicing of mortgage loans secured by real property. The loans are sold to permanent investors, and servicing is usually retained by the seller for the life of the loan in exchange for a fee.

Mortgage Broker-

A firm or individual who receives a commission for bringing the borrower and lender together. A mortgage broker does not service loans.

Mortgage Insurance-

Insurance written by an independent mortgage insurance company (MIC) to protect the mortgage lender against loss incurred by a mortgage default. The insurance enables the lender to lend a higher percentage of the property value. The federal government writes this form of insurance through the FHA and VA.

Mortgage Loan-

An extension of credit using real property as the lender's security.

Mortgage Note-

A written promise to pay a sum of money at a stated interest rate during a specified term. This instrument is secured by a mortgage or deed of trust.

Mortgagee-

The lender.

Mortgagor-

The borrower.

National Flood Insurance Act-

A federal law established to provide flood insurance to homeowners whose houses are in specially designated flood hazard areas. The program is administered by the Federal Insurance Administration.

Negative Amortization –

An increase in the principal balance of the loan resulting from the addition of deferred interest.

Net Profit or Loss-
> Income for a given period that remains after deducting all expenses.

Net Worth-
> The difference between total assets and liabilities of an individual or corporation.

Notary Public-
> One who is authorized by the state or federal government to administer oaths and to attest to the authenticity of signatures.

Note-
> A borrower's written promise to repay a sum certain, plus interest at a stated rate to the lender in specified amounts on specified dates.

Obsolescence-
> Loss of value due to changes in demand for a property when its usefulness and desirability are impaired when contrasted with modern properties.

Origination Fee-
> The amount charged for services performed by the company that handles the initial application and processing of a loan.

Overtime-
> Daily hours of work in excess of the number established by contract or law for which wage earners normally receive extra pay.

Partnership-
> An association of two or more persons for business purchases.

Payee-
> The individual named in an instrument as the recipient of the sum shown.

Payor-
> The party who delivers funds in a transaction.

Per Diem-
> A term meaning "by day" used to compute an allowance or charge that has been established on a daily basis.

Personal Property-
> All property subject to ownership which is not fixed or immovable. Personal property may be tangible or intangible. Tangible personal property consists of physical objects, whereas intangible personal property consists of human rights.

Planned Unit Development (PUD)-
> A planned development which offers flexibility in the design of a subdivision. Usually contains a mixture of land uses such as cluster housing, single-family homes, common areas, and light commercial or office zoning. Usually includes roads, schools, recreational facilities and service areas.

Plat-
> A map showing the dimensions of a piece of real estate based upon the legal description.

Point-
> One percent of the principal amount of a loan.

Power of Attorney-
> A witnessed and acknowledged document that authorizes a person to act as the agent (attorney-in-fact) for another person in legal matters. A general power of attorney authorizes the agent to act for the principal in all matters. A special power of attorney authorized the agent to do only certain specified things.

Preliminary Title Report-
> A report issued by the title company prior to settlement of a real estate purchase. The report provides a legal description of the property and gives the current status of title as it pertains to any defects, liens, easements or covenants.

Prepaid Interest-
> Interest paid before becoming due.

Prepayment-
> Any amount paid to reduce the principal of a mortgage loan in advance of the due date or in excess of the stipulated amortization.

Prepayment Penalty-
> A fee imposed by a lender for the early payoff of a mortgage.

Prime Rate-
> The interest rate charged to an institutional lender's most creditworthy customers.

Principal Balance-
> The outstanding balance of a debt exclusive of interest and any other charges.

Principal, Interest, Taxes and Insurance (PITI)-
> A total monthly payment amount to cover principal and interest on a mortgage plus taxes and insurance.

Processing-
The preparation of a mortgage loan application and supporting documents for consideration by a lender or insurer.

Profit and Loss Statement-
A written statement that covers a period of time and reflects sales, costs of goods sold, expenses and net profit or loss.

Promissory Note-
An unconditional written promise to pay a sum of money to a stated person for specified terms.

Prorate-
To divide among two or more parties proportionately according to share, interest or liability (such as taxes, insurance or rent).

Purchase Money Mortgage-
A mortgage given by a buyer to a seller as part of the purchase consideration.

Quality Control-
Policies and procedures used to determine and maintain a desired level of quality. Also, a department within a bank which audits the loan portfolio to ensure quality.

Quitclaim Deed-
A deed that transfers only such interest, title or right a grantor may have at the time the conveyance is executed. Contains no warranties of ownership.

Real Estate-
Land and anything permanently affixed to it, such as buildings, fences, and those things attached to the building, such as light fixtures, plumbing and heating fixtures, or other such items which would be personal property if not attached.

Real Estate Owned (REO)-
A term that applies to all real estate directly owned by a bank through foreclosure.

Real Property-
Immovable property such as land, buildings, improvements, appurtenances and air space.

Real Property Transaction-
>A transaction for which a security interest is or will be retained or acquired in real property. Defined by the law of the state in which it is located.

Realtor-
>A real estate broker or an associate who holds active membership in a local real estate board affiliated with the national association of realtors.

Reconveyance-
>The conveying of title back to the original owner by use of a deed of reconveyance or mortgage that acknowledges the note is paid in full.

Recordation-
>Public notice that a lien has been created against certain property described in a mortgage. Usually made in the public record of the county or other jurisdiction in which the property is located.

Refinancing-
>The repayment of a debt from the proceeds of a new loan using the same property as security.

Regulation Z-
>Truth in lending. Regulation that requires full disclosure in writing of all costs connected with the credit portion of a purchase including the annual percentage rate (apr).

Rescission-
>Cancellation of a contract. A loan may be cancelled by one party if the other party is at fault, or, in certain transactions, by the borrower under a right granted by the federal truth in lending act/regulation z. Any money that changed hands prior to rescission must be returned to the party that provided it.

Reserves-
>Funds set aside for a particular purpose, usually to protect the security of outstanding mortgage loans.

Residential Mortgage-
>A loan for which real estate is given as collateral. The collateral is usually a single owner-occupied home or two-to-four dwelling units.

Residential Real Property-
> Improved real property used or intended for residential purposes. Includes single family homes, dwellings for two to four families and individual condominiums and cooperatives.

Savings Bank-
> An institution that accepts interest-bearing time deposits for investment in mortgages and high-grade securities.

Second Mortgage-
> A real estate mortgage subordinate to the first mortgage.

Secondary Financing-
> Financing real estate with loans that are subordinate to the first mortgage. Second mortgages or junior liens.

Secondary Mortgage Market-
> A system for the sale and purchase of real estate mortgages. It contrasts with the primary mortgage market where mortgages are originated. For example, a lender originates loans as a primary lender for sale to Fannie Mae, who is part of the secondary mortgage market.

Secured Loan-
> A loan that requires the borrower to pledge collateral to protect the creditor's interest.

Senior Real Estate Analyst (SREA)-
> The highest designation of an appraiser who is a member of the society of real estate appraisers. The society's other major designations are senior residential appraiser (SRA) and senior real property appraiser (SRPA).

Separate Property-
> The property which one person owns free from any rights or control of others, such as the property owned by a married woman independent of her husband.

Servicing-
> The collection of payments of interest and principal, and sometimes taxes and insurance on a mortgage loan.

Settlement-
> Closing. The Conclusion of a real estate transaction by completing all necessary documentation, making necessary payments and transferring title where appropriate.

Single Family Property-
> A property intended for ownership and occupancy by one family.

Simple Interest-
> A method of interest calculation using a flat percentage of the principal balance on an annual basis.

Small Business Administration (SBA)-
> An independent government agency created in 1953 to help small businesses. The SBA makes loans directly to or guarantees those loans made to small businesses.

Subordination Agreement-
> An agreement by which an encumbrance is made subject (junior) to a junior encumbrance. For example, a loan on vacant land is made subject to a subsequent construction loan.

Survey-
> The measurement and description of land by a registered surveyor.

Swing Loan-
> A loan that enables a borrower to purchase real estate where the proceeds of sale to another property will be used to repay the loan. Also called a bridge loan.

Take Out Commitment-
> An agreement by a lender to place a long-term (take out) loan on real property after completion of construction.

Take Out Loan-
> A long-term permanent loan that replaces a short-term construction loan.

Tax Lien-
> A claim against property for the amount of unpaid real estate or federal income taxes.

Tenancy in Common-
> The holding of real property by two or more persons each owning an undivided (not necessarily equal) interest without right of survivorship. Should be distinguished from joint tenancy.

Term-
> The period of time between the commencement date and maturity date of a note, mortgage, legal document or other contract.

Title-
> Documentation of the rightful ownership of property.

Title Exception-
> A specified item in a title policy which the title company does not insure.

Title Insurance Policy-
> An insurance policy that warrants the validity of title to real estate. Insures against losses arising through defects of title or any liens or encumbrances.

Title Search-
> An examination of public records to disclose past and current facts which might affect title to a given piece of real estate.

Title1-
> The section of the FHA insurance program for home improvements and mobile homes.

Tract-
> A parcel of land divided into smaller parcels called lots.

Transferee-
> A person or corporation to whom property is transferred.

Transferor-
> A person or corporation who conveys or transfers property.

Trust-
> A fiduciary relationship in which a trustee holds legal title to property for the benefit of another person (the beneficiary) who holds equitable title to the property.

Trust Deed-
> An instrument which takes the place of a mortgage in many states. The legal title to real property is placed in one or more third party trustees to secure the repayment of money or the performance of other conditions. When the debt is paid, the trustee conveys the title to the owner.

Trustee-
> A person or trust institution that holds title to property in trust for another as security for performance of an obligation.

Truth-in-Lending-
> See regulation Z.

Underwriting-
> The analysis of risk and the determination of an appropriate rate and term for a borrower's mortgage loan.

Unencumbered Property-
> Property that is free and clear of assessments, liens, easements and exceptions of all kinds.

Unsecured Loan-
> Funds extended with no pledge of collateral, or for which the value of the collateral is less that the loaned amount, or for which the security is not physically controlled by the lender for the full loan term.

Usury Rate-
> An interest rate greater than that permitted by state law.

Variable Interest-
> Interest rates that fluctuate up or down according to measurable market conditions.

Vendee-
>A purchaser.

Vendor-
>A seller.

Vesting-
>Present ownership. Rights, absolute and fixed.

Veteran's Administration (VA)-
>A loan to an eligible veteran that is partially guaranteed by the veteran's administration under the servicemen's readjustment act of 1944, as amended.

Waiver-
>The voluntary relinquishment of a right, privilege or advantage.

Warehousing-
>The pledging of the loan under an interim financing arrangement, usually with a bank, pending final disposition of the loan to an investor.

Warranty Deed-
>A deed used in some states to convey real property. Contains the usual covenants of warranty of title.

Whole Loan-
>A term in the secondary mortgage market to indicate that the full amount of a loan is available for sale with no portion of participation retained by the seller.

Yield-
>The amount of income returned from an investment expressed as a percentage. For example, discount points plus interest rates equal the yield.

Zoning-
>A legislative process by which restrictions are placed upon the use of land.

360 Day Year/365 Day Year-
>The base used for calculations of daily interest. A 360 day year is used on conventional loans; a 365 day year is used on government loans.

ALTA	AMERICAN LAND TITLE ASSOCIATION
AML	ADJUSTABLE MORTGAGE LOAN
APR	ANNUAL PERCENTAGE RATE
ARM	ADJUSTABLE RATE MORTGAGE
CAR	CALIFORNIA ASSOCIATION OF REALTORS
CC&Rs	COVENANTS, CONDITIONS & RESTRICTIONS
CLTA	CALIFORNIA LAND TITLE ASSOCIATION
CRA	COMMUNITY REINVESTMENT ACT
ECOA	EQUAL CREDIT OPPORTUNITY ACT
FCRA	FAIR CREDIT REPORTING ACT
FDIC	FEDERAL DEPOSIT INSURANCE CORPORATION
FED	FEDERAL RESERVE SYSTEM
FHA	FEDERAL HOUSING ADMINISTRATION
FHLMC	FEDERAL HOME LOAN MORTGAGE CORPORATION (FREDDIE MAC)
FNMA	FEDERAL NATIONAL MORTGAGE ASSOCIATION (FANNIE MAE)
FRM	FIXED RATE MORTGAGE
GNMA	GOVERNMENT NATIONAL MORTGAGE ASSOCIATION
GPM	GRADUATED PAYMENT MORTGAGE
HMDA	HOME MORTGAGE DISCLOSURE ACT
HOW	HOME OWNER'S WARRANTY
HUD	DEPARTMENT OF HOUSING AND URBAN DEVELOPMENT
HUD 1	SEE RESPA
LTV	LOAN – TO – VALUE
MBA	MORTGAGE BANKERS ASSOCIATION
MIP	MORTGAGE INSURANCE PREMIUM
MMI	MUTUAL MORTGAGE INSURANCE
NAR	NATIONAL ASSOCIATION OF REALTORS
OTS	OFFICE OF THRIFT SUPERVISION
P&I	PRINCIPAL AND INTEREST
P&L	PROFIT AND LOSS
PITI	PRINCIPAL, INTEREST, TAXES, & INSURANCE
PMI	PRIVATE MORTGAGE INSURANCE
PR	PRELIMINARY TITLE REPORT
PUD	PLANNED UNIT DEVELOPMENT
REG Z	REGULATION Z (TRUTH-IN-LENDING)
REO	REAL ESTATE OWNED
RESPA	REAL ESTATE SETTLEMENT PROCEDURES ACT
SAIC	SAVINGS ASSOCIATION INSURANCE CORPORATION
S&L	SAVINGS AND LOAN ASSOCIATION
SBA	SMALL BUSINESS ADMINISTRATION

SREA	SOCIETY OF REAL ESTATE APPRAISERS
SREA	SENIOR REAL ESTATE ANALYST
SRPA	SENIOR REAL PROPERTY APPRAISER
TIL	TRUTH – IN – LENDING
VA	VETERANS ADMINISTRATION
VIR	VARIABLE INTEREST RATE